Teach® Yourself

Essential Spanish Grammar

Juan Kattán-Ibarra

For UK order enquiries: please contact Bookpoint Ltd,
130 Milton Park, Abingdon, Oxon OX14 4SB.
Telephone: +44 (0) 1235 827720. *Fax:* +44 (0) 1235 400454.
Lines are open 09.00–17.00, Monday to Saturday, with a 24-hour
message answering service. Details about our titles and how to
order are available at www.teachyourself.com

For USA order enquiries: please contact McGraw-Hill Customer
Services, PO Box 545, Blacklick, OH 43004-0545, USA.
Telephone: 1-800-722-4726. *Fax:* 1-614-755-5645.

For Canada order enquiries: please contact McGraw-Hill Ryerson
Ltd, 300 Water St, Whitby, Ontario L1N 9B6, Canada.
Telephone: 905 430 5000. *Fax:* 905 430 5020.

Long renowned as the authoritative source for self-guided
learning – with more than 50 million copies sold worldwide –
the *Teach Yourself* series includes over 500 titles in the fields of
languages, crafts, hobbies, business, computing and education.

British Library Cataloguing in Publication Data: a catalogue record
for this title is available from the British Library.

Library of Congress Catalog Card Number: on file.

First published in UK 2000 as *Teach Yourself Spanish Grammar*
by Hodder Education, part of Hachette UK, 338 Euston Road,
London NW1 3BH.

First published in US 2000 by The McGraw-Hill Companies, Inc.

This edition published 2010.

The *Teach Yourself* name is a registered trade mark of
Hodder Headline.

Copyright © 2000, 2003, 2010

Typeset by MPS Limited, A Macmillan Company.

Printed in Great Britain for Hodder Education, an Hachette UK
Company, 338 Euston Road, London NW1 3BH.

The publisher has used its best endeavours to ensure that the URLs
for external websites referred to in this book are correct and active
at the time of going to press. However, the publisher and the
author have no responsibility for the websites and can make no
guarantee that a site will remain live or that the content will remain
relevant, decent or appropriate.

Hachette UK's policy is to use papers that are natural, renewable
and recyclable products and made from wood grown in sustainable
forests. The logging and manufacturing processes are expected to
conform to the environmental regulations of the country of origin.

Impression number   10 9 8 7 6 5 4 3 2 1

Year   2014 2013 2012 2011 2010

Contents

Meet the author

I am an experienced teacher of Spanish and the author of a number of best-selling Spanish courses. I began my career teaching Spanish in the United Kingdom in 1975, at Ealing College in London, and also acted as an external examiner in Spanish for various London examinations boards.

My first Spanish course was published in London in 1978, in a writing career which has lasted until today, and I have written, or co-written, courses in the **Teach Yourself** series including **Complete Spanish, Perfect your Spanish, Complete Latin American Spanish, Essential Spanish Grammar, Speak Spanish with Confidence** and **Phone Spanish,** and courses for other publishers including the BBC and McGraw-Hill. I am now a full-time author and very much look forward to being your guide in the journey you are just about to begin into Spanish grammar. **¡Vamos!**

Juan Kattán-Ibarra

Only got a minute?

If you are looking for an accessible and comprehensive guide to Spanish grammar with practical exercises to reinforce your learning, *Essential Spanish Grammar* offers you precisely that. Unlike most grammar books, this one is centred on usage, so the grammar you learn is not dealt with in isolation but is linked to your communicative needs. Do you need to ask the way or tell someone how to get to a place? Do you want to be able to make a hotel booking or order food in a restaurant? These are real-life situations which require you to handle not just certain vocabulary but also specific grammatical forms, and it is these forms which constitute the base of the grammar you are going to learn. Perhaps you are already familiar with some Spanish grammar but are uncertain about how to use it. With this approach to grammar, you will be able to put the new language structures to immediate use, allowing you to communicate with Spanish speakers in a number of useful contexts.

In each of the 23 units that make up the book, language usage and grammar are clearly defined. Explanations are simple, and all examples have an English translation. The grammar section constitutes the core of the unit, and it is your understanding of and familiarity with the new forms introduced here that will allow you to use the language appropriately. Language, however, normally functions beyond single unconnected sentences, so every unit includes examples of usage within a wider context, followed by practical exercises and tests to reinforce your learning and assess what you have learned.

Perhaps you already know some Spanish – but if not, here are a few expressions:

sí *yes*

no *no, not*

por favor *please*

(**muchas**) **gracias** *thank you (very much)*

¡hola! *hello!*

¡adiós! *goodbye!*

5 Only got five minutes?

If you are a beginner in Spanish looking for a companion to your Spanish course, or are an intermediate or advanced student who wants to consolidate what you have learned on your own or in a class then this is the right course for you. *Essential Spanish Grammar* covers all the language you need to interact with Spanish speakers in a wide range of situations.

Unlike traditional grammar courses, this book is organized following the kinds of things you might want to say in given situations in Spanish, for example describing someone or something, expressing existence and availability, expressing location, possession, obligation and needs, making requests and offers, etc. Each of the 23 units in this course focuses on two or more language functions such as the previous ones, with the grammar contents deriving directly from these. The language forms, then, will not be learned in isolation, as they are in traditional grammar books, but in association with particular usages.

The functional content of the course has been organized in such a way as to allow the grammatical contents to follow a progression which starts with the more basic forms and moves gradually towards more complex constructions. Unit 1, for example, which focuses on asking and giving personal information, brings in the Spanish for *I*, *you*, *he*, *she*, etc., **ser** *to be*, masculine and feminine forms of nouns, different ways of asking questions, etc., all within the same context. In Unit 9, you will learn to talk about the present, and will be introduced to the forms of the present tense and other useful constructions used for referring to the present. Similarly, in Unit 18, you will learn the forms of the simple past and other forms you might need when talking about past events. To express possibility and doubt, in Unit 21, you will be introduced to the subjunctive, a special form of the verb which is common in Spanish but little used in English. Special attention is given to the contrast between forms which English speakers tend to confuse, such as **ser** and **estar** *(to be)*, the preterite and the imperfect tenses, the present indicative and the present subjunctive, conditional sentences of different kinds, etc. Information is also given, where appropriate, on differences between Peninsular and Spanish American usage. Although these are few and do not in any way affect communication, it is important that you are aware of them.

The two key elements in the book, grammar and usage, are listed on the contents pages and on the opening page of each unit, which is then followed by a list of **Key sentences** and a **Grammar summary**. The grammar explanations are kept simple, and all the sentences used are given with an English translation. An **In context** section with dialogues and brief texts related to the unit theme is followed by a **Practice** section, where you will be able to use what you have learned. Help with vocabulary is given after most texts, but you can also refer to the **Spanish–English** or **English–Spanish vocabulary** lists at the end of the book. In each unit, you will find **insights** with brief explanations and hints on how best to approach the material. Most of the information given in these notes relates to language, but there are also insights into Spanish and Spanish American culture. A **Test yourself** section at the end of each unit will allow you to assess what you have learned and decide whether you are ready to go on to the next unit or whether you need some further revision.

You may be wondering whether the grammar covered in this book will allow you to interact with speakers in any part of the Spanish-speaking world, and whether there are any differences between the forms used in Spain and those found in Spanish America. You may be surprised to know that, in fact, with more than 350 million native speakers in 21 countries, including Spain, the African continent and the Americas, the grammar of Spanish is one and the same. Minor differences in usage are easily identifiable and they do not affect communication in any way. Furthermore, these special features are not, as you might think, linked to particular countries but rather to whole regions or areas. Parts of Andalusia in southern Spain, the Canary Islands, off the coast of north-west Africa, and

Spanish-speaking Latin America, have certain characteristics in common. Spanish throughout the world differs more in terms of pronunciation, intonation and vocabulary than in relation to its grammar, just as with English in different parts of the world. British, American and Australian people, for instance, sound different, and some of their vocabulary is also different. Spelling, on the other hand, is exactly the same in all Spanish-speaking countries, and you will find none of the differences that you encounter between British and American English, such as *travelling/traveling, colour/color, centre/center, cheque/check*, etc.

A number of factors have contributed to linguistic unity in the Spanish-speaking world. Most important has been the role of the Real Academia Española, the Royal Spanish Academy, an official body, with national academies in each Spanish-speaking country, whose main function is to dictate norms with regard to Spanish usage, especially in the area of grammar, vocabulary and spelling. No less important has been the part played by literature and other forms of serious writing. Spain has fed on Spanish American literature, perhaps even more so than Spanish Americans have done on Spanish literary texts. This was particularly true during the Spanish-American literary boom of the Sixties, when Spain was still under the Franco dictatorship. Prior to that, at the end of the Spanish Civil War in 1939, when Franco took over, many hundreds of Spaniards, among them many intellectuals, fled to Spanish America and made a permanent home in countries such as Mexico, Argentina or Chile, from where they carried on their work. Three decades later, in the Seventies, a number of Spanish-American writers fleeing military dictatorships in their countries made their way to Spain, where they continued to write. The media, especially the press and, more recently, the Internet, with the need to reach a wider public than that of a single country, have also contributed to the unity of the Spanish language.

It is this unity of Spanish, and with it the fact that you will be able to communicate with Spanish speakers wherever you are, that has led millions of people like you throughout the world to adopt Spanish as their second or third language. Spanish is now the second most studied language after English, in places as far apart as Europe, Asia or Brazil. In the United States, it is the main foreign language, but this country is also home to about 34 million people of Hispanic origin who normally communicate in Spanish in their homes. The number of Spanish speakers, native and non-native, is increasing rapidly, pushed partly by the growth in the Hispanic population, but also by the expansion of international trade, travel and tourism and an increased interest in Spanish and Spanish-American culture, including music, dance, cinema, literature, etc. Learning Spanish and Spanish grammar will give you the chance not just to communicate with Spanish speakers in different parts of the world, but also to enjoy Spanish and Spanish-American life and culture in those areas that most interest you.

10 Only got ten minutes?

Whether you are new to Spanish or have already studied the language on your own or in a class and are looking to improve your capacity to communicate accurately with native speakers, then *Essential Spanish Grammar* has much to offer you. If you are a beginner, it will teach you all the essential language forms that you will need in order to use the language accurately in a wide range of situations. If you already have some knowledge of the language, it will help you to reinforce what you have learned and take you beyond the more basic constructions to more complex ones, thus increasing your ability to interact with Spanish speakers, wherever they are.

If you have never studied Spanish before, you may be wondering how different it is from English and how difficult it will be. The fact is that, for English speakers, Spanish is not a difficult language to learn. There are a number of similarities between the two languages, especially in the area of vocabulary, but also in their grammar, which will make the task of learning Spanish much easier. Similarities and differences in the grammar, which is the main focus of this book, are summed up briefly in the following two sections.

Some similarities between Spanish and English

The word order of subject (**yo** I) – verb (**hablo** *speak*) – object (**español** *Spanish*), for example, is the same in Spanish and English, although generally Spanish shows more flexibility in this area, as it allows for a shift in word sequence in order to focus attention on a certain word or element within the sentence, as in **Hablo español yo**, which is perfectly possible. The implied meaning here is that I speak Spanish, not English or French or another language.

Some of the tenses in the two languages are used in much the same way and, with a few exceptions, words like *the*, *a(n)*, *this/these, that/those, my, your* are also used similarly, except that in Spanish such words must agree with the accompanying noun and will change for number (singular and plural), and some also for gender (masculine and feminine), as in **el/este chico** *the/this boy*, **la/esta chica** *the/this girl*, **los/estos chicos** *the/these boys/children*, **las/estas chicas** *the/these girls*. There are many similarities in vocabulary, too, and many words derived from Latin are much the same: **confortable** *comfortable*, **excelente** *excellent*, **presente** *present*, **profesor** *teacher, professor*, etc. Similarities such as these will help to enhance your capacity to understand the language, particularly in its written form. Similarities in word formation will also help to increase your passive vocabulary: **in**cap**az** *incapable*, **inter**acción *interaction*, **para**médico *paramedic*; **gratitud** *gratitude*, **art**ista *artist*, **catol**icismo *catholicism*, etc.

Some differences between Spanish and English

MASCULINE AND FEMININE FORMS

Nouns (words which name things) – for example, **libro** *book*, **casa** *house* – have gender in Spanish, that is, they are either masculine or feminine. The word **casa** is feminine, while **libro** is masculine. Sometimes the ending of a word can tell you whether it is masculine or feminine. Most words which end in **-o** are masculine and most of those ending in **-a** are feminine, but there are exceptions: **el día** *day* is masculine and **la mano** *hand* is feminine. Words ending in **-r**, **-l** and **-ma/-ta/-pa** are usually masculine: **el color** *colour*, **el hotel** *hotel*, **el clima** *climate*, **el planeta** *planet*, **el mapa** *map*; words ending in **-ción**, **-dad** and **-umbre** are feminine: **la estación** *station*, **la ciudad** *city*, **la muchedumbre** *crowd*. Words ending in **-ista** can be masculine or feminine: **el/la dentista** *dentist*. Some words have different forms for masculine and feminine: **el yerno** *son-in-law*, **la nuera** *daughter-in-law*. A few others change their meaning according to their gender: **el cura** *priest*, **la cura** *cure*. More information on gender can be found in the **Grammar reference** at the back of the book.

SINGULAR AND PLURAL

With the exception of a few words which have a separate plural form, for example *child – children*, English forms the plural by adding *-s* to the word: *car – cars*. Spanish adds **-s** to words ending in a vowel, but **-es** to those which end in a consonant: **el coche** *car* – **los coches** *cars*, **el señor** *gentleman* – **los señores** *gentlemen*.

GENDER AND NUMBER AGREEMENT

As explained earlier, many grammatical words change for number (singular or plural) and/or gender (masculine or feminine), depending on the gender or number of the word that goes with them, as in **un libro** *a book*, **unas casas** *some houses*. Adjectives (words which describe something or someone), such as **bonito** *beautiful* and **caro** *expensive*, change for gender and number. Such words usually follow the word that they describe: **un país bonito** *a beautiful country* (literally *a country beautiful*), **una ciudad bonita** *a beautiful city*, **unos hoteles caros** *some expensive hotels*, **unas vacaciones caras** *some expensive holidays*.

SPANISH VERBS

If you look up Spanish verbs in a dictionary, you will see that they fall into three main categories: most end in **-ar** (e.g. **hablar** *to speak*), while others end in **-er** (e.g. **comer** *to eat*) or **-ir** (e.g. **vivir** *to live*). The English verb system is much simpler than the Spanish one, as Spanish verbs change, not only according to the type of verb (**-ar**, **-er**, **-ir**), but also for person (**yo** *I*, **tú** *you*, **él** *he*, **ella** *she*, etc.) and tense (present tense, future tense, etc.). Most verbs follow a fixed pattern in their conjugation and are called *regular verbs*, but a number of them behave in a different way and are known as *irregular verbs*. It should not be difficult for you to learn the pattern of regular verbs, but irregular ones you will have to learn separately and must try to remember their forms. Some verbs are irregular in one tense, for example the present tense, but not in another.

NO NEED FOR I, YOU, HE, SHE ...

Subject pronouns (words like *I*, *you*, *he*, *she*, etc.) cannot be omitted in English, as the verb form alone, for example *spoke*, does not indicate the person you are referring to. In Spanish, however, the person of the verb is shown in its ending, so words like *I*, *we*, *they*, etc. are usually omitted: **hablé** *I spoke*, **hablamos** *we spoke*, **hablaron** *they spoke*, etc. When the pronouns are used, it is usually for emphasis or to avoid possible ambiguity, as **usted** *you* (formal, one person), **él** *he* and **ella** *she* share the same endings (e.g. **él/ella/ usted trabaja** *he/she works*, *you work*). **Ustedes** *you* (formal, more than one person) and **ellos** *they* also have the same endings. **Usted** and **ustedes** are often included for politeness.

FOUR DIFFERENT FORMS FOR YOU

Peninsular Spanish has four different forms for *you*, two for addressing one person and two for addressing more than one person: **tú** (informal or familiar) is used to address family, friends and younger people in general, even if you have never met them before; **usted** (formal or polite form) is used to address older people, one's superiors or people in official situations; **vosotros** (informal or familiar) is used to address more than one person; **ustedes** (formal or polite form) is used to address more than one person. Again, the ending of the verb will indicate the person, as shown here by the different translations of *you ate*: **comiste** (informal, singular), **comió** (formal, singular), **comisteis** (informal, plural), **comieron** (formal, plural).

Spanish Americans do not use **vosotros** or the verb forms corresponding to this, as **ustedes** is used in both formal and informal address. This usage is also found in parts of Andalusia in southern Spain and in the Canary Islands.

In Argentina, Uruguay and Paraguay, and some other areas of Spanish America, **tú** is replaced by **vos**. In the appropriate units of this book, you will find information on the verb forms that go with **vos**.

SAYING NO

To negate something, Spanish does not use the equivalent of *don't*, *doesn't*, *won't*, etc. In Spanish, you simply put the word **no** before the verb to make a negative sentence: **No hablo español** *I don't speak Spanish*.

ASKING QUESTIONS

To ask questions in Spanish, you can use the same word order as in a statement (**¿Usted habla español?** *You speak Spanish?*) or you can place the verb in first place (**¿Habla usted español?** *Do you speak Spanish?*). Alternatively, you can use either **¿verdad?** (*right, true?*) or **¿no?** at the end of the statement (**Usted habla español, ¿verdad?/¿no?** *You speak Spanish, don't you?*). Like English, Spanish also uses question words such as **¿qué?** *what?/which?*, **¿dónde?** *where?*, etc. (**¿Qué idioma hablas?** *What language do you speak?*). Note that all questions in Spanish carry two question marks, one (upside down) at the beginning of the sentence and one at the end.

Learning strategies

The above are only a few of the grammar points you are going to encounter as you progress in the course. There are many others which, for reasons of space, cannot be mentioned here. This brief insight into the contents of the book is only the first step towards gaining the competence in Spanish that you are probably aiming at. The second step is the book itself, with its unit-by-unit treatment of all the essentials of Spanish grammar. The third step is your own approach to the material which is being presented and what you can do to enhance your own learning. Try planning your own strategy to make the most of what this course has to offer you, to expand your competence in Spanish even further and to satisfy your own needs. The focus here is on grammar rather than vocabulary or some other aspect of the language, and there are a number of things you can do to practise this. For example, you can place flashcards around your house with words you want to learn, such as the forms of irregular verbs. Or use the flashcards to write brief sentences practising a particular point, such as demonstratives (**Este es Carlos** *This is Carlos*, **Esta es María** *This is Maria*) or possessives and descriptive words (**Mi casa es pequeña** *My house is small*). You can take them with you when you go out and look at them on the bus or train while you travel to work or school. With longer sentences, as in the **Key sentences** sections in this book, where each sentence has a translation next to it, study both the Spanish and the English first, then cover up the English translations and try to produce the English equivalents of the Spanish. If you find that relatively easy, go on to cover the Spanish sentences and produce the Spanish equivalents of the English. You will probably find this more difficult. Trying to recall the context in which words and phrases were used may help you to learn them better.

One way of practising and memorizing verbs, regular or irregular ones, is to write or think of a sentence and then replace the person of the verb (and perhaps some other element within the sentence), for example **yo** *I* or a name such as Carmen, by a different person, changing the verb as appropriate: **(Yo) vivo en Inglaterra** *I live in England*, **Carmen vive en Madrid** *Carmen lives in Madrid*, **Alfonso y Silvia viven en Buenos Aires** *Alfonso and Silvia live in Buenos Aires*, etc. You can do this exercise with a number of words or expressions, for example changing adjectives from masculine into feminine or singular into plural (e.g. **Francisco es alto** *Francisco is tall*, **Sofía es alta** *Sofia is tall*), or replacing a word indicating location by another word of the same kind (e.g. **Está al lado de la catedral** *It's next to the cathedral*, **Está enfrente de la farmacia** *It's opposite the chemist's*), etc.

Try to adopt your own personal techniques to further your Spanish. Make use of the Internet, for example, to find more information on Spanish grammar or to establish contact with Spanish speakers in order to practise the language. In the **Taking it further** section at the back of the book, you will find more hints on what to do, including information on resources such as newspapers, magazines, radio and television.

Spanish, an international language

By taking up Spanish, you will be joining millions of other people around the world who have decided to do so. Spanish is one of the most widely spoken languages; it is the native language of more than 350 million people in 21 countries, including Spain, the North African cities of Ceuta and Melilla, the Canary Islands (off the north-west coast of Africa), Equatorial Guinea (a former Spanish colony on the west coast of Africa) and Spanish America (19 countries in all). In most of the 21 countries, Spanish is an official language, either on its own or alongside other languages such as Aymara (Bolivia), Quechua (Bolivia, Peru and Ecuador), Guarani (Paraguay), English (Puerto Rico) and French (Equatorial Guinea). Spanish is also spoken in Andorra (a principality in south-western Europe) alongside Catalan, which is the official language, and in Gibraltar, where the official language is English. The United States is home to around 45 million people of Hispanic origin from countries like Mexico, Puerto Rico (a self-governing commonwealth in association with the United States, whose people have United States citizenship), Cuba and Dominican Republic, among others. Spanish is used within the family by about 34 million of them, making it one of the largest Spanish-speaking countries, well ahead of most Latin American countries.

The origins of Spanish

The roots of **el español** (also referred to as **el castellano** Castilian) – like those of Portuguese, French, Italian, etc. – can be found in Latin, the language of the Romans. However, Arabic rule in large parts of the Peninsula between 710 and 1492 also left an important imprint in the Spanish language, mainly in vocabulary. Many everyday words such as **aceite** oil, **aceituna** olive, **hasta** until, **taza** cup and many place names are derived from Arabic. Starting in the 16th century, a number of words from the conquered territories in the Americas began to find their way into Spanish: **chocolate,**

tomate, cacao, patata and **papa** are just some of them. Old and then modern French, especially from the 17th century onwards, also had an influence on Spanish, and in more recent times, English has been a major contributor. Dozens of English words are in current use in Spanish, some in adapted form, others not: **fútbol, tenis, béisbol, jersey, suéter, ticket, film, suspense, sandwich, marketing, email, chatear,** etc.

Other languages spoken in Spain

Alongside Spanish (**el castellano**), other languages are spoken in the Peninsula: **el catalán** has about nine million speakers in all, in Catalonia, Valencia, the Balearic Islands and parts of Aragon (it is also spoken in northern Catalonia, **Catalogne du Nord**, in France); **el gallego** is spoken in Galicia, with around two and a half million speakers; **el vasco** (or **euskera**) is spoken by about one million people in the Basque country. Not all of these are native speakers, as some, especially in the case of Basque, have acquired the language in later years and have no native-speaker competence. Like Castilian, Catalan and Galician are derived from Latin. Basque is not, and its origins are uncertain. Each of these languages has a co-official status in the regions in which they are spoken, with Castilian remaining the official national language. Other minority languages, such as **Bable** in Asturias and **Aragonés** in Aragon, enjoy special protection.

The predominance of Castilian

The predominance of Castilian over other languages spoken in the Peninsula dates back to the end of the 15th century when the old kingdoms of Castile and Aragon, united under Isabel de Castilla and Fernando de Aragón, brought a large part of the Peninsula under their dominion, and with it the gradual penetration of Castilian into the domains of the Crown, until it became established as the language of Spain.

Introduction

Essential Spanish Grammar has been designed as a reference book for those who, with or without the help of a teacher, need to revise all the essentials of Spanish grammar. It will also be useful as a companion to your Spanish course. A particular feature of the book is its two-fold approach to the language, from a communicative perspective as well as from a purely grammatical one.

The communicative element of the course draws its contents from your own needs as a non-native speaker of Spanish, covering all the most important language uses, which in turn are linked to the grammatical constructions that you will need in order to express them.

On the contents page, each unit lists both language uses and grammatical terms, which will allow you to approach the book from either perspective. If you are using this as a reference book to study or revise particular grammatical points, you will be able to do this by looking them up in the index at the back of the book.

Whether you are new to Spanish or already have some knowledge of it, I will be guiding you through all the essentials of the language, starting with the most basic forms and moving on to more advanced ones, giving you all the elements you need to communicate with Spanish speakers correctly and with confidence.

How to use this book

The following procedure is suggested for working through each unit:

Read the section headed **In this unit you will learn ...**, which gives information about the language uses that are studied in the unit, for example how to say who you are and state your nationality, among other language functions in Unit 1. Then read the **Language points**, which list the constructions associated with those language uses, for example subject pronouns and present tense of **ser** *to be* in Unit 1. You can then study the **Key sentences** and their English translations, which are intended to ease your way into the **Grammar summary** which follows. The language content of the unit is explained here in terms which you should find easy to follow; each point is illustrated by means of further examples, all with their English translations. The vocabulary has been kept simple, so that you can focus your attention on the grammar rather than on the meanings of single words. Try fixing the new language constructions in your memory by writing further examples of your own. Use the **Spanish–English vocabulary** and the **English–Spanish vocabulary** to find new words to adapt the sentences in the unit. In the grammar section, as in other parts of the unit, you will find **Insights** containing further information on language points, as well as useful hints on how to deal with some of them. A few of these notes refer to cultural aspects related to Spain or Spanish America.

Language always functions within a context, so the purpose of the **In context** section, which follows the **Grammar summary**, is to show you how the grammar you have learned in the unit can be used. Read the dialogues and other texts here, paying special attention to the points highlighted in earlier parts of the unit. **Key words** are listed under each dialogue or text.

To help you consolidate what you have learned, each unit includes a **Practice** section, containing both grammatical and communicative exercises. Go through these without looking at the preceding notes, checking your answers in the **Key to the exercises** if necessary. Each unit ends with a **Test yourself** section, a form of self-assessment of the key elements in the unit. The answers to the test will be found in the **Answer key**. If most or all of your answers are right, and you feel confident with the new language, proceeed to the next unit in a similar way. However, if you still feel uncertain, go back through the unit again, checking also the

Grammar reference, where you may find further information. The list of Irregular verbs may also be of help. If you wish to expand on what you have learned, consult the Taking it further section, where you will find references to other grammar books as well as other useful information related to Spanish, such as websites, access to media, including newspapers, television and radio, language courses and organizations.

Although most words used throughout the units are listed in the Spanish–English vocabulary and English–Spanish vocabulary at the end of the book, a good pocket dictionary should help you with those which are not, and will also be useful when building up sentences or texts of your own.

The alphabet

a	a	Ana	ñ	eñe	mañana
b	be	Bilbao	o	o	Colombia, poco
c	ce	Cuba, gracias	p	pe	Perú
d	de	día	q	cu	que, quinto
e	e	Elena	r	erre, ere	perro, Río, París
f	efe	Francia	s	ese	Susana
g	ge	Gloria, Algeciras	t	te	Tarragona
h	hache	hasta	u	u	Murcia
i	i	Isabel	v	uve	Venezuela
j	jota	Juan	w	uve doble	Washington
k	ca	kilo	x	equis	taxi
l	ele	Londres	y	i griega	yo, Paraguay
m	eme	María	z	zeta	Cádiz
n	ene	no			

Until fairly recently, ch and ll were considered separate letters of the alphabet, but this is no longer the case. You may still find separate entries for them in some monolingual dictionaries, but most recent bilingual dictionaries treat ch within c and ll within l.

Many speakers, however, still consider them as separate letters so you should be aware of their names:

| ch | che | Chile |
| ll | elle | calle |

Pronunciation guide

The aim of this pronunciation guide is to offer hints which will enable you to produce sounds recognizable to Spanish speakers. It cannot by itself teach you to pronounce Spanish accurately. The best way to acquire a reasonably good accent is to listen to and try to imitate native speakers. Listed below are the main elements of Spanish pronunciation and their approximate English equivalent. Only information on those sounds which may cause difficulty to English speakers has been included.

VOWELS

a	like the **a** in *answer* but shorter (British English)	
	like the **u** in *but* (American English)	Ana
e	like the **e** in *red*	Elena
i	like the **ea** in *mean*	Rita
o	like the **o** in *cost*	poco
u	like the **oo** in *moon*	luna

CONSONANTS

b *and*	in initial position and after **n** are	Barcelona,
v	pronounced the same, with lips closed, like the **b** in *bar*	invierno
b *and*	in other positions are pronounced with the	Sevilla, Alba
v	lips slightly apart	
c	before **a, o, u**: like the **c** in *car*	coche
	before **e** and **i**: like the **th** in *think*	gracias, Valencia

(in Spanish America, Southern Spain and the Canaries, like the s in *sink*)

g	before **a, o, u**: like the **g** in *get*	Málaga
	before **e** and **i**: like the **ch** in *loch*	Gibraltar
gu	before **e** and **i**: like the **g** in *get*	Guernica
h	is silent	Honduras
j	like the **ch** in *loch*	Jamaica
ll	like the **y** in *yes*	paella
	(in Argentina, more like the **s** in *television*)	
ñ	like the **ni** in *onion*	mañana
qu	like the **k** in *keep*	que
r	between vowels or at the end of a word, like the **r** in *very*	caro, calor
	in initial position, strongly rolled	Roma
rr	always strongly rolled	Tarragona
v	like **b** (see **b** above)	
w	(in foreign words) like Spanish **b** and **v** (see above) or English **w**	wáter, Taiwán
x	between vowels: like the **x** in *box*	taxi
	before a consonant: as above or as **s** in Peninsular Spanish in a few words, like the **ch** in *loch*	México
y	like the **y** in *yes*	
	(in Argentina, more like the **s** in *television*)	mayo
z	like the **th** in *think*	Zaragoza, Cádiz
	(in Spanish America, Southern Spain and the Canaries, like the **s** in *sink*)	

The pronunciation of **c** before **i** and **e**, as in **gracias** and **Valencia**, and **z**, as in **Zaragoza** and **Cádiz**, are both pronounced like an **s** in Spanish America (as well as in parts of Southern Spain and the Canaries). This can be said to be the main difference in pronunciation between Latin American Spanish and that spoken in most parts of Spain.

STRESS AND ACCENTUATION

a Words which end in a vowel, **n** or **s** stress the last syllable but one: **Inglaterra** *England*; **toman** *you/they take*; **Estados Unidos** *United States*.

b Words which end in a consonant other than **n** or **s** stress the last syllable: **Madrid**; **español** *Spanish*; **aparcar** *to park*.

c A written accent overrides the above two rules; the vowel with the written accent is stressed: **allí** *there*; **invitación** *invitation*; **inglés** *English*; **difícil** *difficult*; **González**.

d A number of words are stressed on the third-from-last syllable, in which case the stressed vowel carries a written accent: **América** *America*; **histórico** *historical*; **rápido** *quick, fast*.

e One-syllable words do not normally carry an accent (see exceptions in **f** below): **dio** *he/she/you gave*; **fui** *I went/was*; **pan** *bread*; **¡ven!** *come!*.

f A written accent is used to differentiate meanings between pairs of words which are spelt the same: **de** *of* – **dé** *give* (but **deme/denos** *give me/us*); **el** *the* – **él** *he*; **mi** *my* – **mí** *me*; **se** *(one/him/her/your) self* – **sé** *I know*; **si** *if* – **sí** *yes*; **te** *(for/to) you* – **té** *tea*; **tu** *your* – **tú** *you*.

g Many educated speakers and Spanish grammar books use accents to differentiate words such as **este/éste** *this/this one*, **ese/ése** *that/that one*. The **Real Academia Española** (the body which regulates the spelling and usage of the Spanish language) has ruled that an accent on these words is not required, unless there is ambiguity, which is rarely the case. In this book, they have been used without accents.

h Question words carry an accent: **¿cómo?** *how?*; **¿cuál?** *which?*; **¿cuándo?** *when?*; **¿cuánto?** *how much?*; **¿dónde?** *where?*; **¿por qué?** *why?*; **¿qué?** *what?*; **¿quién?** *who?* Accents are also used in exclamations: **¡qué bonito!** *how pretty!*; **¡quién sabe!** *who knows?*

i Words ending in **-án, -én, -és, -ín** and **-ón** in the singular lose this accent when a syllable is added to form the plural, thus following rule **a** above: **alemán/alemanes** *German/s*; **jabón/jabones** *soap*. Similarly, words ending in **-án, -és, -ín** and **ón** in the masculine lose the accent in the feminine form: **alemán/alemana** *German* (m./f.); **escocés/escocesa** *Scottish* (m./f.).

ABBREVIATIONS

The following abbreviations have been used in this book: m./masc. *masculine*, f./fem. *feminine*, fam. *familiar* (or inf. *informal*), pol. (or *formal*) *polite*, sing. *singular*, pl. *plural*, L.Am. *Latin America*, Am.E. *American English*.

1

Asking for and giving personal information

In this unit, you will learn how to:
- *say who you are*
- *state your nationality*
- *say where you are from*
- *say what your occupation is*
- *give similar information about other people*
- *ask for personal information*

Language points
- *subject pronouns*
- *ser in the present tense*
- *gender of nouns*
- *plural of nouns*
- *adjectives indicating nationality*
- *interrogative sentences*
- *negative sentences*

Key sentences

The key sentences and grammar notes which follow will show you how to ask for and give simple personal information in Spanish. Look at the sentences and their English translation first then read the **Grammar summary** for an explanation of how the language works.

SAYING WHO YOU ARE

Soy Antonio/Ana.	*I'm Antonio/Ana.*

STATING YOUR NATIONALITY

Soy español/española.	*I'm Spanish. (man/woman)*

SAYING WHERE YOU ARE FROM

Soy de Madrid/Salamanca.	*I'm from Madrid/Salamanca.*

SAYING WHAT YOUR OCCUPATION IS

Soy arquitecto/a.	*I'm an architect. (man/woman)*
Soy estudiante.	*I'm a student.*

GIVING SIMILAR INFORMATION ABOUT OTHER PEOPLE

Él es Luis/chileno/profesor.	*He's Luis/Chilean/a teacher.*
Ella es de Barcelona/Londres.	*She's from Barcelona/London.*

ASKING FOR PERSONAL INFORMATION

¿Es usted Gloria?	*Are you Gloria? (formal)*
Usted es española, ¿no?	*You are Spanish, aren't you? (formal/fem.)*
¿Eres inglés o americano?	*Are you English or American? (informal/masc.)*
No eres de aquí, ¿verdad?	*You're not from here, are you? (informal)*

....

Insight

Spanish has three words to designate an American:
americano/a (male/female), **norteamericano/a** (male/female)
North American and **estadounidense** (male or female) *from
the United States* (**Estados Unidos**). The latter is the least

frequent and it is usually found in the press. Note also that words for nationality are not written with capital letters in Spanish.

Grammar summary

1 SUBJECT PRONOUNS (I, YOU, HE, SHE, ETC.)

To say *I*, *you*, *he*, *she*, etc. in Spanish, we use the following set of words:

Singular	
yo	*I*
tú	*you (familiar)*
usted	*you (polite)*
él	*he*
ella	*she*

Plural	
nosotros/as	*we (masc./fem.)*
vosotros/as	*you (familiar, masc./fem.)*
ustedes	*you (polite)*
ellos	*they (masc.)*
ellas	*they (fem.)*

Insight

Nosotras *we* is used by females when there are no males involved. Vosotras *you* is used to address two or more females.

Familiar and polite forms of address
Notice that Spanish uses familiar and polite forms of address. The familiar forms (**tú** and **vosotros**) are used very extensively in Spain

today, even among people who have never met before. However, in business and official situations, it may generally be safer to use the polite form to start with and then wait and see what the other person is using and do likewise. In writing, **usted** and **ustedes** are normally found in abbreviated form as **Vd.** and **Vds.** or as **Ud.** and **Uds.**

Spanish-American usage

Spanish Americans do not use the familiar plural **vosotros.** Instead, they will use **ustedes,** without differentiating between familiarity and formality. Consequently, the verb forms to address a group of people will be those corresponding to **ustedes.** In the singular, the distinction between **tú** and **usted** still remains.

Omission of subject pronouns

Generally, subject pronouns are omitted in Spanish, except at the start of a conversation, to add emphasis or to avoid ambiguity, as with **él, ella, usted** (and their plural equivalents) which always share the same verb forms.

Él es español.	*He's Spanish.*
Ella es española.	*She's Spanish.*
Usted es español.	*You're Spanish.*

2 SER *(TO BE)*

Ser is the verb most frequently used in Spanish when giving basic personal information, such as your name, nationality, place of origin and occupation. Here is **ser** fully conjugated in the present tense:

Singular	
yo soy	*I am*
tú eres	*you are (familiar)*
usted es	*you are (polite)*
él, ella es	*he, she is*

nosotros/as somos	*we are (masc./fem.)*
vosotros/as sois	*you are (familiar, masc./fem.)*
ustedes son	*you are (polite)*
ellos, ellas son	*they are (masc./fem.)*

Insight

Sois is not used in the Spanish-speaking countries of Latin America, where **son** is used in both formal and informal address: **¿Ustedes son españoles?** *Are you Spanish?*

For other uses of **ser**, see Units 2, 3, 5, 6, 11 and the **Grammar reference**.

3 GENDER OF NOUNS

Masculine or feminine?
All nouns in Spanish are either masculine or feminine. Nouns which refer to people, such as those indicating professions or occupations, will normally agree in gender with the person referred to. The following simple rules will help you to form the feminine of nouns denoting professions:

▶ Change the **-o** to **-a**.

| **Él es abogado.** | *He's a lawyer.* |
| **Ella es abogada.** | *She's a lawyer.* |

▶ Add **-a** to the consonant.

| **Juan es profesor.** | *Juan is a teacher.* |
| **María es profesora.** | *María is a teacher.* |

▶ Nouns which end in **-e** do not normally change for masculine and feminine.

| **Pedro es estudiante.** | *Pedro is a student.* |
| **Carmen es estudiante.** | *Carmen is a student.* |

But there are exceptions:

Él es dependiente.	*He's a shop assistant.*
Ella es dependienta.	*She's a shop assistant.*
Él es jefe de ventas.	*He's a sales manager.*
Ella es jefa de ventas.	*She's a sales manager.*

▶ Nouns which end in **-ista** never change for masculine and feminine.

| **Él/Ella es dentista.** | *He's/She's a dentist.* |

With certain professions, you may still hear the masculine form used with reference to women, for example:

| **Él/Ella es médico.** | *He's/She's a doctor.* |

However, new attitudes towards women in Spanish society are bringing about changes in this area of language usage, so you are more likely to come across:

| **Él es doctor.** | *He's a doctor.* |
| **Ella es doctora.** | *She's a doctor.* |

Note that Spanish does not use the equivalent of *a* before a word indicating a profession or occupation, unless the noun is qualified:

| **Es profesora de español.** | *She's a Spanish teacher.* |

But:

| **Es una profesora excelente.** | *She's an excellent teacher.* |

A few nouns which designate people, among them the following ones, have different forms for males and females.

el actor – la actriz	actor – actress
el alcalde – la alcaldesa	mayor
el rey – la reina	king – queen
el poeta – la poetisa	poet
el héroe – la heroína	hero – heroine

While it is not always possible to determine the gender of a noun from its ending, there are a number of endings which can tell us whether a word is masculine or feminine. Words which end in -ción, -sión, -dad, -ie and -tud are normally feminine: **estación** station, **decisión** decision, **ciudad** city, **serie** series, **juventud** youth. Words that end in -aje, -ema, -ismo and -miento are normally masculine: **aterrizaje** *landing*, **dilema** *dilemma*, **periodismo** *journalism*, **casamiento** *marriage*.

There is more on the gender of nouns in Unit 2 and in the **Grammar reference**, paragraph 2.

4 PLURAL OF NOUNS

As in English, nouns in Spanish can have singular and plural forms. The plural of nouns is normally formed by adding -s to the singular form, unless the word ends in a consonant, in which case you add -es.

Él es arquitecto.	*He's an architect.*
Ellos son arquitectos.	*They're architects.*
Soy doctor.	*I'm a doctor.*
Somos doctores.	*We're doctors.*

See also the **Grammar reference**, paragraph 2.

5 ADJECTIVES INDICATING NATIONALITY

Masculine or feminine?
Adjectives of nationality, like many adjectives in Spanish, have masculine and feminine forms. To form the feminine from

a masculine adjective of nationality or origin, change -o to -a or add -a to the consonant, as in:

John es británico.	*John is British.*
Sarah es británica.	*Sarah is British.*
Peter es inglés.	*Peter is English.*
Ann es inglesa.	*Ann is English.*

Insight

The word **inglesa** follows the normal stress pattern of Spanish, whereby words which end in a vowel, **-n** or **-s** stress the last syllable but one. Words of this kind are not written with an accent. The stress in **inglés** falls on the last syllable, therefore it needs a written accent.

Singular and plural

The plural of adjectives, like that of nouns, is normally formed by adding -s to the singular form, unless the word ends in a consonant, in which case you add -es.

John es británico.	*John is British.*
John y Sarah son británicos.	*John and Sarah are British.*
Peter es inglés.	*Peter is English.*
Peter y Ann son ingleses.	*Peter and Ann are English.*

Notice that when the adjective refers to both male and female, the masculine form is used.

Adjectives which end in -i and -ú add -es to form the plural.

Él es paquistaní.	*He's Pakistani.*
Ellos son paquistaníes.	*They're Pakistani.*
Ella es hindú.	*She's Hindu.*
Ellas son hindúes.	*They're Hindu.*

Insight

In some Spanish-speaking countries, the word **hindú** is used instead of **indio/a** *Indian* to designate someone from India.

Adjectives which end in -z change -z into -c and add -es.

Paco es andaluz.   *Paco is Andalusian.*
Paco y Antonio son andaluces.   *Paco and Antonio are Andalusian.*

6 ASKING QUESTIONS

It is possible to form questions in Spanish in several ways:

- ▶ Using the same word order as in a statement, but with a rising
  intonation.

    ¿Usted es española?   *Are you Spanish?*

- ▶ Reversing the order subject–verb.

    ¿Es usted irlandés?   *Are you Irish?*

- ▶ Adding either **¿verdad?** (literally, *true?*) or **¿no?** to the
  statement.

    Usted es escocés, ¿verdad?   *You're Scottish, aren't you?*
    Ella es americana, ¿no?   *She's American, isn't she?*

7 NEGATIVE SENTENCES

Negative sentences are formed simply by using the word **no** before
the verb.

¿ *No* es usted español?   *Aren't you Spanish?*
No, *no* **soy español.**   *No, I'm not Spanish.*

Notice the double negative, as in English, in the second sentence.

8 ASKING FOR AND GIVING INFORMATION ABOUT MARITAL STATUS

To ask for and give information about marital status, use the verb
estar (also meaning *to be*). **Estar** is normally used when referring

to states or conditions, such as the state of being single or married (see Unit 3).

¿Está soltero/a o casado/a?	*Is he/she single or married?*
Está soltera.	*She's single.*

But note:

Es un hombre casado.	*He's a married man.*
Es una mujer divorciada.	*She's a divorced woman.*

Definitions such as the above require **ser** rather than **estar**.

Latin Americans tend to use **ser** to express marital status.

Carlos es casado.	*Carlos is married.*

In context

1 Study these conversations between people who have just met and are getting to know each other. The first exchange is formal and the second one informal.

a Señor	¿Es Vd. española?
Señora	Sí, soy española, ¿y Vd.?
Señor	Soy mexicano. Soy de Guadalajara.
Señora	Yo soy de Madrid.

sí *yes*
y *and*

b Carlos	Hola. ¿Cómo te llamas?
Carmen	Me llamo Carmen, ¿y tú?
Carlos	Yo soy Carlos López. ¿Eres de Madrid?
Carmen	No, no soy de Madrid. Soy de Salamanca.

hola *hello*
¿Cómo te llamas? *What's your name? (fam.)*

Insight

Me llamo ... means literally *I call myself ...*, from **llamarse** *to call oneself*. To ask someone's name in a formal way, use the phrase **¿Cómo se llama usted?**

2 Look at this piece of writing which gives personal information:

Me llamo Alfonso González, soy español, de Sevilla. Soy estudiante de medicina ...

Practice

1 You are writing to a Spanish-speaking correspondent for the first time. Try putting the following information into Spanish.

    a Say what your name is.
    b Say your nationality.
    c Say what town or city you are from.
    d Say what your occupation is.
    e Say whether you are single or married.

2 At a party, you are introduced to someone who only speaks Spanish. Can you fill in your questions in this dialogue?

    – Hola, ¿__?
    – Me llamo Antonio.
    – ¿ __?
    – No, no soy español. Soy argentino.
    – ¿ __?
    – Sí, soy de Buenos Aires.
    – ¿ __?
    – Sí, soy estudiante. Estudio inglés y alemán.

3 What do these people do for a living? Match the names with the occupations listed below and write sentences saying what they do. Use the appropriate gender in each case.

> **médico/a estudiante taxista mecánico/a peluquero/a camarero/a (mesero/a, L.Am.)**

a Antonio Morales

b Silvia Pérez

c Alfredo Muñoz

d Juan González

e Javier Díaz

f Francisco Mella

TEST YOURSELF

1 *Fill in the missing subject pronouns.*
   – __ es español, ¿verdad?
   – Sí, __ soy español, pero mi mujer no, __ es argentina. Y __, ¿de dónde sois?

2 *Replace each of the following by a suitable subject pronoun.*
   a Carmen y yo **b** María **c** Andrés y usted **d** José **e** Patricia y tú

3 *Fill in the appropriate form of ser.*
   – ¿De dónde __ ustedes?
   – __ de Bristol. Y tú, ¿de dónde __?

4 *Give the feminine for each of these occupations.*
   a ingeniero **b** escritor **c** dependiente **d** actor

5 *Give the feminine for each of these nationalities.*
   a español **b** mexicano **c** francés **d** alemán **e** andaluz

6 *Give the plural for each of these nationalities.*
   a americano **b** árabe **c** irlandés **d** andaluz **e** marroquí **f** hindú

7 *Give three alternatives in Spanish for this question.*
   Are you English? (formal/fem.)

8 *Translate this conversation into Spanish.*
   – Are you a lawyer?' (inf./masc.)
   – No, I'm not a lawyer, I'm a dentist.

9 *Translate this conversation into Spanish.*
   – Is she single or married?
   – She's divorced.

10 *Fill in the blanks with suitable words.*
   – ¿Cómo __ llamas?
   – __ llamo Emilio. Soy __ Granada.

Check the **Answer key** if you feel uncertain about any of your answers. If most of them were correct, it means you are now able to give some important information about yourself and others. If any of your answers were wrong, make sure you revise the relevant sections of the unit before you go on to Unit 2.

2

Identifying people, places and things

In this unit, you will learn how to:
* *introduce people*
* *greet people when being introduced*
* *identify people, places and things*

Language points
* *demonstrative adjectives and pronouns*
* *ser in introductions and identification*
* *definite articles*
* *question words* ¿quién?, ¿cuál?, ¿qué?
* *possessives:* mi, tu, su

Key sentences

To introduce people and to identify people, places and things, you can use the Spanish equivalent of words such as *this*, *that*, *these*, *those*.

Questions leading to identification, for example *Who's that man?*, *What's that?*, require the use of question words.

The key sentences and grammar notes which follow will show you how to express these ideas in Spanish.

INTRODUCING PEOPLE

Esta es Carmen/mi mujer. *This is Carmen/my wife.*
Este es Raúl/mi hermano. *This is Raúl/my brother.*

GREETING PEOPLE WHEN BEING INTRODUCED

Encantado/a. *Pleased to meet you. (man/woman)*
Mucho gusto. *Pleased to meet you.*
Hola. *Hello.*

....
Insight
The word **encantado**, literally *delighted*, said by a man, will change to **encantada** when said by a woman. **Mucho gusto**, literally *much pleasure*, is invariable. In more informal situations, use **hola** *hello*.
....

IDENTIFYING PEOPLE, PLACES AND THINGS

¿Quién es esa señora/ese señor? *Who's that lady/gentleman?*
Es la señora Ruiz/el señor Bravo. *It's Mrs Ruiz/Mr Bravo.*
¿Cuál es tu oficina/habitación? *Which is your office/room?*
Es la número 202. *It's number 202.*
¿Qué es esto/eso? *What's this/that?*
Es un despertador. *It's an alarm clock.*

....
Insight
Note the use of **la** *the* (fem.) before **señora** *Mrs*: **la señora Ruiz**. Before **señor** *Mr*, use **el** *the* (masc.): **el señor Bravo**. In direct address, **la** and **el** are not needed: **Buenos días, señorita Lara** *Good morning, Miss Lara*.
....

Grammar summary

1 DEMONSTRATIVES (THIS/THAT, THESE/THOSE)

Look at the preceding examples once again and study the Spanish equivalent of *this*, *these* and *that*, *those*. Unlike English, which only distinguishes between singular and plural, Spanish also makes a distinction between masculine and feminine.

Forms of demonstratives
This, these (next to you)

este **señor (masc.)**	*this gentleman*
esta **señora (fem.)**	*this lady*
estos **señores (masc.)**	*these gentlemen*
estas **señoras (fem.)**	*these ladies*

That, those (near you)

ese **hotel (masc.)**	*that hotel*
esa **habitación (fem.)**	*that room*
esos **hoteles (masc.)**	*those hotels*
esas **habitaciones (fem.)**	*those rooms*

Spanish also differs from English in having a separate set of words to identify or point at someone or something which is far from you. In English, however, the translation would still be *that, those*.

aquel **chico (masc.)**	*that boy*
aquella **chica (fem.)**	*that girl*
aquellos **chicos (masc.)**	*those boys*
aquellas **chicas (fem.)**	*those girls*

Adjectives and pronouns
In all the previous examples, the demonstratives have been followed by nouns (e.g. **este señor, ese hotel, aquel chico**), in which case words such as **este, ese, aquel** are functioning as adjectives.

But they may also be used to refer to a noun without mentioning it specifically, for example **este** (*this one*), **ese** (*that one*), **aquel** (*that one over there*). In this case, they act as pronouns.

Insight

Demonstrative pronouns are sometimes written with an accent, to distinguish them from adjectives. The Spanish Royal Academy (Real Academia Española), which is the body that regulates language usage in the Spanish-speaking world, has ruled that the written accent on demonstrative pronouns may be omitted, unless there is ambiguity, which is rarely the case. In this book, they have been used without the accent, but you may still find them with accents in some grammar books and literary texts, e.g. **éste** *this one*.

Neuter demonstratives
Neuter forms are used when we are not referring to a specific noun.

¿Qué es *esto*?	*What's this?*
¿Qué es *eso*?	*What's that?*
¿Qué es *aquello*?	*What's that (over there)?*
Quiero *esto/eso*.	*I want this/that.*

2 SER *(TO BE) IN INTRODUCTIONS AND IDENTIFICATION*

Notice the use of **ser** (**es** for singular and **son** for plural) for identifying people, places and things.

Ese *es* **el señor García.**	*That is Mr García.*
Este *es* **mi pueblo.**	*This is my town.*
Aquellas *son* **mis llaves.**	*Those are my keys.*

If we are introducing or identifying ourselves, we need to use **soy** in the singular and **somos** in the plural.

Soy **Paco Martínez.**	*I'm Paco Martínez.*
Soy **la señora Santos.**	*I'm Mrs Santos.*
Somos **los señores García**	*We're the Garcías.*

Notice also the use of **ser** when enquiring about someone or something.

¿Quién es **esa señorita?**   *Who's that young lady?*
¿Cuál es **el coche?**   *Which is the car?*

For the full forms of **ser**, see Unit 1.

3 DEFINITE ARTICLES (THE)

As we saw in Unit 1, all nouns in Spanish are either masculine or feminine and, as in English, there are singular and plural forms. Likewise, the definite article (*the*) has different forms, depending on the gender (masculine or feminine) and number (singular or plural) of the noun it qualifies.

el **hotel** (masc. sing.)   *the hotel*
la **habitación** (fem. sing.)   *the room*
los **hoteles** (masc. pl.)   *the hotels*
las **habitaciones** (fem. pl.)   *the rooms*

But before a feminine noun beginning with a stressed **a-** or **ha-**, we must use **el** and not **la**.

el **agua**   *water*
el **arte**   *art*
el **hambre**   *hunger*

The noun, however, is still feminine. Notice:

el agua fría   *cold water*
las aguas   *waters*
las artes marciales   *martial arts*

There is more on the use of the definite article in the **Grammar reference**.

4 *QUESTION WORDS* QUIÉN, CUÁL, QUÉ

To ask questions in order to identify people, places and things, we may need words such as **¿quién?** (*who?*), **¿cuál?** (*which?*, *what?*) and **¿qué?** (*what?*).

Quién – quiénes
Quién translates into English as *who*.

¿Quién **es aquel muchacho?**	*Who's that boy?*
¿Quién **es aquella muchacha?**	*Who's that girl?*

If we are referring to more than one person, we must use the plural form **quiénes** followed by the plural form of the verb.

¿Quiénes **son esas personas?**	*Who are those people?*
¿Quiénes **son esos niños?**	*Who are those children?*

Cuál – cuáles
The most usual translation of **cuál** into English is *which*.

¿Cuál **es la maleta?**	*Which is the suitcase?*
¿Cuál **es el equipaje?**	*Which is the luggage?*

The Spanish equivalent of *Which are ...?* is **¿Cuáles son ...?**.

¿Cuáles son **los billetes?**	*Which are the tickets?*
¿Cuáles son **las cartas?**	*Which are the letters?*

Notice also the use of **cuál – cuáles** in sentences where English would normally require the use of *what*.

¿Cuál **es el problema?**	*What's the problem?*
¿Cuáles **son las ventajas?**	*What are the advantages?*
¿Cuál **es tu dirección/email?**	*What's your address/e-mail?*
¿Cuál **es tu número de teléfono?**	*What's your telephone number?*

Qué
Qué translates normally as *what*.

¿Qué **es eso?**	*What's that?*
¿Qué **es esto?**	*What's this?*

But when it functions as an adjective, it sometimes translates as
which.

¿Qué **libro es?**	*Which book is it?*
¿Qué **habitación es?**	*Which room is it?*

Notice the use of the accent in all interrogative words: **¿quién?**,
¿cuál?, **¿qué?**, etc.

' 5 *POSSESSIVE ADJECTIVES* MI, TU, SU

The Spanish equivalent of *my* (as in *my friend*) is **mi**, which varies
in number, depending on whether the noun which follows is
singular or plural. There is no variation for masculine or feminine.

Esa es *mi* **amiga Isabel.**	*That is my friend Isabel.*
Estos son *mis* **amigos chilenos.**	*These are my Chilean friends.*

To say *your*, use **tu** (informal) or **su** (formal). Like **mi** above, **tu**
and **su** add an -s when followed by a plural noun.

¿Es ese *tu* **coche?**	*Is that your car?*
¿Son esas *sus* **llaves?**	*Are those your keys?*

Su/s also stands for *his/her/its*.

¿Cuál es *su* **email?**	*What's his/her e-mail?*
¿Cuáles son *sus* **libros?**	*Which are his/her books?*

For the full forms and usage of possessive adjectives and pronouns, see Unit 6.

6 OTHER WAYS OF INTRODUCING PEOPLE

Here are some alternative ways of introducing people:

Informal

Te presento a Juan.	*May I introduce Juan?*
¿Conoces a Ana?	*Do you know/Have you met Ana?*

Formal

Le presento a María.	*May I introduce María?*
¿Conoce Vd. a Isabel?	*Do you know/Have you met Isabel?*

Insight

Note the use of the preposition **a** after **presentar** *to introduce*. This use of **a** before the name of a person or a noun referring to a person, for example **mi marido/mujer** *my husband/wife*, is a special feature of Spanish, which is known technically as 'personal **a**'. Its use is explained in Unit 12.

In context

1 Study these conversations in which people are being introduced. The first exchange is informal; the second one is formal.

a Cristina	¿Qué tal, Isabel?
Isabel	Hola Cristina, ¿cómo estás?
Cristina	Bien, gracias. Esta es Gloria, mi amiga argentina.
Isabel	Hola.
Gloria	Hola.

¿Qué tal? *How are you? (informal)*
¿Cómo estás? *How are you? (informal)*
Bien, gracias. *Fine, thank you.*

b Señora Gómez	Buenas tardes, señor Ramos. ¿Cómo está Vd.?
Señor Ramos	Muy bien, ¿y Vd.?
Señora Gómez	Bien, gracias. Este es José, mi marido.
Señor Ramos	Mucho gusto, señor.
Señor Gómez	Encantado.

¿Cómo está Vd.? *How are you? (formal)*
Muy bien. *Very well.*

Insight

Spanish has two verbs meaning *to be*, **ser** and **estar**, which are clearly differentiated by native speakers. In this and the previous unit, you have become familiar with some of the uses of **ser**. **Estar** is used to indicate a state, as in **¿Cómo está usted?** *How are you?* (formal), but it has a number of other uses which are explained later in the course.

2 Getting to know people.

Rodolfo	¿Quién es aquella chica?
Alvaro	¿Cuál?
Rodolfo	Aquella chica de azul.
Alvaro	Esa es Marta. Es guapa, ¿eh?
Rodolfo	Sí, muy guapa.

de azul *in blue*
guapo/a *pretty, good looking*

Practice

1 Fill in the gaps in these sentences with suitable question words. Choose from the following: ¿qué?, ¿cuál/cuáles?, ¿quién/quiénes?

    a ¿__ es ese señor?
    b ¿__ es la idea?
    c ¿__ son esos chicos?
    d ¿__ es esto?
    e ¿__ es tu habitación?
    f ¿__ son las maletas?

2 Carmen is introducing her family to some friends. Fill in the gaps in the dialogue with suitable words and phrases.

Carmen	Hola José, ¿__?
José	Bien, gracias.
Carmen	Te __ a mi familia. __ es Juan, mi marido.
José	Mucho __.
Juan	Encantado.
Carmen	__ es Julia, mi hermana, y __ son mis hijos, Pablo y Luis.

TEST YOURSELF

1 *Add the correct ending to each of these demonstratives.*

   a Est__ es mi hermano Alberto, est__ es Sofía, est__ son mis padres y est__ son mis amigas Gloria y María.

   b – ¿Es es__ tu casa?

      – No, mi casa es aqu__.

   c – Perdone, ¿qué es est__?

      – Es una paella, un plato español.

   d – Por favor, ¿es es__ el autobús para Málaga?

      – No, el autobús para Málaga es aqu__.

2 *Fill in the blanks with* **el, la, los** *or* **las**.

   a __ pensión, __ tema, __ posibilidad

   b __ decisiones, __ gratitud, __ realismo

   c __ agua, __ artes, __ hambre

   d __ libertad, __ juventud, __ habitaciones

3 *Translate these sentences into Spanish.*

   a What's your e-mail, Mrs Rojas?

   b Which are your friends? (inf.)

   c Who is that lady?

      – She's my mother.

   d What's that?

      – These are my tickets.

These tests assess your knowledge of three important points: demonstratives, gender of nouns and question words. There aren't very many demonstratives and question words, so you should have got most of them right. If you did, you can now go on to Unit 3, in which you will learn how to describe people, places and things, and to talk about the weather.

3

Describing people, places and things

In this unit, you will learn how to:
- *describe people, places and things*
- *describe the weather*
- *ask what someone or something is like*

Language points
- **ser** *in descriptions*
- **estar** *in descriptions*
- *adjectives*
- *question word* **cómo**
- **hacer** *in descriptions of the weather*
- **tener** *in descriptions*

Key sentences

The key sentences and grammar notes which follow will show you how to use **ser** and **estar** (*to be*) in the description of people, places and things. You will also learn to talk about the weather using a construction with **hacer** (literally *to do, make*).

DESCRIBING PEOPLE, PLACES AND THINGS

Roberto es alto/simpático.	*Roberto is tall/nice.*
Las playas son buenas/limpias.	*The beaches are good/clean.*
La comida es excelente/abundante.	*The food is excellent/plentiful.*

DESCRIBING PEOPLE, PLACES AND THINGS AT A POINT IN TIME

Está muy guapa/elegante.	*She is/looks very pretty/elegant.*
La ciudad está sucia/fea.	*The city is/looks dirty/ugly.*
Esta leche/carne no está buena.	*This milk/meat is off.*

DESCRIBING THE WEATHER

Hace (mucho/un poco de) frío/calor.	*It's (very/a little) cold/warm.*

ASKING WHAT SOMEONE OR SOMETHING IS LIKE

¿Cómo es el personal/hotel?	*What's the staff/hotel like?*
¿Cómo es el tiempo/clima?	*What's the weather/climate like?*

Insight

In Unit 2, you learned to ask people how they are by saying **¿Cómo está/s?** *How are you?*, in which **estar** is used for enquiring about a state. To ask what someone or something is like, you use **ser** instead of **estar**. Compare these two sentences:

¿Cómo está tu novio/a?	*How is your boy/girlfriend?*
¿Cómo es tu novio/a?	*What is your boy/girlfriend like?*

Grammar summary

1 SER *AND* ESTAR *(TO BE)*

There are two ways of saying *to be* in Spanish – **ser** and **estar** – and the uses of each are clearly differentiated by the native speaker, as you will see from the explanations and examples that follow. See also the **Grammar reference**.

2 SER *USED IN DESCRIPTION*

Ser is the verb most frequently used in description. In this context, it is generally used with adjectives which refer to:

a Characteristics which are considered as permanent, e.g. physical and mental characteristics.

Víctor es **delgado.**	*Victor is thin.*
Mercedes es **inteligente.**	*Mercedes is intelligent.*

b Characteristics which, although subjective, may be considered as true by the speaker.

El español es **fácil.**	*Spanish is easy.*
El árabe es **difícil.**	*Arabic is difficult.*

c Characteristics which are considered as universal.

La Tierra es **redonda.**	*The Earth is round.*
El oro es **un metal.**	*Gold is a metal.*

d Certain states or conditions such as **inocente** *innocent*, **culpable** *guilty*, **pobre** *poor*, **feliz** *happy*, **desgraciado** *unhappy*.

Ella es **inocente.**	*She's innocent.*
Ellos son **felices.**	*They're happy.*
Son **países pobres.**	*They're poor countries.*

For other uses of **ser**, see Units 5, 6 and 11 and the **Grammar reference**.

3 ESTAR *USED IN DESCRIPTION*

Estar is not normally used in description, except with adjectives which refer to a state or condition.

Cecilia está **triste.**   *Cecilia is (looks) sad.*
Ricardo está **contento.**   *Ricardo is happy.*

Estar is also found in sentences with adjectives which refer to a state or condition which is the result of an action.

¿Está **listo/a?**   *Is it ready?*
Está **terminado/a.**   *It is finished.*
Están **bebidos/as.**   *They are tipsy* (literally, *drunk*).

Forms such as **terminado** and **bebido** are known as *past participles* which, as in the examples above, can function as adjectives (see section 4 below). To form the past participle, add **-ado** to the stem of **-ar** verbs and **-ido** to that of **-er** and **-ir** verbs. You will find more on the use of past participles in Units 11 and 17.

Some adjectives may be used with either **ser** or **estar**. Ser refers to the nature of what is being described, while **estar** denotes a state or condition at a particular point in time.

Jorge es elegante.   *Jorge is elegant. (always)*
Jorge está elegante.   *Jorge is (looks) elegant. (now)*
Mónica es guapa.   *Mónica is pretty. (general characteristic)*

Mónica está guapa.   *Mónica is (looks) pretty. (now)*

It is not correct to say – as some textbooks do – that **ser** always refers to permanent characteristics, while **estar** refers to states which are transitory. The following examples contradict that rule:

Mi madre está muerta.   *My mother is dead.*
Cádiz está en Andalucía.   *Cadiz is in Andalusia.*

Present tense of **estar**
Here is **estar** fully conjugated in the present tense.

Singular	Plural
estoy *I am*	**estamos** *we are*
estás *you are* (fam.)	**estáis** *you are* (fam.)
está *you are* (pol.)	**están** *you are* (pol.)
he/she/it is	*they are*

Insight

The informal plural form **estáis** is not used in the Spanish-speaking countries of Latin America, where **están** is used in both formal and informal address: **¿Por qué están tan enfadados?** *Why are you so annoyed?*

For other uses of **estar**, see Units 5 and 8 and the **Grammar reference**.

4 ADJECTIVES

To be able to describe things, you need adjectives. In Spanish, we can distinguish the following types of adjectives.

• ADJECTIVES WHICH AGREE IN NUMBER AND GENDER WITH THE NOUN

Most Spanish adjectives fall into this category; within this group, we have most of those ending in -o, for example **bajo** *short*. Adjectives ending in -ol, -or, -és and -uz – for example **español** Spanish, **trabajador** *hard-working*, **francés** *French*, **andaluz** *Andalusian* – also fall into this group.

These adjectives form the feminine by changing -o into -a (e.g. **pequeño**, **pequeña** *small*) or by adding -a to the consonant (e.g. **encantador**, **encantadora** *enchanting*). The plural is formed by adding -s to the vowel (e.g. **pequeños**) or -es to the consonant (e.g. **encantadores**).

• ADJECTIVES WHICH AGREE ONLY IN NUMBER

Within this group are most adjectives ending in a consonant, for example **fácil** *easy*, **azul** *blue*, **feliz** *happy*. Other adjectives in this category are those ending in -a (e.g. **hipócrita** *hypocritical*) and -e (e.g. **grande** *big*).

To form the plural, add -s to the final vowel (e.g. **grande** – **grandes**) or **-es** to the consonant (e.g. **fácil** – **fáciles**). But if the word ends in **-z**, change the **z** to **c** and then add **-es** (e.g. **feliz** – **felices**).

• ADJECTIVES WHICH ARE INVARIABLE
A few adjectives do not change for number or gender. Among these, we find some adjectives describing colour, especially those which may also function as nouns. Examples of these are **naranja** *orange*, **violeta** *violet* and **rosa** *pink, rose*.

Agreement of adjectives
As a general rule, in the presence of one or more masculine nouns, use the masculine form of the adjective, e.g. **libros y periódicos españoles** *Spanish books and newspapers*.

In the presence of one or more feminine nouns, use the feminine form of the adjective, e.g. **escuelas y universidades americanas** *American schools and universities*.

If there are nouns of different gender, you will need to use the masculine form of the adjective, e.g. **hombres y mujeres mexicanos** *Mexican men and women*.

Short forms
A few adjectives have short forms: **grande** *large, big* shortens to **gran** before a masculine or feminine singular noun.

un coche grande	*a big car*
un gran **coche**	*a big car*
una ciudad grande	*a big city*
una gran **ciudad**	*a big city*

When **grande** precedes the noun, it often translates into English as *great*.

un gran **hombre**	*a great man*
una gran **mentira**	*a great lie*

Bueno *good* and **malo** *bad* drop the ending -o when they come before a masculine noun.

un libro *bueno*	*a good book*
un *buen* **libro**	*a good book*
un día *malo*	*a bad day*
un *mal* **día**	*a bad day*

Other adjectives in this category, whose position is normally before the noun are: **santo** *saint* (**San Juan** *Saint John*); **primero** *first* (**primer día** *first day*); **tercero** *third* (**tercer piso** *third floor*); **ninguno** *none* (**ningún problema** *no problem*). If the accompanying noun is feminine, use the full form: **Santa Ana** *Saint Ana*, **primera vez** *first time*, etc.

Intensive forms

To intensify the meaning of a descriptive adjective, we can add to it the suffix **-ísimo** (masculine) or **-ísima** (feminine). Adjectives which end in a vowel must drop the vowel before adding **-ísimo/a**. See what happens to **difícil** *difficult*, **caro** *expensive* and **sabroso** *tasty*.

Es dificil*ísimo.*	*It's very difficult.*
Es carís*imo.*	*It's very expensive.*
La comida está sabros*ísima.*	*The food is very tasty.*

Notice the following spelling changes when adding **-ísimo/a**.

▶ Adjectives which end in **-co** *(e.g.* **rico** *rich)* change the **c** to **qu** before adding this suffix.

   Él es ri*qu***ísimo.**   *He's very rich.*

▶ Adjectives which end in **-ble** (e.g. **amable** *kind)* change **-ble** into **-bil** before adding **-ísimo**.

   Ella es ama*bil***ísima.**   *She's very kind.*

As there are a number of adjectives which cannot take -ísimo/a, it is best not to use this suffix if you're not sure. Instead, you can use an intensifier such as **muy** *very*, **demasiado** *too* or **bastante** *quite*.

Es *muy* **barato.**	*It's very cheap.*
Está *demasiado* **caliente.**	*It's too hot.*
Él es *bastante* **raro.**	*He's quite strange.*

Position of adjectives
Adjectives often follow the noun they describe.

Es un problema *difícil.*	*It's a difficult problem.*
Es una chica *alta.*	*She's a tall girl.*

Descriptive adjectives are sometimes placed before the noun to show emphasis, affection or some other desired effect.

Es una *buena* **idea.**	*It's a good idea.*
Es una *pequeña* **casa.**	*It's a small house.*

Insight

The position of an adjective, either following or preceding the noun it qualifies, may change its sense or meaning. Among these, we find **grande** (see example under Short forms above); **pobre: un hombre pobre** *a poor man* (not rich), **¡Pobre hombre!** *Poor man!*; **nuevo: un coche nuevo** *a new car*, **un nuevo coche** *another car*; **solo: una persona sola** *a lonely person*, **una sola persona** *only one person*; **viejo: un amigo viejo** *an old (aged) friend*, **un viejo amigo** *an old (long-standing) friend*.

For comparison of adjectives, see the **Grammar reference**.

5 *QUESTION WORD* CÓMO

Cómo normally translates into English as *how*, as in questions enquiring about the state or condition of someone or something.

| ¿Cómo **está Fernando?** | *How's Fernando?* |
| ¿Cómo **están ellos?** | *How are they?* |

But in questions asking what someone or something is like, **cómo** translates into English as *what*.

| ¿Cómo **es Fernando?** | *What's Fernando like?* |
| ¿Cómo **son ellos?** | *What are they like?* |

To enquire about a state or condition, use **estar**; to ask questions regarding characteristics, use **ser**.

6 HACER *IN DESCRIPTIONS OF THE WEATHER*

To describe the weather, Spanish normally uses the verb **hacer** (literally, *to do*, *make*) in the third person singular plus a noun.

Hace **(mucho) frío.**	*It's (very) cold.*
Hace **(demasiado) calor.**	*It's (too) hot.*
Hace **(un poco de) viento.**	*It's (a little) windy.*

....
Insight
To ask what the weather is like, use phrases like the following: **¿Hace frío?** *Is it cold?*, **¿Qué tiempo hace en julio?** *What's the weather like in July?*, **¿Cómo está el tiempo?** *What's the weather like?* or simply **¿Qué tal el tiempo?** *What is/was the weather like?*, in which the verb is understood.
....

7 OTHER WAYS OF DESCRIBING THE WEATHER

Although the weather is normally described with **hacer**, e.g. **Hoy hace calor** *Today it's warm*, the climate in general may be described with **ser** *to be* or **tener** *to have*.

| **El clima es (muy) caluroso/frío.** | *The climate is (very) hot/cold.* |
| **Tiene un clima húmedo/**
templado. | *It has a wet/mild climate.* |

In the following expressions, **estar** is used for describing the weather at a particular point in time.

Hoy está **nublado/cubierto.**	*Today it's cloudy/overcast.*
Está **lloviendo/nevando.**	*It's raining/snowing.*

Note also the use of **llover** *to rain* in **Llueve mucho** *It's raining a lot.*

8 TENER *IN DESCRIPTION*

Another verb often used in description is **tener** *to have*: **tiene** *you have, he/she/it has*, **tienen** *you/they have*.

Ella tiene ojos verdes/el cabello largo.	*She has green eyes/long hair.*
Esta ciudad tiene mucho encanto.	*This city has a lot of charm.*

For the full forms of **tener**, see Units 4 and 6.

9 *DESCRIBING THINGS IN TERMS OF THE MATERIAL THEY ARE MADE OF*

Es de madera/metal.	*It's made of wood/metal.*
Son de lana.	*They're made of wool.*
Es de plata/oro.	*It's silver/gold.*

In context

1 Describing someone.

A ¿Quién es ese señor?
B Es el nuevo profesor de español.
A ¿Cómo es?

B Es simpático, pero es muy estricto.
A ¿Es un buen profesor?
B Sí, es un profesor excelente.

nuevo *new*
estricto *strict*

QV

2 Read this extract from an e-mail describing a place.

Querido Jorge,

Esta es mi primera visita a Cadaqués. Es un lugar precioso y el hotel es estupendo, aunque es un poco caro. Hace muchísimo calor ...

mi primera visita *my first visit*
un lugar precioso *a very nice place*
aunque *although*

QV

Notice the position of the ordinal number **primera: Esta es mi primera visita a Cadaqués.** Ordinal numbers normally precede the noun they qualify.

_____

Practice

1 Can you describe each of the following? Use full sentences and appropriate adjectives from the list.

elegante	gordo
delgado	bajo
alto	triste
redondo	limpio

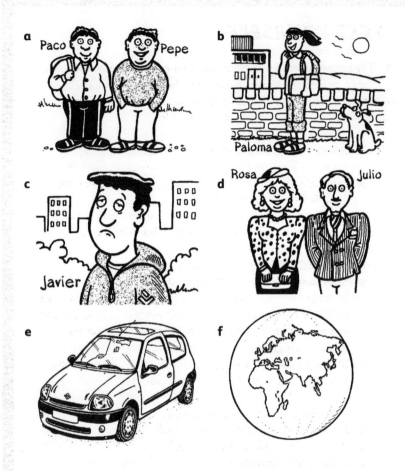

2 In an e-mail to a Spanish-speaking friend, you describe a town you are visiting for the first time. Use the following phrases and an appropriate verb from the list to write a paragraph about the place.

estar ser tener hacer
una ciudad muy bonita   la gente muy simpática y el clima
bastante bueno   no demasiado calor   el hotel excelente
un restaurante muy bueno y dos bares   también una playa
estupenda   (yo) muy contento/a aquí

Now try describing your own town.

TEST YOURSELF

1 *Fill in the gaps with the correct form of either* **ser** *or* **estar**.
  a Carmen __ muy sociable, pero hoy __ enfadada.
  b La comida en este restaurante normalmente __ muy
    buena, pero esta paella __ horrible.
  c ¿Cómo __ tu jefe?
    Mi jefe no __ muy simpático, pero mis colegas sí,
    ellos __ simpatiquísimos. (Yo) __ muy contenta aquí.
  d Su casa no __ muy grande, pero __ bastante cómoda,
    aunque hoy no __ muy limpia.

2 *Complete each sentence with the adjective in brackets,*
changing the ending where appropriate.
  a El chino y el japonés son bastante __ (difícil).
  b Esta novela de García Márquez es muy __ (bueno).
    Es un muy __ (bueno) libro. Él es un __ (grande) escritor.
  c La ciudad es __ (precioso), las playas son __ (estupendo)
    y la gente muy __ (amable), pero los hoteles son un
    poco __ (caro).
  d María y Pablo no son __ (español), son __ (mexicano).
    María es una persona __ (encantador).

3 *Translate these sentences into Spanish.*
  a It's cold today and it's a little windy.
  b What's the weather like in Chile?
  c It has a mild climate.
  d It's very warm today, isn't it?

Don't be discouraged if you encountered difficulties with
question 1. The uses of **ser** and **estar** will come up again in later
units. A summary of their main uses will be found in the **Grammar
reference**. If you are satisfied with your performance in the tests, go
on with your course. Otherwise check the relevant sections of this
unit again.

4

Expressing existence and availability

In this unit, you will learn how to:
- *express existence*
- *express availability*
- *express quantity*

Language points
- **hay**
- **tener** *in the present tense*
- *indefinite articles*
- **cuánto**
- **alguien** *and* **nadie**
- **alguno** *and* **ninguno**
- **algo** *and* **nada**
- *other verbs expressing existence and availability*

Key sentences

This unit focuses on the use of **hay** *there is/are, is/are there?* for expressing existence, and the use of **tener** *to have* to express availability.

Have a look at these key sentences and their English translations before going on to the **Grammar summary**.

EXPRESSING EXISTENCE

¿*Hay* **un/algún banco por aquí?**	*Is there a bank around here?*
Hay **uno en la esquina.**	*There's one on the corner.*
No *hay* **ninguno.**	*There aren't any./There isn't one.*
¿*Hay* **una/alguna farmacia cerca?**	*Is there a chemist's nearby?*
Hay **dos en la calle Mayor.**	*There are two on the high street.*
No *hay* **ninguna.**	*There aren't any./There isn't one.*

EXPRESSING AVAILABILITY

¿*Tienen* **una habitación para esta noche?**	*Have you got a room for tonight?*
Tenemos **una doble solamente.**	*We only have a double.*
¿*Tiene* **un coche para el fin de semana?**	*Have you got a car for the weekend?*
En este momento no *tengo* **ningún coche.**	*At the moment, I don't have any cars.*

EXPRESSING QUANTITY

¿Cuántos coches/Cuántas personas *hay*?	*How many cars/people are there?*
Hay **tres solamente.**	*There are only three.*
¿Cuánto dinero *tienes*?	*How much money have you got?*
Tengo **cien euros.**	*I have 100 euros.*

Grammar summary

1 HAY *(THERE IS/ARE, IS/ARE THERE?)*

To say *there is/are* and *is/are there?*, Spanish uses the single word **hay**. In negative sentences, **no** precedes the word **hay**.

¿*Hay* **un hotel por aquí?**	*Is there a hotel around here?*
Hay **uno/dos.**	*There is/are one/two.*

¿Hay **alguno?**	*Is there one?*
No *hay* **ninguno.**	· *There aren't any.*

Insight

Hay is the third person of the present tense of **haber,** one of whose functions is to express existence, as in the examples above. **Hay,** like **habrá** *there will be,* **había** *there was/were,* etc., can only be used in the singular, even when the word it refers to is in the plural: **Había muchas personas** *There were a lot of people.* For the use of **alguno** and **ninguno,** see paragraph 7 below.

2 TENER *(TO HAVE)*

One of several functions of **tener** *to have* is the expression of availability. **Tener** is irregular in the first person singular of the present tense, but it is also a stem-changing verb: the **e** of the stem **ten-** changes into **ie** in the second and third person singular and third person plural.

Singular		Plural	
tengo	*I have*	**tenemos**	*we have*
tienes	*you have (fam.)*	**tenéis**	*you have (fam.)*
tiene	*you have (pol.)*	**tienen**	*you have (pol.)*
	he/she/it has		*they have*

¿*Tiene* **Vd. cambio?**	*Have you got any change?*
Lo siento, no *tengo.*	*I'm sorry, I haven't.*
¿*Tienen* **Vds. una habitación individual/doble?**	*Have you got a single/double room?*
Sí, *tenemos.*	*Yes, we have.*

Insight

As in English, **tener** *to have* is also used to express possession: **Tiene una casa muy bonita** *He/She has a very beautiful house,* **No tengo coche** *I haven't got a car* (see Unit 6, paragraph 4). It is also used in a number of expressions in which English uses *to be*: **¿Cuántos años tienes?** *How old are you?*, **Tengo 30 (años)** *I'm 30 (years old)*, **Tengo frío/calor/ sed/hambre** *I'm cold/hot/thirsty/hungry*, etc.

3 INDEFINITE ARTICLES (A/AN)

The word for *a* is **un** for masculine nouns and **una** for feminine nouns.

Masculine

¿Hay un **supermercado por aquí?** *Is there a supermarket around here?*
No, pero hay un **mercado.** *No, but there's a market.*

Feminine

¿Tienes una **cerveza fría?** *Have you got a cold beer?*
¿Tiene Vd. una **mesa?** *Have you got a table?*

The plural forms **unos, unas** are translated into English as *some*.

unos **restaurantes** *some restaurants*
unas **habitaciones** *some rooms*

Spanish does not use the equivalent of English *a* when you indicate your own or someone else's occupation (see Unit 1).

Paco es camarero. *Paco is a waiter.*
Yo soy recepcionista. *I'm a receptionist.*

Insight

Note also that Spanish does not use the indefinite article after **medio/a** *half* or *before* **otro/a** *another (one)*: **medio kilo** *half a kilo*, **media docena** *half a dozen*, **otro día** *another day*.

4 QUESTION WORD CUÁNTO

¿Cuánto? agrees in number (singular and plural) and gender (masculine and feminine) with the noun it refers to.

¿Cuánto **tiempo tenemos?**	*How much time have we got?*
¿Cuánta **fruta hay?**	*How much fruit is there?*
¿Cuántos **invitados hay?**	*How many guests are there?*
¿Cuántas **personas hay?**	*How many people are there?*

¿**Cuánto?** may replace a noun when this is understood.

¿Cuántos **libros hay?**	*How many books are there?*
¿Cuántos **hay?**	*How many are there?*
¿Cuánta **gente hay?**	*How many people are there?*
¿Cuánta **hay?**	*How many are there?*

Here are some words and phrases which may be used in reply to the question ¿**cuánto/s?.**

Hay **mucho/a/un poco.**	*There is a lot/a little.*
Hay **muchos/as/pocos/as.**	*There are many/a few.*
Hay **muchísimos/as/** poquísimos/as.	*There are many/very few.*
Hay **suficiente(s).**	*There is/are enough.*
Hay **bastante(s).**	*There is/are plenty.*

5 ALGUIEN *(SOMEBODY/SOMEONE, ANYBODY/ANYONE)*

Alguien is an invariable pronoun which is used in positive and interrogative sentences.

¿**Hay** alguien **allí?**	*Is there anyone there?*
Hay alguien **en la puerta.**	*There's someone at the door.*
Alguien **llama.**	*Someone's calling.*

6 NADIE *(NOBODY/NO ONE)*

Nadie is a negative word which may follow the verb in a double negative construction, as in:

Allí no hay nadie.	*There's nobody there.*
En la puerta no hay nadie.	*There's nobody at the door.*

Nadie may also precede the verb, acting as the subject of a sentence.

Nadie **tiene fuego.**	*No one has a light.*
Nadie **tiene tiempo.**	*No one has time.*

Notice that in this construction, the negative **no** must be omitted.

7 ALGUNO *(SOME/ANY)*

Alguno varies in gender and number according to the noun it modifies (acting as an adjective) or the noun it refers to (acting as a pronoun). Its forms are **algún, alguno, algunos, alguna, algunas**. **Algún** is used before a singular masculine noun.

¿Hay *algún* **banco por aquí?**	*Is there a bank around here?*
¿Hay *algún* **museo en la ciudad?**	*Is there a museum in the city?*

Alguno/s, alguna/s
¿Tiene Vd. *alguno*?	*Have you got any?*
Tenemos *algunos* **billetes solamente.**	*We only have a few tickets.*
Ya hay *algunas* **personas en la reunión.**	*There are already some people at the meeting*

In singular sentences, **algún, alguno, alguna** may be replaced by **uno/a**.

¿Hay *algún* **café por aquí?**	*Is there a café around here?*
¿Hay *un* **café por aquí?**	*Is there a café around here?*

8 NINGUNO *(NO/ANY/NONE/NOBODY)*

Ninguno is a negative word which normally occurs in the singular as **ningún** (before masculine nouns), **ninguno** or **ninguna**. This negative word may follow the verb in a double negative construction.

No hay *ningún* **bar.**	*There isn't a bar.*
No hay *ninguno.*	*There isn't one/any.*
No tenemos *ninguna* **reserva.**	*We have no reservation.*
No tenemos *ninguna.*	*We don't have one/any.*

Ninguno may sometimes precede the verb.

| *Ningún* **banco tiene cajero** **automático.** | *No bank has a cashpoint.* |
| *Ninguno* **tiene cajero automático.** | *None of them has a cashpoint.* |

Insight

Note the use of 'personal **a**' (Unit 12) before **alguien, nadie** and **alguno, ninguno**, when they refer to people, in sentences like these:

| **¿Conoces a alguien/alguno** **de ellos?** | *Do you know anyone/any* *of them?* |
| **No conozco a nadie/ninguno** **de ellos.** | *I don't know anyone/any* *of them.* |

9 ALGO *(SOME/ANY/SOMETHING/ANYTHING)*

Algo is an invariable pronoun which normally follows the verb.

Hay *algo* **de dinero.**	*There is some money.*
¿Hay *algo* **de comer?**	*Is there anything/something to eat?*
¿Necesitas *algo*?	*Do you need anything/something?*

10 NADA *(NOTHING/ANY)*

Nada is a negative word which normally follows the verb in a double negative construction.

No tengo *nada* **de dinero.**	*I haven't got any money.*
No hay *nada* **de carne.**	*There isn't any meat.*
No hay *nada.*	*There is nothing.*

Note the use of **de** *of* before the noun in the first two examples, literally *nothing of money/meat*.

Insight

Other common negative words worth learning at this stage are: **nunca** *never*, **tampoco** *neither, not either*, **ni ... ni** *neither ... nor*: **Nunca hay tiempo para eso** *There's never any time for that*, **Aquí tampoco tienen habitaciones** *They don't have any rooms here either*, **No hace ni frío ni calor** *It's neither cold nor warm*.

11 *OTHER VERBS EXPRESSING EXISTENCE AND AVAILABILITY*

Existence and availability may also be expressed with **existir** *to exist*, **contar con** *to have* and **disponer de** *to have*. Overall, these are less frequent than **hay** and **tener**, and tend to be used in more formal contexts.

En Madrid *existen* **buenos museos.**	*In Madrid there are good museums.*
¿*Con* **cuánto dinero contamos?**	*How much money do we have?*
No *disponen de* **tiempo.**	*They don't have time.*

In context

1 Study this conversation between a tourist and a hotel receptionist.

Recepcionista	Buenos días.
Turista	Buenos días. ¿Tiene alguna habitación?
Recepcionista	¿Para cuántas personas?
Turista	Para dos.
Recepcionista	¿Para cuántas noches?
Turista	Para cuatro noches.
Recepcionista	Tenemos una interior solamente. Exterior no tenemos ninguna.

para *for*
una (habitación) interior *a room at the back*
una (habitación) exterior *a room facing the street*

2 Read this text describing the facilities available at a hotel.

El Hotel Don Carlos es un hotel de cuatro estrellas. El hotel tiene cien habitaciones dobles, treinta individuales y cuatro suites. Todas las habitaciones tienen baño privado, teléfono y televisión.

En el Hotel Don Carlos hay tres restaurantes y dos bares. También hay una piscina muy grande y una sauna. El hotel tiene aparcamiento propio para los clientes. Además, hay una sala de convenciones muy cómoda y moderna para trescientas personas.

todos/as *all*
el baño privado *private bathroom*
propio/a *own*
además *besides*
una sala de convenciones *a conference room*

Notice the use of **para** in the following phrases:

para dos personas	*for two people*
para cuatro noches	*for four nights*
para los clientes	*for the clients*
para 300 personas	*for 300 people*

Practice

1 You have just arrived in a Spanish-speaking town and you want to find out about some of the facilities in and around the hotel where you are staying.

    a Ask if the hotel has a restaurant.
    b Ask if there is a swimming pool.

c A couple of friends are arriving today, so ask the receptionist if he has a double room.

d Ask if the hotel has a car park.

e Ask if there is a supermarket nearby.

f Ask if there are museums in the town.

2 You are describing your own town and your neighbourhood to a Spanish-speaking acquaintance. Say what places of interest there are and what facilities you can find. Look up new words in your dictionary if necessary.

Ejemplo: **Hay un museo de arte.**

3 You have been visiting friends at the house below and, on your return home, you describe this in a letter to a Spanish-speaking friend. Fill in the gaps with **hay** or the correct form of **ser** or **tener**, as appropriate. More than one form may be correct in some cases.

La casa de Laura y José (1) .... muy agradable, y (2) .... unas vistas espectaculares. La casa no (3) .... demasiado grande, (4) .... tres habitaciones solamente, pero (5) .... muy cómoda. En el salón (6) .... una biblioteca con algunos libros muy interesantes, y (7) .... un cuadro moderno muy bueno. En el dormitorio (ellos) (8) .... una pequeña colección de libros en inglés.

José (9) .... un excelente cocinero y la casa (10) .... una cocina muy bien equipada. Laura prefiere el jardín y ella (11) .... un jardín precioso.

La ciudad (12) .... pequeña, pero (13) .... algunos museos muy buenos y una catedral muy bonita. El museo principal (14) .... una buena colección de pintura española.

unas vistas *views*
una biblioteca *bookshelf*
un cuadro *picture*
un(a) cocinero/a *cook*
prefiere *she prefers (from* **preferir***)*
la pintura *painting*
el dormitorio *bedroom*

TEST YOURSELF

1 *Fill the gaps with the appropriate form of* **tener.**

   a – ¿__ (tú) tiempo para un café?

      – Perdona, pero no __ (yo) tiempo. Estoy muy ocupado.

   b – ¿__ (ustedes) un coche disponible (*available*) para mañana?

      – No __ (nosotros) ninguno.

   c – ¿Cuánto equipaje (*luggage*) __ (vosotros)?

      – __ (nosotros) una maleta solamente.

   d – El hotel Astoria __ una gran piscina y todas las habitaciones __ aire acondicionado.

2 *Fill in the gaps with the appropriate form of* **algo, alguien, alguno, nada, nadie** *or* **ninguno.**

   a – Perdone, hay __ restaurante por aquí?

      – No, por aquí no hay __.

   b – ¿Hay __ gasolinera cerca?

      – No, no hay __.

   c – ¿Hay __ de comer en la nevera (*fridge*)?

      – No hay __.

   d – ¿Hay __ en casa?

      – No hay __, la familia está de vacaciones (*on holiday*).

3 *Translate the dialogues into Spanish.*

   a – How much money do you have? (inf., sing.)

      – I have nothing.

   b – How many people are there?

      – There aren't many.

   c – How much petrol do we have?

      – We have plenty.

   d – How many guests are there?

      – There are very few.

Tener, like *to have* in English, is an important verb, so make sure you got the answers to question 1 right before you continue. The constructions in questions 2 and 3 are no less important. For a revision of *there is/are*, go back to paragraph 1. For the Spanish equivalent of *some, any, somebody, anybody*, etc., see paragraphs 5–10.

5

Expressing location

In this unit, you will learn how to:
- *ask and say where a place or a thing is*
- *ask and say how far a place is*
- *ask and say where an event is taking place*

Language points
- **dónde**
- **estar** *to indicate position and distance*
- **ser** *to say where an event is taking place*
- *words and phrases denoting position and distance*

Key sentences

To say where something or someone is or how far a place is, Spanish normally uses the verb **estar** *to be*.

To say where an event is taking place, you need to use **ser** *to be*.

To learn more about this, look at the key sentences and the grammar notes which follow.

ASKING AND SAYING WHERE A PLACE OR A THING IS

¿Dónde está el banco?　　*Where is the bank?*
Está en la esquina.　　*It's on the corner.*

| ¿Dónde están las llaves? | *Where are the keys?* |
| Están en la mesa. | *They are on the table.* |

ASKING AND SAYING HOW FAR A PLACE IS

¿A qué distancia está Toledo?	*How far is Toledo?*
Está a setenta kilómetros.	*It's 70 kilometres away.*
¿Está muy lejos el museo?	*Is the museum very far?*
Está cerca, a cinco minutos de aquí.	*It's nearby, five minutes from here.*

ASKING AND SAYING WHERE AN EVENT IS TAKING PLACE

¿Dónde es la fiesta?	*Where is the party?*
Es en casa de Fernando.	*It's at Fernando's house.*
¿Dónde son los cursos de español?	*Where are the Spanish courses?*
Son en la universidad.	*They are at the university.*

Grammar summary

1 *USING* ESTAR *TO ASK AND GIVE INFORMATION ABOUT POSITION AND DISTANCE*

a To ask where a place or a thing is, you can use **dónde** *where*, followed by **estar** *to be*, followed by the third person singular or plural.

¿Dónde está **el hotel?**	*Where is the hotel?*
¿Dónde está **la catedral?**	*Where is the cathedral?*
¿Dónde están **los teléfonos?**	*Where are the telephones?*

....

Insight
In questions, ¿dónde? must be written with an accent.
Without an accent, it is used in sentences like the following:
No tiene donde vivir *He/She has nowhere to live*, **Esta es la**

(Contd)

empresa donde trabajo *This is the company where I work.*
A word derived from **¿dónde?** is **¿adónde?**, which indicates
movement towards a place, not position: **¿Adónde vas?**
Where are you going to?

b To say where a place or a thing is, use **estar** followed by a
prepositional phrase – for example **al lado de la estación** *next
to the station*, **enfrente del museo** *opposite the museum* – or an
adverb such as **allí** *there*, **arriba** *upstairs*, etc.

El hotel *está al lado de* **la estación.**	*The hotel is next to the station.*
La catedral *está allí, enfrente del* **museo.**	*The cathedral is there, opposite the museum.*
Los teléfonos **están arriba.**	*The telephones are upstairs.*

Insight

To say where *you* are, use sentences like the following: **Estoy
en casa de mi hermano** *I'm at my brother's house*, **Estamos
de vacaciones en París** *We're on holiday in Paris*. To ask
people where they are, as you might do when calling a mobile
phone, you can say: **¿Dónde estás/estáis?** *Where are you?*
(fam., sing./pl.).

c To ask how far a place is, use phrases like the following:

¿A qué distancia *está(n)*?	*How far is it/are they?*
¿Está(n) **cerca/lejos?**	*Is it/Are they near/far?*
¿A cuántos kilómetros de aquí *está(n)*?	*How many kilometres from here is it/are they?*

d To say how far a place is, use **estar** followed by the preposition
a and an expression indicating distance, or by the words **cerca** or
lejos.

Está(n) **a cinco minutos/una hora.**	*It is/They are five minutes/an hour away.*
Está(n) **a sólo doscientos metros.**	*It is/They are only 200 metres away.*

Está(n) **muy cerca/bastante lejos.**　　*It is/They are very near/ quite far.*

2 USING SER TO ASK AND SAY WHERE AN EVENT IS TAKING PLACE

To ask where an event is taking place, you can use **dónde** followed by **ser** to be.

¿Dónde es **la reunión?**　　*Where is the meeting?*
¿Dónde son **las clases?**　　*Where are the classes?*

To say where an event is taking place, use **ser** and a phrase indicating a venue.

La reunión *es* **en el salón de reuniones.**　　*The meeting is in the conference room.*
Las clases *son* **en el aula número dos.**　　*The classes are in classroom number two.*

Insight

The use of **ser** to indicate a venue is fairly common in Spanish. In formal contexts, especially in writing, you will find alternative verbs such as **tener lugar** to take place, **realizarse** *to take place, carry out:* **La boda tendrá lugar este sábado** *The wedding will take place this Saturday,* **La ceremonia se realizará al mediodía** *The ceremony will take place/be carried out at midday.*

See also paragraph 15 of the **Grammar reference**.

3 WORDS AND PHRASES USED FOR INDICATING POSITION AND DISTANCE

To indicate position, you need adverbs – e.g. **dentro** *inside*, **delante** *in front* – or a prepositional phrase (a preposition + an adverb or a noun) – e.g. **dentro de la casa** *inside the house*, **delante del teatro** *in front of the theatre*.

a Adverbs of place (*here, there, inside*, etc.)

Some common adverbs of place are: **aquí** *here*, **ahí** *there*, **allí** *there*, **dentro** *inside*, **fuera** *outside*, **arriba** *up/upstairs*, **abajo** *down/downstairs*, **cerca** *near*, **lejos** *far*, **delante** *in front*.

La obra de teatro es *aquí*.	*The play is here.*
Tu pasaporte está *ahí/allí*.	*Your passport is there.*
El perro está *dentro*.	*The dog is inside.*
El taxi ya está *fuera*.	*The taxi is already outside.*
El baño está *arriba/abajo*.	*The bathroom is upstairs/downstairs.*
El parque está *cerca/lejos*.	*The park is near/far.*
Antonio está *delante*.	*Antonio is in front.*

Insight

Ahí indicates closer proximity than **allí**. Two other adverbs of this kind are **acá** *here* and **allá** *there*, which are generally more common in Latin America than the alternative words **aquí** and **allí**. In Spain, **acá** and **allá** are felt to be more imprecise, although you will hear them used with the word **más** *more* in **más acá** and **más allá**, especially with verbs of movement: **Muévelo más acá/allá** *Move it this way/further away*.

b Prepositions and prepositional phrases (*in, on, at, next to*, etc.)

Examples of single prepositions indicating position are: **bajo** *underneath*, **contra** *against*, **en** *in, on, at*, **entre** *between*, **sobre** *on, on top of*. Among prepositional phrases indicating position, there are the following: **al lado de** *next to*, **a la izquierda** *on the left*, **a la derecha** *on the right*, **al final de** *at the end of*, **al fondo de** *at the back of*, **cerca de** *near*, **lejos de** *far*, **debajo de** *underneath*, **encima de** *on top of/above*, **delante de** *in front of*, **detrás de** *behind*, **dentro de** *inside*, **fuera de** *outside*, **enfrente de/frente a** *opposite*, **por aquí** *nearby*.

Está *al lado de* **mi casa,** *a la derecha/izquierda*.	*It's next to my house, on the right/left.*
Están *al final/fondo* **del pasillo.**	*They are at the end of the corridor.*
Está *debajo de/bajo* **la mesa.**	*It's under/underneath the table.*

Está *contra/en* **la pared.**	*It's against/on the wall.*
Están *entre* **el colegio y la iglesia.**	*They're between the school and the church.*
Está *sobre/en* **la silla.**	*It's on the chair.*
Está *delante/detrás* **del cine.**	*It's in front of/behind the cinema.*
Están *enfrente de* **la plaza.**	*They are opposite the square.*

To indicate distance, use words and expressions like **cerca** *near*, **lejos** *far*, **a** + distance, etc. (see paragraph 1 above).

¿Está *cerca/lejos*?	*Is it near/far?*
¿A qué distancia está?	*How far is it?*
Está *a cinco minutos/una hora.*	*It's five minutes/an hour away.*
Están *a doscientos metros/un kilómetro de aquí/distancia.*	*It's 200 metres/one kilometre from here/away.*

....

Insight

If you are travelling in Latin America, you are very likely to hear the word **cuadra** *block* in phrases such as **Está a dos cuadras de** *aquí It's two blocks from here*. This word is not used in Spain, where an alternative is **Está a dos calles/manzanas de aquí.**

....

4 OTHER VERBS DENOTING LOCATION

Encontrarse, hallarse (to be, to be situated)
These two verbs are used in more formal contexts, especially in writing. Both are reflexive (see Unit 9); **encontrarse** is also a stem-changing verb (see Unit 8).

¿Dónde se *encuentra* **Perú?**	*Where's Peru?*
Se *encuentra* **en Sudamérica.**	*It's in South America.*
¿Dónde se *encuentran/hallan* **las islas?**	*Where are the islands?*
Se *encuentran/hallan* **en el Atlántico.**	*They are in the Atlantic.*

Estar situado (to be situated)
In this expression, **situado** must agree in gender (masculine or feminine) and number (singular or plural) with the noun it refers to.

| **La ciudad está situada al norte.** | *The city is (situated) in the north.* |
| **Los Andes están situados en Sudamérica.** | *The Andes are (situated) in South America.* |

In context

1 Looking for a bank.

> **Turista**   Perdone, ¿hay algún banco por aquí?
> **Guardia**   Sí, hay uno en la calle Mayor.
> **Turista**   ¿Dónde está la calle Mayor?
> **Guardia**   Es la segunda calle a la izquierda. El banco está al lado del cine.
> **Turista**   Muchas gracias.
> **Guardia**   De nada.

QV

la segunda calle *the second street*
el guardia *policeman*

2 On the way to the airport.

> **Conductor**   Perdone, ¿cuál es la carretera para el aeropuerto?
> **Transeúnte**   Es la próxima a la derecha.
> **Conductor**   ¿A qué distancia está el aeropuerto más o menos?
> **Transeúnte**   Está a unos veinte kilómetros.
> **Conductor**   Muchas gracias.
> **Transeúnte**   De nada.

QUICK VOCAB

el conductor *driver*
el transeúnte *passer-by*
de nada *you're welcome*
unos *about*

Practice

1 You are trying to find your way around a Spanish town. What questions would you need to ask to get these replies? Look at the map, then ask the questions.

a Está en la calle Real, al lado de la plaza.
b Sí, hay dos, uno está en la calle Mayor, al lado de Correos, y el otro está en la calle Miramar, enfrente de la gasolinera.
c Está detrás del cine.
d Está en la próxima esquina, a la derecha, enfrente de la plaza.

2 How would you reply to these questions? Look at the map and answer.

a ¿Hay algún banco por aquí?
b ¿Dónde está la gasolinera?
c ¿Dónde está el museo?
d ¿Dónde está el hotel Sol?

TEST YOURSELF

1 *Translate these questions and answers into Spanish.*
  a Where is the museum?
  b Where are the toilets?
  c It's at the end of this street, on the right.
  d They are downstairs, next to the bar.

2 *Choose the correct verb.*
  a La marcha (*march*) <u>está/es</u> en la plaza de Mayo.
  b La exposición (*exhibition*) <u>está/es</u> en el Museo de Arte Contemporáneo.

3 *Translate these sentences into English.*
  a El mercado está un poco lejos. Está detrás de la estación.
  b La terminal de autobuses está a dos calles de aquí, a la izquierda, enfrente de la estación.
  c Tu pasaporte está ahí, dentro de la maleta negra.

4 *Each of these sentences contains two mistakes. Can you correct them?*
  a ¿Que distancia está Málaga?
  b Tus zapatos son debajo la cama.

The construction with **estar** to enquire and give information about location is extremely frequent in Spanish, and it is very important that you get this right. Check your answers in the **Answer key** and go back to the **Grammar summary** again if necessary. Otherwise, go on to Unit 6, which focuses on the expression of possession.

6

....

Expressing possession

In this unit, you will learn how to:
- *express possession*
- *ask questions regarding possession*

Language points
- *possessive adjectives and pronouns*
- *using* de *to indicate possession*
- ser *used with a possessive*
- *expressing possession with* tener
- *definite article to express possession*
- pertenecer

Key sentences

We can express possession in a variety of ways in English, for example: *That is my house, It's mine, Whose car is that?, It's Peter's, Have you got a computer?, I don't have one.* Spanish also has a number of ways of expressing possession. These involve some of the constructions learned in previous units.

EXPRESSING POSSESSION

Esta es *mi/su* **bicicleta.**
Tus/Sus **llaves están aquí.**
Nuestras/Vuestras **maletas son esas.**

This is my/his/her bicycle.
Your/His/Her keys are here.
Our/Your suitcases are those ones.

El dinero es *mío/tuyo.*   *The money is mine/yours.*
La carpeta *de Ana* **es la azul.**   *Ana's file is the blue one.*
Tenemos/Tienen **una casa.**   *We/They have a house.*

ASKING QUESTIONS REGARDING POSSESSION

¿De quién **es este periódico?**   *Whose newspaper is this?*
¿A quién pertenece **la propiedad?**   *Who does the property belong to?*
¿Tiene Vd./Tienes **coche?**   *Have you got a car?*

Grammar summary

1 *POSSESSIVE ADJECTIVES AND PRONOUNS (MY, MINE, YOUR, YOURS, ETC.)*

To express possession, we may, as in English, use possessives. Spanish has two sets of possessives: short forms such as **mi** *my*, **tu** *your* (familiar) and long forms such as **mío** *mine*, **tuyo** *yours* (familiar).

a Short forms
Short forms function as adjectives and they all agree in number (singular or plural) with the noun they accompany, but only those ending in -o in the masculine singular (**nuestro, vuestro**) agree in gender (masculine or feminine). Note that this agreement is with the thing *possessed*, not with the possessor.

mi	**mis**	*my*
tu	**tus**	*your* (familiar)
su	**sus**	*your* (formal), *his/her/its*
nuestro/a	**nuestros/as**	*our*
vuestro/a	**vuestros/as**	*your* (familiar)
su	**sus**	*your* (formal), *their*

Esta es *mi* **agenda.**   *This is my diary.*
¿Has visto *mis* **llaves?**   *Have you seen my keys?*

| *Nuestro* **hijo llegó ayer.** | *Our son arrived yesterday.* |
| *Vuestra idea* **es estupenda.** | *Your idea is great.* |

b Long forms

Long forms can function as pronouns, in place of a noun which is understood, or as adjectives. They all agree in number (singular or plural) and gender (masculine or feminine) with the thing possessed.

mío/a	**míos/as**	*mine*
tuyo/a	**tuyos/as**	*yours* (familiar)
suyo/a	**suyos/as**	*yours* (formal), *his/hers/its*
nuestro/a	**nuestros/as**	*ours*
vuestro/a	**vuestros/as**	*yours* (familiar)
suyo/a	**suyos/as**	*yours* (formal), *theirs*

In these examples, the possessive pronoun is preceded by a definite article (**el, la, los, las**).

Me encanta su jardín, pero *el*	*I love his/her garden, but ours is*
nuestro **es más grande.**	*larger.*
¿Son estas sus maletas?	*Are these your suitcases?*
No, *las nuestras* **son esas.**	*No, ours are those (ones).*

But no definite article is needed when the possessive pronoun is introduced by **ser** *to be* or when **ser** is understood, except after a preposition (words like **en** *in*, **con** *with*).

¿Es *tuyo* **ese dinero?**	*Is this money yours?*
Sí, (es) *mío.*	*Yes, it's mine.*
¿La fiesta será en *tu* **casa?**	*Will the party be in your house?*
Sí, será en *la mía.*	*Yes, it will be in mine.*

Long forms, acting as pronouns, can be used with the neuter article **lo** in sentences like these, in which the exact meaning will be established by the context.

Lo suyo **con Elisa es sólo una aventura.**	*His affair with Elisa is just an adventure.*
Lo tuyo **está en tu habitación.**	*Your things are in your room.*
Lo nuestro **es algo muy especial.**	*Our relationship is something very special.*

In these examples, long forms are acting as adjectives and are used without a definite article.

Es un amigo mío.	*He's a friend of mine.*
Ayer murió una tía suya.	*An aunt of his/hers died yesterday.*
Muy señor/a mío/a	*Dear Sir/Madam*
Muy señores nuestros	*Dear Sirs*

Long forms acting as adjectives can be used for emphasis instead of short forms. For example:

El **problema** *mío/nuestro* **es el siguiente.**	*My/Our problem is the following one.*

Instead of:

Mi/Nuestro **problema es el siguiente.**	*My/Our problem is the following one.*

2 USING DE (OF) TO INDICATE POSSESSION

Another frequent way of expressing possession in Spanish is by using the construction **de** + name.

| la casa de **Mónica** | *Mónica's house* |
| el libro de **José** | *José's book* |

This construction with **de** is also used in order to avoid the ambiguity that may arise with third-person possessive adjectives and pronouns, **su** and **suyo**.

Compare:

su **apartamento**	*your (formal)/his/her/their apartment*
el apartamento de ella/ellos	*her/their apartment*
un primo suyo	*a cousin of yours (formal)/his/hers/theirs*
un primo de él/ella	*a cousin of his/hers*

3 ¿DE QUIÉN ...? *(WHOSE ...?)*

To say *Whose is it?*, use the expression **¿De quién es?** For *Whose are they?*, use **¿De quién son?** To answer, use the construction **ser + de +** person/personal pronoun or **ser +** possessive.

¿De quién **es este bolígrafo?**	*Whose is this ballpoint pen?*
Es de Sofía/ella.	*It's Sofía's/hers.*
¿De quién **son esos libros?**	*Whose books are those?*
Son de Antonio/de él.	*They are Antonio's/his.*
¿De quién **es esto?**	*Whose is this?*
Es mío/nuestro.	*It's mine/ours.*

Insight

The construction **¿de quién ...?** translates literally *of whom ...?* with **de** indicating possession, as in **Es de Sofía**, literally, *It is of Sofía.*

4 *EXPRESSING POSSESSION WITH* TENER *(TO HAVE)*

Tener *to have* indicates possession in sentences such as these.

| *Tienen* **mucho dinero.** | *They have a lot of money.* |
| *Tiene* **una casa en el campo.** | *He/She has a house in the country.* |

| ¿Tienes **coche**? | *Do you have a car?* |
| **No, no** *tengo.* | *No, I don't have one.* |

Insight

Note the ommission of the indefinite article **un** *a* before the word **coche**. This also occurs with words like **padre** *father*, **madre** *mother*, **novio/a** *boy/girlfriend*, etc. when these are used in a general sense. If the noun is qualified, then the indefinite article must be restored: **Tiene un coche estupendo** *He/She has a great car.*

5 DEFINITE ARTICLES TO EXPRESS POSSESSION

The possessive is often substituted by a definite article when the object of the sentence is an item of clothing or a part of the body.

Ella se lavó *las* **manos.**	*She washed her hands.*
Él se quitó *los* **zapatos.**	*He took off his shoes.*
Nos quitamos *las* **chaquetas.**	*We took off our jackets.*

Insight

In the previous examples, the possessives *her*, *his* and *our* are understood. The word **se** in the first and second sentence, literally *herself/himself*, and **nos**, which can be said to mean *ourselves*, indicate that the action expressed by the verb is done by the subject to himself or herself. Words such as **se**, **nos**, etc., are known as *reflexive pronouns*. For an explanation of this, see Unit 9, paragraph 1.

6 PERTENECER *(TO BELONG)*

Although this use is much less frequent, possession may also be expressed with **pertenecer** *to belong*.

¿A quién *pertenece* **esta casa?**	*Who does this house belong to?*
Pertenece **a un señor muy rico.**	*It belongs to a very rich gentleman.*
¿A quién *pertenecen* **esos edificios?**	*Who do those buildings belong to?*
Pertenecen **a una firma inglesa.**	*They belong to an English firm.*

Pertenecer is conjugated like **conocer** *to know*: **pertenezco, perteneces, pertenece,** etc. (see unit 8, paragraph 2)

Insight

In the construction above, **pertenecer** must be used in the third person singular (**pertenece**) or plural (**pertenecen**), depending on the number (singular or plural) of the noun it refers to. Note that the question translates literally as *To whom does/do (it/they) belong?*

One other much less frequent way of asking about possession or ownership is by using the word **dueño/a** or **propietario/a,** both meaning *owner.*

¿Quién es *el/la dueño/a* **de esta propiedad?**	*Who is the owner of this property?*
¿Quién es *el/la propietario/a* **del hotel?**	*Who is the hotel owner?*

In context

1 A hotel porter is helping a tourist with her luggage.

Portero	¿Cuál es su equipaje?
Turista	El mío es aquel.
Portero	¿Este maletín también es suyo?
Turista	No, no es mío, es de mi amiga. El mío es el negro.
Portero	¿Dónde está su coche?
Turista	Está en el aparcamiento.

2 Talking about the family.

Marisol	¿Cómo están tus hijos?
Isabel	Muy bien, ¿y los tuyos?
	(Contd)

Marisol	Bien. Ahora están en casa de sus abuelos.
Isabel	Los míos están en la piscina con sus amigos.

3 Alfonso has received the following e-mail from his friend Roberto.

Alfonso:

Hoy es el cumpleaños de mi mujer y tenemos una pequeña fiesta en nuestro nuevo apartamento. Tú eres nuestro invitado de honor. No faltes. Nuestra dirección es Ismael Valdés Vergara 640 B.

Roberto

el invitado de honor   *guest of honour*

....

Insight

Note the use of possessive pronouns preceded by the definite article in dialogues 1 and 2. In each case, the noun in brackets is understood: **El (equipaje) mío es aquel, El (maletín) mío es el negro, ¿Y los (hijos) tuyos?, Los (hijos) míos están en la piscina.**

....

Practice

1 Fill in the gaps with a possessive or other suitable words expressing possession.

  a Perdone Vd., ¿es suya esta carta?
  – Sí, es __.
  b ¿ __ quién son esos libros?
  – Son __ Carlos.
  c Buenas tardes, señor Díaz, ¿cómo está __ familia?

d Hola María, te presento a __ marido. Y estos son __ hijos, Pablo y Carmen.

e Estas no son mis cosas. Las __ son esas.

f ¿Es esa la casa __ Cristina y José?
  – No, la __ es la que está en la esquina.

g ¿A quién __ esa empresa?

h ¿Es tuyo el piso?
  – No, es __ mi padre.

2 Mario received the following e-mail from a friend. Fill in the gaps with a suitable possessive.

Querido Mario:
Muchas gracias por (1) __ email y muchas gracias también por (2) __ invitación para este verano. Desgraciadamente me es imposible ir, porque en agosto llega Mónica, una gran amiga (3) __, de Nueva York.
¿Cómo están (4) __ padres? Los (5) __ están muy bien.
Ahora están de vacaciones en (6) __ apartamento de la playa.
Y (7) __ novia, ¿cómo está? ¿Cómo se llama? No recuerdo (8) __ nombre.
Mario, (9) __ nuevo número de teléfono es el 91 675 4321.
Pero yo no tengo el (10) __. ¿Cuál es tu número?

3 Write sentences about Juan, Ana/Luis and you, using **tener**.

  a Juan **tiene tarjetas de crédito.** (tarjetas de crédito)
  b Ana y Luis __ . (tarjetas de crédito)
  c Yo __ . (tarjetas de crédito)
  d Juan __ . (una casa)
  e Ana y Luis __ . (una casa)
  f Yo __ . (una casa)
  g Juan __ . (coche/carro, L. Am.)
  h Ana y Luis __ . (coche/carro)
  i Yo __ . (coche/carro)

	Juan	Ana/Luis	tú
	✓	✗	?
	✗	✓	?
	✓	✓	?

TEST YOURSELF

1 *Fill in the gaps with the Spanish of the possessives in brackets.*

  a __ piso está en el centro de la ciudad. (*our*)

  b __ familia vive en Barcelona. (*my*)

  c ¿Cuál es __ nuevo número de teléfono? (*your*, formal)

  d __ casa es preciosa. (*your*, fam., talking to more than one person)

  e __ novelas son muy buenas. Aquí tengo la última __. (*his*, *his*)

2 *Translate these sentences into Spanish.*

  a This money is yours, isn't it? (fam./sing.)

  b No, that money isn't mine, it's José's.

  c This is Carmen. She's a friend of mine.

  d Here's your passport, Mrs Johnson, and here's yours, sir.

  e Whose jacket is that? Is it María's?
    – Yes, it's hers.

Question 1 above deals with short possessive forms, while question 2 focuses mainly on long forms. Did you get them right? If you need to revise these, go back to paragraphs 1–3 of the **Grammar summary** or check paragraph 7 of the **Grammar reference**.

7

Expressing obligation and needs

In this unit, you will learn how to:
- *express obligation and needs*
- *ask questions with regard to obligation and needs*

Language points
- **tener que**
- **necesitar**
- **deber**
- **hay que**
- **hacer falta**
- **ser necesario**
- *present tense of -ar and -er verbs*

Key sentences

We can express obligation and need in English in a variety of ways, for example: *I have to go, We must tell them, She needs to work more, One has to accept it, What do you have to do?* Spanish also has a number of ways of expressing obligation and need, as you will see from the following examples and grammar notes.

EXPRESSING OBLIGATION AND NEED

Tengo/Tienen que salir.	*I/They have to go out.*
Debo/Debemos estar allí a las 6:00.	*I/We must be there at 6.00.*

Necesita/Necesito hablar con Vd.   *He/She needs/I need to talk*
                                      to you.

EXPRESSING OBLIGATION AND NEED IN IMPERSONAL TERMS

Hay que hacer un esfuerzo.   *One needs to make an effort.*
No hace falta decírselo.   *We/You don't need to tell him/her.*
Es necesario esperar.   *It's necessary to wait.*
Se necesita tener paciencia.   *One needs to have patience.*

ASKING QUESTIONS WITH REGARD TO OBLIGATION AND NEED

¿Qué tienes/tenéis que hacer?   *What do you have to do?*
¿Qué debo/debemos decir?   *What must I/we say?*
¿Qué necesitas/necesitan?   *What do you/they need?*
¿Hace falta/Hay que comprar algo?   *Do we need to buy anything?*

Grammar summary

1 TENER QUE *(TO HAVE TO)*

Tener que is the verb most frequently used in the expression of obligation and need. As in English, it is used with an infinitive.

¿Qué *tienes que* **hacer?**   *What do you have to do?*
Tengo que **trabajar.**   *I have to work.*
¿Qué *tenéis que* **comprar?**   *What do you have to buy?*
Tenemos que **comprar pan.**   *We have to buy bread.*

Tener que, like all the rest of the verbs in this unit, can be used with reference to the present, as in the examples above, but also to the past and the future: **Tuve que salir** *I had to go out*, **Tendré que trabajar más** *I will have to work more*.

For the full forms of **tener** in the present tense, see Unit 4.

2 NECESITAR *(TO NEED) AND PRESENT TENSE OF -AR VERBS*

To say what we need or what we need to do, we may use **necesitar** *to need*, followed by a noun (e.g. **Necesito dinero** *I need money*), a pronoun (e.g. **Necesito esos** *I need those*) or an infinitive (e.g. **Necesito hablar con él** *I need to speak to him*). **Necesitar** is a regular verb whose infinitive ends in **-ar**. Verbs which finish in **-ar** are known as first conjugation verbs.

Here are the present tense forms of **necesitar**. Bear in mind that the endings will be the same for all regular -ar verbs.

Singular		Plural	
necesito	*I need*	**necesitamos**	*we need*
necesitas	*you need* (fam.)	**necesitáis**	*you need* (fam.)
necesita	*you need* (pol.)	**necesitan**	*you need* (pol.)
	he/she/it needs		*they need*

¿**Cuánto tiempo** *necesitas*?	*How much time do you need?*
Necesito **un mes.**	*I need a month.*
¿*Necesitan* **Vds. hablar con alguien?**	*Do you need to talk to somebody?*
Necesitamos **hablar con Vd.**	*We need to talk to you.*

3 DEBER *(MUST, TO HAVE TO)* AND PRESENT TENSE OF *-ER VERBS*

Deber is followed directly by an infinitive. It is a regular verb whose infinitive ends in **-er**. Verbs which finish in **-er** are known as second conjugation verbs.

Here are the present tense forms of **deber**. Bear in mind that the endings will be the same for all regular **-er** verbs.

Singular		Plural	
debo	*I must, have to*	**debemos**	*we must, have to*
debes	*you must, have to* (fam.)	**debéis**	*you must, have to* (fam.)
debe	*you must, have to* (pol.)	**deben**	*you must, have to* (pol.)
	he/she/it must, has to		*they must, have to*

¿Qué debo **hacer?**	*What must I do?*
Debes **decir la verdad.**	*You must tell the truth.*
Debemos **volver.**	*We must come back.*
Deben **esperar.**	*They must wait.*

Insight

Deber expresses stronger obligation than **tener que**; it is used less frequently and its use tends to be circumscribed to contexts in which the obligation stems from the speaker him/herself.

4 *EXPRESSING OBLIGATION AND NEED IN IMPERSONAL TERMS*

To express obligation and need in an impersonal way, use the following constructions:

a Hay que + infinitive

Hay que **tener mucho cuidado.**	*One has to be very careful.*
No hay que **hacer nada.**	*You don't have to do anything.*

b Hacer falta + infinitive/noun

Hace falta **estudiar mucho.**	*You need/One needs to study a lot.*
Hace falta **mucho dinero.**	*You need/One needs a lot of money.*
No *hace falta* **repetirlo.**	*You don't/One doesn't need to repeat it.*
– ¿Compro más pan?	*– Shall I buy more bread?*
– No, no *hace falta.*	*– No, it's not necessary.*

c Se + necesita + infinitive/noun

Se necesita **ser muy capaz.**	*You need to be very capable.*
Se necesita **dependienta.**	*We need a shop assistant./Shop assistant needed.*

d Ser necesario

You can use this expression on its own or with an infinitive. By and large, however, this construction is much less frequent than the equivalent English expression *to be necessary*.

Es necesario abrir la ventana.	*It's necessary to open the window.*
¿Es necesario hacerlo?	*Is it necessary to do it?*
No, no es necesario.	*No, it's not necessary.*

5 EXPRESSING STRONG NEED

To express strong need, you can use the following expressions with **ser** *to be*: **ser preciso** *to be necessary*, **ser imprescindible, ser esencial, ser indispensable, ser fundamental** *to be essential/vital*.

Es preciso recordarle.	*It's necessary to remind him/her.*
Es imprescindible viajar.	*It's essential to travel.*
Es esencial tenerlo aquí.	*It's essential to have him/it here.*
Es indispensable ir solo.	*It's essential to go alone.*
Es fundamental no decir nada.	*It's vital not to say anything.*

In context

1 Enquiring about a visa.

Secretaria	Buenos días. ¿Qué desea?
Viajero	¿Qué tengo que hacer para conseguir un visado?
Secretaria	¿Qué pasaporte tiene Vd.?
Viajero	Español.
Secretaria	Tiene que rellenar esta solicitud y traer su pasaporte con tres fotografías.
Viajero	¿Necesito traer una carta de mi empresa?
Secretaria	¿Es un viaje de negocios?
Viajero	Sí, es un viaje de negocios.
Secretaria	Sí, en ese caso debe traer una carta de su empresa.

conseguir *to get*
rellenar una solicitud *to fill in a form*
la empresa *firm*
un viaje de negocios *a business trip*
en ese caso *in that case*

QUICK VOCAB

2 Elena, a secretary, describes her duties in an e-mail to a friend.

... hay que estar en la oficina a las 9:00. Primero tengo que leer el correo de mi jefe y contestar los emails y las cartas más urgentes. A veces debo asistir a reuniones y tomar notas y de vez en cuando tengo que salir para ir al banco o para visitar a algún cliente ...

el correo *mail, post*
a veces *sometimes*
asistir *to attend*
tomar notas *to take notes*
de vez en cuando *from time to time*

Notice the use of **para** in these phrases:

para **conseguir un visado**	*to (in order to) get a visa*
para **ir al banco**	*(in order) to go to the bank*
para **visitar a algún cliente**	*(in order) to visit some client or other*

For an explanation of the use of the preposition **a** in **visitar a algún cliente** *to visit a client*, see Personal **a**, Unit 12 of **Grammar summary**.

Practice

1 Here are some sentences expressing obligation and need. Fill in the gaps in each word with the missing letters.

   a T _ n _ _ o _ que salir muy pronto.
   b _ _ y que estar allí al mediodía.
   c No d _ _ _ s decir nada.
   d ¿Qué n _ _ e _ _ t _ Vd.?
   e _ a _ e f _ l _ _ hablar español.
   f Es n _ c _ s _ _ _ o trabajar mucho.
   g Se _ e _ e _ _ t _ secretaria que hable español.
   h Es i _ _ r _ s _ i _ d _ _ l _ estudiar más.

2 Eloísa's problems need sorting out. What does she have to do to solve them? Match each problem with a suitable solution.

a Estoy muy delgada.
b Mi madre no está bien.
c No tengo suficiente dinero.
d No estoy muy contenta en mi trabajo.
e Mi inglés no es muy bueno.
f La casa está sucia.

1 Tienes que hacer un esfuerzo y estudiar más.
2 Es necesario limpiarla.
3 Debes buscar otro.
4 Hay que llamar al médico.
5 Tienes que comer más.
6 Tienes que trabajar.

TEST YOURSELF

1 *Fill in the gaps with the correct form of the verbs in brackets.*

    a __ (yo) estudiar más español. (tener que)

    b ¿Qué __ (tú) hacer esta noche? (tener que)

    c __ (vosotros) volver pronto a casa. (tener que)

    d __ (nosotros) estar alertas. (deber)

    e __ (Vd.) dormir más. Está muy estresada. (necesitar)

2 *Translate these sentences into Spanish.*

    a You mustn't say anything. (use the **tú** form)

    b You don't need to buy anything. (use **hacer falta**)

    c One has to be very punctual (**puntual**). (use **haber que**)

    d One needs to wait. (use **ser necesario**)

    e What do you need? (use the **Vds.** form of **necesitar**)

Regardless of general rules, the way people express obligation and needs varies from to person to person and according to context, so the verbs in brackets above are not the only ones possible in each sentence. Take this test a little further and see whether you can replace some of the verbs in brackets by others suitable to the context.

8

....

Talking about the present

In this unit, you will learn how to:
- *describe states which are true in the present*
- *refer to events which are present but not in progress*
- *refer to events taking place in the present*
- *express timeless ideas*
- *ask questions regarding present states and events*

Language points
- *present tense of* -ir *verbs*
- *irregular verbs*
- *stem-changing verbs*
- estar + *gerund*
- llevar + *gerund*
- hacer *in time phrases*

_____

Key sentences

In this unit dealing with the present, you will have a chance to review some of the constructions learned in previous units, such as the present tense of -ar and -er verbs, which you learned in Unit 7. The key sentences and grammar notes which follow will take you a step further by showing you how to use the present tense of verbs ending in -ir, as well as other verbs which do not follow a fixed pattern. You will also learn other constructions used in Spanish for talking about the present.

DESCRIBING STATES WHICH ARE TRUE
IN THE PRESENT

Hoy hace calor/frío.   *It's warm/cold today.*
Elena está enferma/cansada.   *Elena is ill/tired.*

REFERRING TO EVENTS WHICH ARE PRESENT
BUT NOT IN PROGRESS

Escucha ese ruido.   *Listen to that noise.*
Alguien llama/viene.   *Someone's calling/coming.*

REFERRING TO EVENTS TAKING PLACE IN THE PRESENT

El niño duerme/está durmiendo.   *The child is sleeping.*
Estudio./Estoy estudiando.   *I'm studying.*

EXPRESSING TIMELESS IDEAS

Es difícil/caro.   *It's difficult/expensive.*
No me gusta/importa.   *I don't like it/mind.*

ASKING QUESTIONS REGARDING PRESENT STATES
AND EVENTS

¿Cómo estás/están?   *How are you/they?*
¿Oyes ese ruido?   *Do you hear that noise?*
¿Qué pasa/está pasando?   *What's wrong/is happening?*

Grammar summary

1 *PRESENT TENSE OF* -IR *VERBS*

Verbs whose infinitive ends in **-ir**, for example **vivir** *to live* and **escribir** *to write*, are known as third conjugation verbs. Here are the present tense forms of **vivir**.

Singular		Plural	
vivo	*I live*	**vivimos**	*we live*
vives	*you live (fam.)*	**vivís**	*you live (fam.)*
vive	*you live (pol.)*	**viven**	*you live (pol.)*
	he/she/it lives		*they live*

¿Dónde vives?	*Where do you live?*
Vivo en Londres.	*I live in London.*
¿Subes?	*Are you going up?*
Subo ahora mismo.	*I'm going up right away.*
El banco abre a las 3:00.	*The bank opens at 3.00.*
¿Qué escribes?	*What are you writing?*
Escribo una carta.	*I'm writing a letter.*

(For first and second conjugation verbs, see Unit 7.)

2 IRREGULAR VERBS

There are many verbs in Spanish which do not follow a fixed pattern in their conjugation. They are irregular. In the present tense, some verbs are irregular only in the first person singular. Here is a list of the most common. Those marked with an asterisk (*) are also stem-changing verbs (see section 3 below).

-ar verbs

dar *to give*	doy *I give*

-er verbs

conocer *to know*	conozco *I know*
hacer *to do, make*	hago *I do, make*
parecer *to seem*	parezco *I seem*
pertenecer *to belong*	pertenezco *I belong*
poner *to put*	pongo *I put*
saber *to know*	sé *I know*
tener* *to have*	tengo *I have*
traer *to bring*	traigo *I bring*
ver *to see*	veo *I see*

-ir verbs

conducir *to drive*	conduzco *I drive*
decir* *to say, tell*	digo *I say, tell*
oír *to hear*	oigo *I hear*
salir *to go out*	salgo *I go out*
venir* *to come*	vengo *I come*

Oír has other changes: **i** changes to **y** in the second and third person singular and the third person plural:

oigo	oímos
oyes	oís
oye	oyen

Some verbs, for example **ser** *to be*, **estar** *to be*, **haber** *to have* (auxiliary verb) and **ir** *to go* are highly irregular. (For the present tense of **ser**, see Unit 1; for **estar**, Unit 3; for **haber** Unit 19.) Here are the present tense forms of **ir**.

ir *to go*

voy	*I go*	**vamos**	*we go*
vas	*you go* (fam.)	**vais**	*you go* (fam.)
va	*you go* (pol.)	**van**	*you go* (pol.)
	he/she/it goes		*they go*

¿Adónde vas?	*Where are you going?*
Voy al cine.	*I'm going to the cinema.*
Allí va Manuel.	*There goes Manuel.*

Insight

Verbs derived from those above follow a similar pattern:
deshacer *to undo* > **deshago; componer** *to compose* >
compongo; contradecir *to contradict* > **contradigo;**
desoír *to disregard* > **desoigo,** etc.

For a list of the most common irregular verbs in all tenses, see **Irregular verbs**.

3 STEM-CHANGING VERBS

Some verbs undergo a change in the stem (the main part of the verb without its ending, e.g. **quer-er** *to want*), which occurs only when the stem is stressed. Therefore, the first and second persons plural are not affected by this change. Stem-changing verbs have the same endings as regular verbs. Here is a list of the most common stem-changing verbs in the present tense.

a Verbs which change *e* to *ie*

-ar		-er	
cerrar	*to close, shut*	**encender**	*to light, turn on*
despertar(se)	*to wake up*	**entender**	*to understand*
empezar	*to begin*	**perder**	*to lose*
nevar	*to snow*	**querer**	*to want*
pensar	*to think*	**tener**	*to have*

-ir			
herirse	*to hurt oneself*	**sentir(se)**	*to feel*
preferir	*to prefer*	**venir**	*to come*

Here is one of the above verbs in all its present-tense forms.

pensar *to think*			
pienso	*I think*	**pensamos**	*we think*
piensas	*you think* (fam.)	**pensáis**	*you think* (fam.)
piensa	*you think* (pol.)	**piensan**	*you think* (pol.)
	he/she thinks		*they think*

b Verbs which change *o* to *ue*

-ar		-er	
acostarse	to go to bed	devolver	to return, give back
acordarse	to remember	doler	to hurt, feel pain
comprobar	to check	llover	to rain
contar	to tell, count	moverse	to move
encontrar	to find	poder	to be able
mostrar	to show	soler	to be accustomed to
recordar	to remember	volver	to return
rogar	to ask, beg		

-ir			
dormir(se)	to sleep, go to sleep	morir(se)	to die

Jugar, whose stem has a **u**, also changes into **ue**.

juego	*I play*
juegas	*you play* (fam.)
juega	*you play* (pol.) *he/she/it plays*
juegan	*you/they play*

Here is one of the above verbs in all its present-tense forms.

volver to return

vuelvo	*I return*	**volvemos**	*we return*
vuelves	*you return* (fam.)	**volvéis**	*you return* (fam.)
vuelve	*you return* (pol.)	**vuelven**	*you return* (pol.)
	he/she returns		*they return*

c Verbs which change *e* to *i*

conseguir	*to get*	**reír(se)**	*to laugh*
corregir	*to correct*	**repetir**	*to repeat*
elegir	*to choose*	**seguir**	*to follow, continue*
pedir	*to ask (for)*	**servir**	*to serve*

Notice also the spelling change in the first person singular of the following verbs:

conseguir > consigo   elegir > elijo
corregir > corrijo   seguir > sigo

Insight

Changes in spelling in certain forms of the verb, like those above, allow these verbs to maintain the pronunciation of their stem throughout. Spelling changes also occur in other tenses with other verbs, for example **llegar** *to arrive* > **llegué** *I arrived*, **buscar** *to look for* > **busqué** *I looked for*.

Here is **pedir** in its present-tense forms.

pedir *to ask (for)*

pido	*I ask*	**pedimos**	*we ask*
pides	*you ask* (fam.)	**pedís**	*you ask* (fam.)
pide	*you ask* (pol.)	**piden**	*you ask* (pol.)
	he/she asks		*they ask*

4 ESTAR + *GERUND (TO BE + VERB ENDING IN -ING)*

To say what you are doing at the moment of speaking, you use **estar** followed by a gerund, a construction which is known as present continous. The gerund is formed by adding **-ando** to the stem of **-ar** verbs and **-iendo** to that of **-er** and **-ir** verbs:
hablar > hablando, hacer > haciendo, escribir > escribiendo.

Está hablando con el jefe.	*He/She is speaking to the boss.*
¿Qué estás haciendo?	*What are you doing?*
Estoy escribiendo una carta.	*I'm writing a letter.*

Spelling changes in the gerund

▶ Verbs ending in -ir which change e into ie (see paragraph 3a above) also take i in the gerund, e.g. **venir > viniendo**.

▶ Verbs ending in -ir and certain -er verbs which change o to ue (see paragraph 3b above) take u in the gerund, e.g. **dormir > durmiendo, poder > pudiendo**.

▶ Verbs ending in -ir which change the stem from e to i in the present tense (see paragraph 3c above) also show this change in the gerund, e.g. **pedir > pidiendo**.

Using the present continuous

The present continuous is used:

▶ in contrast to the present tense, to make it perfectly clear that we are referring to an action which is taking place at the time. For example:

¿Qué *estás haciendo?*   *What are you doing?*

instead of:

¿Qué haces?   *What do you do?/What are you doing?*

▶ to emphasize some kind of change in the action in relation with the past:

Estoy viviendo **en California.**   *I'm living in California.*

▶ to refer to an action which has been taking place over a period of time including the present:

Está lloviendo **desde anoche.**   *It's been raining since last night.*

▶ to express disapproval or surprise:

¡Pero qué *estás diciendo!*   *But what are you saying!*

Insight

Generally, the use of the present continuous to refer to
actions which occur at the moment of speaking is less
frequent in Spanish than in English. Spanish tends to use the
simple present instead of the present continous: **¿Qué haces?**
What are you doing?, **Estudio español** *I'm studying Spanish*,
¿Con quién hablas? *Who are you talking to?*

5 OTHER WAYS OF REFERRING TO THE PRESENT

To refer to events which began at some point in the past but which
are still in progress, we can use the following constructions:

a Llevar + gerund

¿Cuánto tiempo llevas trabajando aquí?	*How long have you been working here?*
Llevo un año (trabajando) aquí.	*I've been working here for a year.*
Llevamos dos horas esperando.	*We've been waiting for two hours.*

Insight

Vivir and **trabajar** can be left out in this construction with
llevar + gerund, as the meaning is usually made clear by
the context: **¿Cuánto tiempo llevas (viviendo) en España?**
How long have you been (living) in Spain?, **Luis lleva un año
(trabajando) en la empresa** *Luis has been (working) in the
company for a year*. Note also **¿Cuánto tiempo llevan juntos?**
How long have they been together?

b Hace + time phrase + **que** + present tense

¿Cuánto tiempo hace que vives en Madrid?	*How long have you been living in Madrid?*
Hace seis meses que vivo allí.	*I've been living there for six months.*
Hace dos años que estudio español.	*I've been studying Spanish for two years.*

Note the following alternative to the last two sentences:

Vivo allí desde hace seis meses. *I've been living there for six months.*
Estudio español desde hace *I've been studying Spanish for*
dos años. *two years.*

In context

1 Here is an extract from a postcard describing a holiday.

Querida Carolina:

Te escribo desde Río. Estoy aquí de vacaciones con mi familia. Hace muchísimo calor y estamos todos muy morenos. Río es fantástico. Los chicos están muy contentos. Ahora están jugando con unos amigos mientras yo escribo y escucho música brasileña.
¡Qué tranquila estoy! No te imaginas …

estamos morenos *we are tanned*
brasileño/a *Brazilian*
¡Qué tranquila estoy! *How relaxed I am!*
no te imaginas *you can't imagine*

2 An appointment with the manager.

Cliente	Buenos días. Tengo una cita con el gerente. Me llamo Hugo Pérez.
Secretaria	Un momento, por favor, señor Pérez. El gerente está hablando con unos clientes.
Cliente	¿Y la señora Martínez está?
Secretaria	La señora Martínez ya no trabaja aquí. Está trabajando en una firma en Barcelona. Ah, allí viene el gerente …

Tengo una cita. *I have an appointment.*
ya no *no longer*

Practice

1 Fill in the gaps with the appropriate present tense form of the infinitive in brackets.

    a Carlos __ (jugar) muy bien al tenis. Yo no __ (saber) jugar.
    b En Galicia __ (llover) mucho, pero no __ (nevar).
    c Gloria no __ (entender) bien el español.
    d __ (conocer, yo) mucha gente en España porque __ (ir) allí
    en mis vacaciones.
    e No __ (encontrar, yo) mis llaves. No __ (recordar) dónde
    están.
    f Luis __ (empezar) a trabajar a las 9:00. Nosotros __
    (empezar) a las 9:30.

2 How would you ask Ignacio how long he has been doing each of the following and how would he reply? Use the construction with **hace** and the phrases given.

    a Vivir en Madrid – 10 años
    b Trabajar en la misma empresa – 8 años
    c Estudiar inglés – 5 años
    d Conocer a Isabel – 3 años y medio
    e Jugar al tenis – 2 años
    f Hacer yoga – 6 meses

Now try saying how long you have been doing certain things, for example, studying Spanish or working.

3 Can you say what these people are doing? Match each phrase with the corresponding picture and fill in the correct form of **estar** + gerund.

Ejemplo: 1–c Está escuchando...

1 (escuchar) música
2 (comer) en el campo
3 (cocinar)

4 (leer) el periódico
5 (nadar) en la piscina
6 (jugar) al fútbol

TEST YOURSELF

1 *Fill in the gaps with the correct form of the verbs in brackets.*

   a (Yo) __ en Tarragona, mi hermana __ en Zaragoza, y mis padres __ en Lérida. Y tú, ¿dónde __? (vivir)

   b – Perdone, ¿__ Vd. dónde está el ayuntamiento? (saber)
   – No, (yo) no __. (saber) No __ la ciudad. (conocer)

   c – ¿Qué __ (tú) los fines de semana? (hacer) (Yo) no __ nada especial. (hacer)

   d Normalmente (yo) __ de casa a las 8:00 y mi mujer __ a las 8:30. Y vosotros, ¿a qué hora __? (salir)

   e (Yo) __ a la oficina en autobús. Tú __ en el coche, ¿verdad? (ir)

2 *Translate the following into Spanish.*

   a How long has she been working in London? (use **hace**)

   b Carmen and Agustín have been here for a year. (use **llevar**)

   c How long have you been studying Spanish? (use **llevar** with the **tú** form)

   d He's preparing dinner for his children. (use **estar**)

   e They are playing tennis. (use **estar**). They've been playing for an hour. (use **llevar**).

Did you get all or most of your answers right? If you did, congratulations! You have reached a very important stage in your Spanish, one that will allow you to express yourself in a number of contexts related to the present. If you feel you still need to revise the language associated with this, do so, as it is extremely important that you get the verb forms right before you go on to Unit 9, which will take you one step further in your handling of the present tense.

9

Talking about habitual actions

In this unit, you will learn how to:
- *talk about things you do regularly*
- *say how often you or others do certain things*
- *ask how often people do certain things*
- *ask and state what time something is done*

Language points
- *reflexive verbs*
- *adverbs ending in* -mente
- *frequency adverbs*
- *preposition* a *in time phrases*
- soler + *infinitive*
- acostumbrar + *infinitive*

Key sentences

In this unit, you will learn to talk about things you do regularly, such as your daily routine. This will involve the revision of the present tense, as well as the introduction of new forms of the verb. By the end of this unit, you should also be familiar with the Spanish equivalent of words which express frequency, such as *always*, *never*, *often*.

Look at these examples and then read the grammar notes which follow.

TALKING ABOUT THINGS YOU DO REGULARLY

¿Qué haces los domingos/fines de semana? *What do you do on Sundays/at weekends?*

Leo/Escucho música/Salgo. *I read/listen to music/go out.*

SAYING HOW OFTEN YOU OR OTHERS DO CERTAIN THINGS

Siempre/Nunca llega a la hora. *He/She always/never arrives on time.*

A veces/De vez en cuando nos invitan. *They invite us sometimes/from time to time.*

ASKING PEOPLE HOW OFTEN THEY DO CERTAIN THINGS

¿Viene Vd. aquí a menudo/ siempre? *Do you often/always come here?*

¿Cuántas veces por semana/ mes la ves? *How many times a week/month do you see her?*

ASKING AND STATING WHAT TIME SOMETHING IS DONE

¿A qué hora cenas/te acuestas? *What time do you have dinner/go to bed?*

Ceno/Me acuesto a las 10:00. *I have dinner/go to bed at 10.00.*

¿A qué hora empieza/termina? *What time does he/she/it start/ finish?*

Empiezo/Termino a las 8:00. *I start/finish at 8.00.*

Grammar summary

1 *REFLEXIVE VERBS*

A reflexive verb is one that is normally indicated by -se added to the infinitive, e.g. **levantarse** *to get up*, **lavarse** *to wash*. Se is sometimes translated into English as *oneself*, e.g. **alegrarse** *to enjoy* *oneself*, but often it is not expressed at all. The reflexive pronouns **me, te, se, nos, os, se** could be said to correspond to forms such as *myself, yourself, himself, herself*, etc.

Reflexive verbs, also known as pronominal verbs, are conjugated in the usual way but with a reflexive pronoun preceding the verb.

---

levantarse *to get up*

---

me levanto	*I get up*	**nos levantamos**	*we get up*
te levantas	*you get up* (fam.)	**os levantáis**	*you get up* (fam.)
se levanta	*you get up* (pol.)	**se levantan**	*you get up* (pol.)
	he/she gets up		*they get up*

Los sábados siempre me levanto tarde. — *On Saturdays I always get up late.*
Se levanta y se va al trabajo. — *He/She gets up and goes to work.*
Nos levantamos antes de las 6:00. — *We get up before 6.00.*

Insight

Some verbs have two separate forms, one with the reflexive pronoun **se** attached and one without it. The reflexive pronoun may change meaning sometimes, as in **levantar** *to raise*, **levantarse** *to get up/raise oneself*, or it may simply indicate that with the proper reflexive pronoun you can refer to actions which revert on the subject rather than on someone else, **me levanto** *I get up/raise myself*.

Position of reflexive pronouns
As explained earlier, reflexive pronouns normally precede the verb, but they are attached to the end of infinitives, gerunds (see Unit 8) and positive imperative forms (see Unit 20).

Antes de acostarse lee un rato. — *Before going to bed, he/she reads for a while.*

Afeitándose, se cortó. — *He cut himself while shaving.*
Levántate, es tarde. — *Get up, it's late.*

In a construction with a main verb followed by an infinitive or a gerund, the reflexive pronoun may either precede the main verb or be attached to the infinitive or gerund.

Me voy a duchar./   *I'm going to take a shower.*
  Voy a duchar*me*.
Nos tenemos que ir./   *We have to leave.*
  Tenemos que ir*nos*.

Some common reflexive verbs

There is a large number of reflexive verbs in Spanish. Here is a list of some of the most frequent. The (ie), (ue) or (i) next to the verb shows that its stem changes in the present tense (see Unit 8).

acostarse (ue)	*to go to bed*
acordarse (ue)	*to remember*
afeitarse	*to shave*
alegrarse	*to be glad*
bañarse	*to have a bath*
casarse	*to get married*
cortarse	*to cut oneself*
despertarse(ie)	*to wake up*
dormirse (ue)	*to go to sleep*
equivocarse	*to make a mistake*
hallarse	*to be (situated)*
irse	*to leave*
lavarse	*to wash*
levantarse	*to get up*
marcharse	*to leave*
morirse (ue)	*to die*
moverse (ue)	*to move*
olvidarse	*to forget*
pararse	*to stop*
peinarse	*to comb one's hair*
probarse (ue)	*to try on*
reírse (i)	*to laugh*
sentarse (ie)	*to sit down*
sentirse (ie)	*to feel*

2 ADVERBS ENDING IN -MENTE

In English, we often form adverbs by adding *-ly* to an adjective, as
in *normally* or *frequently*. In Spanish, many adverbs are formed by
adding **-mente** to the feminine form of the adjective.

rápida *rapid* > **rápidamente** *rapidly*
lenta *slow* > **lentamente** *slowly*

Notice that if the adjective carries an accent, the accent is kept in
the adverb.

If the adjective ends in a consonant, simply add **-mente**.

fácil *easy* > **fácilmente** *easily*

When there are two or more consecutive adverbs in **-mente** joined
by a conjunction – e.g. **y** *and*, **pero** *but* – only the final one takes
the ending **-mente**.

Él trabaja rápida y eficientemente.   *He works rapidly and efficiently.*

3 FREQUENCY ADVERBS (USUALLY, NORMALLY, ETC.)

The following adverbs and adverbial phrases are commonly used to say how often one does something:

frecuentemente	*frequently*
generalmente	*generally, usually*
normalmente	*normally*
usualmente	*usually*
a menudo	*often*
a veces	*sometimes*
de vez en cuando	*from time to time*
una vez, dos veces (por semana)	*once, twice (a week)*
siempre	*always*
nunca, jamás	*never*
todos los días (meses, años)	*every day (month, year)*
cada día (semana, mes, año)	*every day (week, month, year)*

Insight

Note that the plural of **vez** is **veces** (**z** becomes **c**), a change which applies to all nouns ending in **-z**.

The word **jamás** *never*, also listed above, is more emphatic and stronger in meaning than **nunca**.

Ella *nunca* **sale de noche.**	*She never goes out at night.*
Van a Sevilla *dos veces* **al año.**	*They go to Seville twice a year.*
La veo *a menudo.*	*I often see her.*
Nunca **me llama.**	*He/She never calls me.*
No me llama *nunca.*	*He/She never calls me.*

Notice the double negative when **nunca** is placed after a verb.

4 PREPOSITION A IN TIME PHRASES

Note the use of the preposition **a** in the expressions **¿a qué hora?**, **a las** (*time*).

¿A qué hora sales de la oficina?	*What time do you leave the office?*
Salgo a las 7:00.	*I leave at 7.00.*

> ## Insight
>
> Here is a reminder of the expressions used for asking and telling the time: **¿Qué hora es?** *What time is it?*, **Es la una/ son las dos** *It's one/two o'clock*, **Son las tres y cuarto** *It's a quarter past three*, **Son las cuatro y veinticinco** *It's twenty-five past four*, **Son las cinco y media** *It's half past five*, **Son las seis menos veinte** *It's twenty to six* (literally, *six minus twenty*), **Son las siete menos cuarto** *It's a quarter to seven.*

5 SOLER + *INFINITIVE*

We can also ask and answer questions about habitual actions by using the construction **soler** (**o > ue**) plus infinitive. **Soler** by itself translates into English as *to be in the habit of, usually.*

¿Qué *suele* **hacer Vd. en el verano?**	*What do you usually do in the summer?*
Suelo **salir de vacaciones.**	*I usually go on holiday.*
¿Dónde *sueles* **comer?**	*Where do you normally eat?*
Suelo **comer en un restaurante.**	*I usually eat in a restaurant.*
Solemos **trabajar hasta muy tarde.**	*We usually work until very late.*

For the use of **soler** and **acostumbrar** in phrases like **Él solía/ acostumbraba trabajar mucho** *He used to work a lot*, see Unit 19.

6 ACOSTUMBRAR + *INFINITIVE*

Like **soler** + infinitive, **acostumbrar** + infinitive translates into English as *to be in the habit of* or *to be accustomed to, to usually* (*do*, etc.). Although not strictly correct in the context of habitual actions, many speakers in Spain and Latin America use this expression with the preposition **a** following the verb: **acostumbrar a** + infinitive.

Acostumbro **levantarme tarde.**	*I usually get up late.*
No *acostumbramos* **hacer eso.**	*We don't usually do that.*

Insight

Acostumbrar is much less frequent and more formal than **soler** and is normally associated with the written language. Overuse of the constructions with **soler** and **acostumbrar** may be considered clumsy. The alternative, of course, is to use a present tense verb with a frequency adverb such as **normalmente, generalmente,** etc.: **Normalmente me levanto tarde, Generalmente como en un restaurante.**

In context

1 Read this extract from a letter in which Ignacio, a student, relates his daily activities to a new friend.

Estudio en un instituto de Granada y tengo clases de lunes a viernes por la mañana y por la tarde. Generalmente me levanto a eso de las 8:00 y me voy al instituto que está muy cerca de casa. Al mediodía vuelvo a casa a comer y a las 3:00 regreso al instituto. A las 6:00 termino las clases y vuelvo nuevamente a casa. A veces salgo con mis amigos …

a eso de *around*
al mediodía *at midday*

Insight

In Spain, the word **instituto** (m.) refers to a secondary school. A more general word for school is **colegio** (m.), while **escuela** (f.) is normally associated with a primary school.

2 Alicia talks to a friend about her daily routine at work.

Cristóbal	¿Qué horario de trabajo tienes?
Alicia	Pues, no tengo un horario fijo, pero normalmente llego a la oficina a las 8:00 y estoy allí hasta las 4:00.
Cristóbal	¿Trabajas también los sábados?
Alicia	No, los sábados no trabajo. Normalmente voy con José, mi marido, al supermercado y por la tarde nos quedamos en casa. De vez en cuando cenamos fuera o vamos al cine.
Cristóbal	¿Y los domingos, qué hacéis?
Alicia	Bueno, los domingos muchas veces vamos a la sierra. Allí tenemos una casa para pasar los fines de semana …

un horario fijo *fixed working hours*
fuera *out*
muchas veces *many times, often*
la sierra *mountains*

Insight

Note the phrase **a eso de las 8:00** *about 8.00*. Other ways of expressing approximate times are: **alrededor de las 8:00, sobre las 8:00, a las 8:00 aproximadamente**. These all mean *about 8.00*.

Practice

1 In a letter to a friend, Marta describes her daily routine during her holidays. Fill in the gaps with a suitable verb from the list, using the appropriate form of the present tense.

ver   escribir   levantarse   ser   salir   llamar   desayunar
leer   volver   hacer   jugar   acostarse   ayudar   oír

En tu última carta me preguntas qué (1) ___ durante mis vacaciones.
Bueno, mira, normalmente (2) ___ a las 8:30, después (3) ___,
generalmente un café y unas tostadas, y luego (4) ___ a mi madre en
casa. A veces (5) ___ al supermercado a hacer la compra. Por la tarde
(6) ___ la radio o (7) ___ la televisión y de vez en cuando (8) ___ al
tenis con algún amigo. También (9) ___ mucho, especialmente revistas.
Por la noche (10) ___ con mis amigos de paseo, y a eso de las 9:00 (11)
___ a casa a cenar. Después (12) ___ cartas o (13) ___ por teléfono a
alguna amiga. Nunca (14) ___ antes de la medianoche.

Now try writing about your own daily routine.

2 What questions would you ask to get these replies? Use the familiar form.

a Normalmente me levanto a eso de las 7:00.
b Salgo de la oficina a las 6:00.
c Tengo clase de 7:00 a 8:00.
d No, no me acuesto tarde.
e Los fines de semana no hago nada especial.
f En mis vacaciones suelo ir a San Sebastián.

3 Here are some of the things Elena normally does during the week. Complete each sentence with an appropriate phrase from the list below, using the present tense.

> **(hablar) por teléfono** **(volver) a casa** **(irse) al trabajo**
> **(soler) ver la televisión** **(preparar) la cena** **(levantarse)**

a ___ a las 7:10.   **b** ___ a las 7:45.

c Por la mañana, en la oficina, __.

d A las 5:00 de la tarde __.

e Después de las 7:00 __.

f Por la noche __.

TEST YOURSELF

1 *Fill in the gaps with the correct form of the verb in brackets.*

    a Normalmente (yo) __ a las 11:00, pero mi marido no __ nunca antes de la medianoche. Los chicos __ a las 9:30. (acostarse)

    b Antes de __ a veces leo un rato. Generalmente (yo) __ a eso de las 11:30. (dormirse)

    c Elena siempre __ a la oficina sobre las 8:30. Normalmente (ella) __ en el coche. (irse – ir)

    d (Yo) __ (despertarse) todos los días bastante tarde, __ (afeitarse), __ (bañarse) rápidamente y __ (salir) para el trabajo.

    e Ricardo __ (alegrarse) cuando sus padres __ (venir) a visitarle.

2 *Rewrite the verbs in these sentences using the verbs in brackets.*

    a Marisol **viene** aquí todos los veranos. (soler)

    b ¿Qué **haces** los fines de semana? (soler)

    c Durante las vacaciones **me olvido** de mis problemas. (soler)

    d Por la noche **escuchan** música o **ven** la televisión. (acostumbrar)

    e Luis y yo **no salimos** tarde por la noche. (acostumbrar)

Did you get most of your answers right? If you did, congratulations! It means you are now familiar with the constructions needed for talking about things you do regularly and you are ready to move on. If you are still uncertain, you may need a little more practice. Go back through the relevant points in the unit and write a few sentences showing the use of the present tense in the context of daily routines.

10

Stating possibility, capacity and permission

In this unit, you will learn how to:
- *state possibility or probability*
- *state capacity*
- *ask questions regarding possibility and capacity*
- *request, give and deny permission*

Language points
- **poder** + *infinitive*
- **saber** + *infinitive*
- **se** *in impersonal sentences*
- **ser posible** + *infinitive*

Key sentences

This unit focuses on the expression of possibility, capacity and permission, through the use of verbs such as **poder** and **saber**.

STATING POSSIBILITY

Puede llover/ser difícil.	*It may rain/be difficult.*
Puede estar en casa/ocupado/a.	*He/She may be at home/busy.*

STATING CAPACITY

No puedo hacerlo/explicarlo.	*I can't do it/explain it.*
No sé nadar/jugar al tenis.	*I can't swim/play tennis.*

ASKING QUESTIONS REGARDING POSSIBILITY AND CAPACITY

¿Puedes venir/volver mañana?	*Can you come/come back tomorrow?*
¿Sabes tocar el piano/jugar al ajedrez?	*Can you play the piano/chess?*

REQUESTING, GIVING AND DENYING PERMISSION

¿Puedo fumar/aparcar aquí?	*May I smoke/park here?*
Aquí no se puede fumar/ aparcar.	*You can't smoke/park here.*

Grammar summary

1 PODER *(CAN, BE ABLE TO, MAY)* + *INFINITIVE*

Poder, a verb whose stem changes from **o** to **ue** in the present tense (**puedo, puedes, puede, podemos, podéis, pueden**), is normally used with an infinitive to express possibility, capacity or permission.

Puede **suceder.**	*It may happen. (possibility)*
No *puedo* **ayudarte.**	*I can't help you. (capacity)*
¿Puedo **pasar?**	*May I come in? (permission)*

Insight

Spanish has no separate verbs to distinguish *can* and *may*. Possibility, capacity and permission are all expressed with **poder**.

2 SABER *(TO BE ABLE TO)* + *INFINITIVE*

Saber (literally *to know*) is used with an infinitive to express capacity or ability.

No *sé* **cocinar.**	*I don't know how to cook.*
Ella no *sabe* **bailar.**	*She doesn't know how to dance.*
¿Sabes **tocar el piano?**	*Do you know how to play the piano?*

Insight

The use of *can* as an alternative to *to know how to* to express ability or capacity, as in *Can you play the piano?*, has no parallel in Spanish. Spanish must use **saber** in this context. The use of **poder**, as in **¿Puedes tocar el piano?**, conveys more the idea of possibility than of ability.

3 SE *IN IMPERSONAL SENTENCES*

Impersonal sentences such as *Is it possible to go in?*, *Can one eat here?* and *One can't listen to music here* are expressed in Spanish through the word **se** followed by **poder** in the third person singular plus an infinitive.

¿Se *puede* **entrar?**	*Is it possible to go in?/Can one go in?*
¿Se *puede* **comer aquí?**	*Can one eat here?*
Aquí no se *puede* **escuchar música.**	*One can't listen to music here.*

Insight

Se has a number of uses in Spanish: it may be used, as above, to form impersonal sentences, translating *one, you, we* (see also Unit 7, **Grammar summary**, paragraph 4), or it may have a reflexive value, as in **Se divierten mucho** *They enjoy themselves very much* (see Unit 9, **Grammar summary**, paragraph 1). For other uses of **se**, see Units 11 and 12.

4 SER POSIBLE *(TO BE POSSIBLE)* + *INFINITIVE*

Possibility may also be expressed in Spanish with the phrase **es posible** plus infinitive, a construction which is much less frequent in Spanish than its English equivalent *it's possible*.

¿Es posible **hablar con el señor Díaz?**	*Is it possible to speak to señor Díaz?*
Lo siento, no es posible.	*I'm sorry, it isn't possible.*
¿Es posible **reservar una habitación por teléfono?**	*Is it possible to book a room on the phone?*
Por supuesto que *es posible.*	*Of course it's possible.*

In context

1 Where can we park?

Conductor	Perdone, ¿se puede aparcar aquí?
Policía	No, señor, aquí no se puede.
Conductor	¿Dónde se puede aparcar?
Policía	En la plaza Mayor, al final de la calle.
Conductor	¿Puedo girar aquí?
Policía	Aquí no, pero puede girar en la próxima calle a la derecha y luego bajar hasta la plaza.
Conductor	Gracias.
Policía	De nada.

Insight

The impersonal sentence **¿Se puede aparcar aquí?**, in which **poder** conveys the idea of *being allowed to*, may also be expressed in personal terms: **¿Puedo aparcar aquí?** *May I park here?* Similarly for **¿Dónde se puede aparcar?**

girar *to turn*
bajar *to go down*
hasta *as far as, to*

2 What can one do in Barcelona?

Turista A ¿Qué se puede hacer en Barcelona?

Turista B Se puede ir a algún museo, al museo de Picasso por ejemplo. También se puede visitar el Barrio Gótico, que es muy bonito. Puede ir al puerto, que está muy cerca de aquí ...

Turista A Y por la noche, ¿qué se puede hacer?

Turista B Por la noche puede Vd. ir a algún espectáculo, al teatro o a la ópera por ejemplo, o tomar una copa en un bar ...

Turista A Y los fines de semana, ¿dónde puedo ir?

Turista B Puede ir a la playa. Sitges no está muy lejos. Se puede ir en tren o en coche ...

QV

el puerto *port*
el espectáculo *entertainment, show*

Practice

1 During a holiday in a Spanish-speaking country, you meet someone. How would you say the following? Use **poder** and **saber** as appropriate.

   a Can you understand my Spanish?
   b Can you speak more slowly? (**más despacio**)
   c Can you repeat, please?
   d Can you play tennis?
   e I can't play today. We can play tomorrow.
   f I can't drive. Can you drive?

2 Paco and Lucía are visiting Barcelona for the first time. Here's a conversation between them and the hotel receptionist. Fill in the gaps using the verbs in brackets in the appropriate form of the present tense.

Paco	Perdone, ¿__ (poder, nosotros) aparcar en esta calle?
Recepcionista	No, en esta calle no se __ (poder) aparcar. Pero __ (poder, Vds.) aparcar detrás del hotel.
Paco	Gracias. Por favor, ¿__ (poder, Vd.) recomendarnos un restaurante?
Recepcionista	__ (poder, Vds.) comer en el restaurante del hotel. Está abierto.
Paco	Gracias. ¿Y dónde __ (poder, yo) hacer una llamada?
Recepcionista	Allí están los teléfonos, señor.

3 Label the signs below with the correct expression from the box.

No entrar   No se puede nadar
No hacer/tomar (L. Am.) fotografías
No aparcar   No se puede girar/doblar a la izquierda
No se puede fumar

a   b   c

d   e   f

TEST YOURSELF

1 *Transform these impersonal sentences into personal ones using the correct form of the verb in italics for the person in brackets.*
   a En Nueva York *se puede* visitar los museos, que son excelentes. (nosotros)
   b En la Metropolitan Opera House *se puede* ver y escuchar a los mejores cantantes del mundo. (tú)
   c En Broadway *se puede* ir a alguna comedia musical. (vosotros)
   d ¿Cómo *se puede* reservar entradas? (yo)
   e *Se puede* reservar entradas por internet. (usted)

2 *Translate these questions into Spanish.*
   a May I come in?
   b Can we leave (**dejar**) our luggage here?
   c Can you play the guitar (**la guitarra**)? (fam.)
   d Can you come this afternoon? (formal)
   e Is it possible to speak to Mrs Rodríguez?

Poder is an important verb, so make sure you've got its forms and usage right before you move on. If you feel you need some further practice, think of contexts where you might need this verb in Spanish and write a few sentences or brief exchanges showing its various uses, for example ¿**Puedes estar aquí a las 6:00? – Lo siento, no puedo.**

11

Describing processes and procedures

In this unit, you will learn how to:
- *describe processes and procedures*
- *ask questions regarding processes and procedures*
- *express the result of an action*

Language points
- *passive and active sentences*
- *passive sentences with* ser + *past participle*
- *passive sentences with* se
- *impersonal* tú *and* ellos
- estar + *past participle*

Key sentences

The main focus of this unit will be the language used in the description of processes and procedures. Ideas such as *The fruit is harvested and then packed and exported* or *Candidates are short-listed and then interviewed* can be expressed in Spanish in a variety of ways, as you will see from the examples and grammar notes which follow.

DESCRIBING PROCESSES AND PROCEDURES

Las verduras se cortan, después se cocinan al vapor ...
The vegetables are cut, then they are steamed ...

La carne es procesada, y luego es embalada y exportada ...
The meat is processed, and then packed and exported ...

ASKING QUESTIONS REGARDING PROCESSES AND PROCEDURES

¿Cómo se prepara una tortilla española?
How do you make a Spanish omelette?

¿Cómo se consigue/obtiene el permiso de trabajo/visado?
How do you get a work permit/ visa?

EXPRESSING THE RESULT OF AN ACTION

El trabajo está terminado. *The job is finished.*
Las luces están apagadas. *The lights are off.*

Grammar summary

1 *PASSIVE AND ACTIVE SENTENCES*

Look at these sentences in English.

The farmers cut the oranges.   *The oranges are cut by the farmers.*

The first is an active sentence with an active verb: *The farmers cut the oranges*. The second sentence is passive: *The oranges are cut by the farmers*. In the passive sentence, *the oranges* is the subject and *the farmers* is the agent carrying out the action expressed by the verb. In Spanish, there are also active and passive sentences.

Los granjeros cortan **las naranjas.** (active)
The farmers cut the oranges.

Las naranjas son cortadas **por los granjeros.** (passive)
The oranges are cut by the farmers.

2 PASSIVE SENTENCES WITH SER + PAST PARTICIPLE

There are two main ways of forming passive sentences in Spanish. As in the last sentence, we may use the verb **ser** plus a past participle. The past participle is formed by adding the ending **-ado** to the stem of **-ar** verbs and **-ido** to the stem of **-er** and **-ir** verbs.

cortar	Es cortado.	*It's cut.*
vender	Es vendido.	*It's sold.*
recibir	Es recibido.	*It's received.*

In this construction, the past participle will change for gender and number:

Las naranjas son cortad*as*.	*The oranges are cut.*
La fruta es vendid*a*.	*Fruit is sold.*
Los productos son recibid*os*.	*Products are received.*

Irregular past participles
Some past participles are irregular. Here is a list of the most common ones.

abrir	*to open*	abierto
decir	*to say, tell*	dicho
escribir	*to write*	escrito
hacer	*to do, make*	hecho
poner	*to put*	puesto
romper	*to break*	roto
ver	*to see*	visto
volver	*to come back*	vuelto

Insight

All verbs derived from the infinitives above follow a similar pattern: **deshacer** *to undo* – **deshecho** *undone*, **prever** *to foresee* – **previsto** *foreseen*, **devolver** *to return (something)* – **devuelto** *returned*, etc.

Using passive sentences with **ser**

You should bear in mind the following points when using passive sentences with *ser*.

▶ The passive with **ser** is found more frequently in written and more formal language.
▶ The passive with **ser** is uncommon in the spoken language, particularly in Spain.
▶ If the agent of the action expressed by the verb is mentioned, use a passive with **ser** and not with se, e.g. **Las naranjas son cortadas por los granjeros.** The preposition **por** *by* introduces the 'agent which carries out the action' (in this case **los granjeros** *the farmers*) which, quite often, is not made explicit: **Por razones de seguridad, el equipaje de mano es revisado cuidadosamente** *For security reasons, the hand luggage is checked carefully.*
▶ Some verbs do not allow the use of the passive with **ser** but, as there is no rule about it, only usage will tell you which ones cannot be used.

Insight

As a non-native speaker, you may be tempted to translate the English passive into Spanish using the construction with **ser**, but given the rather infrequent use of this in colloquial Spanish, its use may seem clumsy to Spanish ears. Unless you are certain, try to replace this by an active sentence or the construction which follows.

3 PASSIVE SENTENCES WITH SE

In Unit 10 you learned the use of **se** with a third person verb in impersonal sentences.

Aquí no se **puede aparcar.**   *One can't park here.*

The same construction – **se** plus third-person verb – is used with a passive meaning.

El libro se **publicó en 1970.**   *The book was published in 1970.*

Using passive sentences with **se**

You should bear in mind the following points when using passive sentences with **se**.

▶ The verb normally agrees in number (singular or plural) with the subject.

Se **fabrica aquí.**	*It's manufactured here.*
Se **fabrican aquí.**	*They're manufactured here.*
Se **produce en España.**	*It's produced in Spain.*
Se **producen en España.**	*They're produced in Spain.*

▶ If the passive subject is a person, as in *Delia and Cristóbal have been invited*, use the singular form of the verb followed by the personal **a** (see Unit 12, **Grammar summary**, paragraph 4): **Se ha invitado a Delia y Cristóbal.**

▶ Passive sentences with **se** are not used when the agent of the action expressed by the verb is present. In such cases, you must use a passive with **ser**.

Los viajeros *son* **recibidos** *por* **un guía ...**	*Travellers are received by a guide ...*

▶ Generally speaking, passive sentences with **se** are more frequent than those with **ser**.

Insight

English passive constructions such as *It is said that ...*, *It is thought that ...*, *It is expected that ...* are often expressed in Spanish with the passive with **se: Se dice que ..., Se piensa/ cree que ..., Se espera que ...**

4 IMPERSONAL TÚ (YOU) AND ELLOS (THEY)

Processes and procedures may also be described using **tú** or **ellos** in an impersonal way.

Pides una solicitud de inscripción, la rellenas y la envías.	*You ask for a registration form, you fill it in and send it.*
Seleccionan a los mejores candidatos y los llaman para una entrevista.	*They select the best candidates and they call them for an interview.*

> **Insight**
>
> Phrases such as **Se dice/piensa/espera que** ... can be expressed with the impersonal third person plural: **Dicen que** ... *They say that* ..., **Piensan/Creen que** ... *They think that* ..., **Esperan que** ... *They expect that* ... The second construction is more common in the spoken language.

5 ESTAR + *PAST PARTICIPLE TO EXPRESS THE RESULT OF AN ACTION*

To enquire and give information about the result of an action, use **estar** and a past participle. The past participle must agree in gender and number with the subject.

¿Está preparada **la cena?**	*Is dinner prepared?*
La ventana está cerrada.	*The window is closed.*
Las tiendas están abiertas.	*The shops are open.*

> **Insight**
>
> This construction with **estar** and a past participle is by no means interchangeable with that of **ser** + past participle. **Estar** signals a state which is the result of an action, while **ser** focuses on the process itself. The agent which carried out the action is not normally expressed in the construction with **estar**.

In context

1 Read these instructions on how to get a visa for a South American country.

Para obtener un visado de estudiante se debe ir personalmente al Consulado donde se rellena un formulario con los datos personales y los motivos del viaje. Se deben llevar tres fotografías tamaño pasaporte y una carta de la institución donde se va a estudiar. El visado debe ser solicitado por lo menos un mes antes de la fecha en que se piensa viajar. Para más información se puede llamar al teléfono 91 396 6907.

los datos personales *personal information*
debe ser solicitado *it must be requested*
por lo menos *at least*
en que se piensa viajar *when you're thinking of travelling*

2 Read this extract from a tourist brochure.

Los viajeros son recibidos en el aeropuerto por un guía y desde allí son trasladados a sus respectivos hoteles donde son atendidos por nuestro propio personal. Las excursiones son organizadas por agencias locales y se pueden pagar en moneda extranjera o moneda local ...

son trasladados *they're transferred*
son atendidos *they're looked after*
se pueden pagar *they can be paid for*
en moneda extranjera *in foreign currency*

Practice

1 Read this passage, which describes the process for the selection of new staff in a Spanish company, and change each of the verb phrases in italics into the more colloquial third person plural of the verb.

Se estudian las solicitudes, *se realiza* una primera selección y *se invita* a los candidatos a participar en una serie de entrevistas, algunas de ellas de carácter informal. Luego de las entrevistas preliminares, *se hace* una segunda selección, en la que *se seleccionan* tres o cuatro candidatos. Después *se llama* a estos candidatos a una entrevista final, de carácter formal, y de entre ellos *se escoge* a una persona.

2 Rewrite these sentences, changing the verbs and verb phrases in italics into the construction of **se** + third person of the verb.

a Primero *cortas* la cebolla muy fina y *la fríes* durante unos minutos. Luego *le pones* un poco de vino.

b La fruta *es seleccionada*, y luego *es llevada* hasta los puertos y desde allí *es enviada* al exterior.

c Los hoteles *son elegidos* cuidadosamente y *son evaluados* periódicamente.

TEST YOURSELF

1 *Change these passive sentences into the active voice using the verbs in brackets.*

   a El español *es hablado* por más de 350 millones de personas. (hablar)

   b La empresa *es administrada* por tres directores. (administrar)

   c Los chicos *son llevados* al colegio por el padre. (llevar)

   d Estos coches *son fabricados* por una empresa china. (fabricar)

2 *Translate these sentences into Spanish using the passive with* se. *You may need to look up some of the words in your dictionary.*

   a The rooms are cleaned in the morning.

   b The towels are changed every day.

   c The reservations are made by internet and confirmed by e-mail.

   d Dinner is served at 8.00.

3 Ser or estar? *Choose the correct verb.*

   a La puerta <u>es/está</u> abierta.

   b Los bancos <u>son/están</u> cerrados.

   c Los viajeros <u>son/están</u> recibidos por un guía.

   d La Semana Santa <u>es/está</u> celebrada en toda España.

If you made a few mistakes in the tests above, try to determine the nature of your errors before you do any revision. Was it the concept of active versus passive voice, or was it simply the forms of the verbs that gave you trouble? Did the choice between **ser** and **estar** constitute a problem? If it did, remember that the construction with **ser** refers to an action, while that with **estar** denotes a state.

12

Expressing wants and preferences

In this unit, you will learn how to:
- *ask and answer questions about wants*
- *ask and answer questions about preferences*

Language points
- **querer** + *noun/pronoun/verb*
- **preferir** + *noun/pronoun/verb*
- *direct object pronouns*
- *personal* a
- *other verbs expressing wants*

Key sentences

In this unit dealing with wants and preferences, you will learn the use of verbs such as **querer** *to want* and **preferir** *to prefer* and the Spanish equivalent of words such as *me, you, him, her*.

ASKING AND ANSWERING QUESTIONS ABOUT WANTS

¿Qué quieres/quiere Vd.?	*What do you want?*
Quiero una camisa/un vestido.	*I want a shirt/dress.*
Quiero (ver) esta/este.	*I want (to see) this one.*

ASKING AND ANSWERING QUESTIONS
ABOUT PREFERENCES

¿Cuál prefieres/prefiere Vd.?	*Which one do you prefer?*
Prefiero el azul/negro.	*I prefer the blue/black one.*
Prefiero (comprar/llevar) ese.	*I prefer (to buy/take) that one.*

Grammar summary

1 QUERER *(TO WANT)* + *NOUN/PRONOUN/VERB*

Querer (e > ie) is the verb most frequently used in Spanish to ask
and answer questions about wants. It may be used with a noun, a
pronoun or a verb. Like **preferir** below, it is a stem-changing verb
(see Unit 8, **Grammar summary**, paragraph 3).

A noun

Quiero *un zumo/jugo* (L.Am.) **de naranja.**	*I want an orange juice.*
Queremos *una habitación.*	*We want a room.*

A pronoun

¿Quieres *algo***?**	*Do you want something?*
Quiero *esto.*	*I want this.*

A verb

Quiero *alquilar* **un coche.**	*I want to hire a car.*
Queremos *ir* **al teatro.**	*We want to go to the theatre.*

Insight

Querer also means *to love*: **¿Me quieres?** *Do you love me?*,
Te quiero mucho *I love you very much.* The alternative verb,
amar, tends to be restricted to formal written language.

2 PREFERIR *(TO PREFER)* + *NOUN/PRONOUN/VERB*

Preferir (e > ie) is the verb most frequently used in Spanish to ask and answer questions about preferences. It may be used with a noun, a pronoun or a verb.

A noun

Prefiero *el tenis.*   *I prefer tennis.*
Él prefiere *el fútbol.*   *He prefers football.*

> **Insight**
>
> Note the use of **el** *the* before **tenis** and **fútbol**. Nouns used in a general sense are preceded by the definite article, just as in **Prefiere la música/la televisión/el cine** *He/She prefers music/ television/cinema.* (But **Quiero/Prefiero escuchar música/ver televisión** *I want/prefer to listen to music/watch television*; in this case, the nouns have not been used in a generic sense.)

A pronoun

Prefiero este.   *I prefer this one.*
– Prefiero pescado.   *– I prefer fish.*
– ¿Cómo lo prefiere?   *– How do you prefer it?*
– Lo prefiero a la plancha.   *– I prefer it grilled.*

> **Insight**
>
> In the previous examples, **lo** *it* replaces the word **pescado**, a masculine word. The feminine form for *it* is **la**: **Prefiero carne y la quiero muy hecha** *I prefer meat and I want it well done.* (See also paragraph 3 below.)

A verb

Preferimos *ir* **a Mallorca.**   *We prefer to go to Mallorca.*
Prefieren *quedarse* **en casa.**   *They prefer to stay at home.*
Luis prefiere *aprender* **inglés.**   *Luis prefers to learn English.*

3 DIRECT OBJECT PRONOUNS

First and second person
Words such as *me, you, him, her, it*, etc., as in *He prefers me,
I prefer you* and *I don't want it*, are called direct object pronouns.
Object pronouns for the first and second person singular are:

Singular			
me	*me*	**Me prefiere.**	*He prefers me.*
te	*you* (fam.)	**Te prefiere.**	*He prefers you.*
Plural			
nos	*us*	**Nos prefiere.**	*He prefers us.*
os	*you* (fam.)	**Os prefiere.**	*He prefers you.*

Third person
Now look at these examples and explanations regarding the use of
third person object pronouns.

¿Cómo quiere el *pescado***?**	*How do you want the fish?*
Lo **quiero frito.**	*I want it fried.*
¿Cómo quiere las patatas?	*How do you want the potatoes?*
Las **quiero fritas.**	*I want them fried.*

In order to avoid the repetition of the nouns **el pescado** and **las
patatas,** we have used instead the pronouns **lo** (masculine, singular)
and **las** (feminine, plural). **Lo** and **las** are direct object pronouns.
Lo refers back to the object **el pescado** and **las** refers back to **las
patatas,** the thing wanted. Direct object pronouns agree in gender
and number with the noun they refer to. Here are the third person
forms:

lo (masc. sing.)   **los** (masc. pl.)
la (fem. sing)   **las** (fem. pl.)

Direct object pronouns can refer to people
In the following sentences, third person object pronouns refer to people rather than things.

Prefiero a Carmen.	*I prefer Carmen.*
La **prefiero.**	*I prefer her.*
Prefiero a Carmen y Elena.	*I prefer Carmen and Elena.*
Las **prefiero.**	*I prefer them.*

Carmen, in the first sentence, and **Carmen y Elena** in the second sentence, are direct objects replaced by **la** (fem. sing.) and **las** (fem. pl.) respectively. The use of **la** and **las** for a human female direct object seems to present no variation throughout the Spanish-speaking world. However, when it comes to human male direct objects there are two main dialectal differences.

Le or **lo**?
In the Spanish-speaking countries of Latin America, as well as in some parts of Spain, you will hear **lo** (singular) and **los** (plural) used for males, as for things. However, in many parts of Spain, you are much more likely to hear **le** (singular) and **les** (plural) used for human males and **lo** (singular) and **los** (plural) used for things. Both usages are correct, but the latter may be easier for you to remember.

Yo *lo* **prefiero.**	*I prefer him/it.*
Yo *le* **prefiero.**	*I prefer him.*
Ella *lo* **quiere.**	*She loves him/it.*
Ella *le* **quiere.**	*She loves him.*

Direct address
In direct address, **lo/le – la** and **los/les – las** stand for **usted** and **ustedes** respectively.

Ellos lo/le prefieren (a Vd.).	*They prefer you.* (masc. sing.)
Yo la quiero aquí.	*I want you here.* (fem. sing.)

Position of direct object pronouns

The normal position of the object pronoun is before the main verb, as shown in the previous examples. However, in phrases where a verb precedes an infinitive or a gerund, the object pronoun may either precede the main verb or be attached to the infinitive or gerund.

Quiero hacer*lo*.	*I want to do it.*
Lo **quiero hacer.**	*I want to do it.*
Estoy terminándo*lo*.	*I'm finishing it.*
Lo **estoy terminando.**	*I'm finishing it.*

Direct object pronouns precede negative imperatives but are attached to positive forms.

No *lo* **haga.**	*Don't do it.*
Hága*lo*.	*Do it.*

Insight

Note that with the addition of the pronoun in **terminándolo** and **hágalo**, the stress has shifted from the last syllable but one to the last but two. The stressed syllable, then, must have a written accent (see **Stress and accentuation, Introduction**).

(For the imperative, see Unit 20.)

4 PERSONAL A

Observe these sentences.

Prefiero *a* **Carmen.**	*I prefer Carmen.*
Quiero *a* **Juan.**	*I love Juan.*

A peculiarity of Spanish is that the preposition **a** is placed before a direct object if the object is a definite person. This use of the preposition **a** is known as 'personal **a**'.

5 OTHER VERBS EXPRESSING WANTS

Desear to wish, want, like
Desear, literally *to wish*, is used in more formal contexts and is much less frequent than **querer**.

¿Desea **Vd. algo?**	*Would you like anything?*
¿Qué *desea***?**	*What would you like?* (in a shop, office, etc.)

Quisiera I'd like, **quisiéramos** we'd like
Quisiera *I would like* and **quisiéramos** *we would like*, from **querer**, is used in place of **quiero** or **queremos** to add more politeness to a request.

Quisiera **una habitación.**	*I'd like a room.*
Quisiéramos **hablar con Vd.**	*We'd like to speak to you.*

Quería I'd like, **queríamos** we'd like
Quería *I would like* and **queríamos** *we would like* are used in much the same way as the two previous forms.

Quería **pedir hora con el doctor/la doctora.**	*I'd like to ask for an appointment with the doctor.*
Queríamos **alquilar un coche.**	*We'd like to hire a car.*

Insight

The word **hora** *appointment* is used with professionals like doctors, dentists, hairdressers, etc. who normally see a number of people over a fixed period at specific times. In other contexts, use the word **cita: Tengo hora con el/la dentista** *I have an appointment with the dentist*, **Tengo cita con mi abogado/a** *I have an appointment with my lawyer.*

In context

1 In a restaurant.

Camarero	¿Qué van a tomar?
Roberto	Yo quiero sopa de verduras y de segundo pescado con ensalada.
Camarero	El pescado, ¿cómo lo quiere? Frito, a la plancha …
Roberto	Lo prefiero a la plancha.
Camarero	¿Y usted, señor?
Juan	Para mí una tortilla de patatas y de segundo quiero chuletas de cerdo.
Camarero	Las chuletas, ¿con qué las quiere?
Juan	Con puré.
Camarero	¿Y para beber?
Roberto	Una botella de vino de la casa.
Camarero	¿Prefieren blanco o tinto?
Roberto	Tinto.
Camarero	De acuerdo. Un momento, por favor.

la sopa de verduras *vegetable soup*
de segundo *as a second course*
el vino de la casa *house wine*
blanco o tinto *white or red*
de acuerdo *all right*

QUICK VOCAB

2 Buying a shirt.

Dependienta	Buenas tardes. ¿Qué desea?
Elisa	Quiero una camisa de esas. ¿Cuánto valen?
Dependienta	Estas las tenemos de oferta a 25 euros. ¿De qué color la quiere?
Elisa	La prefiero en azul.
Dependienta	¿Qué talla tiene?
Elisa	Treinta y ocho.
Dependienta	Aquí tiene Vd. una en azul.
Elisa	Sí, está muy bien. ¿Puedo probármela?
Dependienta	Sí, por supuesto. Pase por aquí, por favor.

QUICK VOCAB

¿Qué desea? *What would you like?*
¿Cuánto valen? *How much are they?*
de oferta *special offer*
¿Puedo probármela? *May I try it on?*
por supuesto *certainly*
pase por aquí *come this way*

Notice the use of direct object pronouns in the following sentences from dialogue 1.

El pescado, ¿cómo lo quiere? Lo refers back to **el pescado**.

Las chuletas, ¿con qué las quiere? Las refers back to **las chuletas**.

Note also the question **¿Puedo probármela?** *May I try it on?*

The verb here is **probarse** *to try on*, a reflexive verb. Both the reflexive pronoun **me** and the direct object pronoun **la** (which refers back to **la camisa**) have been added to the infinitive. An alternative position would be **¿Me la puedo probar?**

Practice

1 You and a travelling companion are booking into a hotel in a Spanish-speaking country. Fill in your part of the conversation with the hotel receptionist.

Recepcionista	Buenas tardes. ¿Qué desean?
Tú	*Say you'd like a double room. Ask if they have any.*
Recepcionista	¿Prefieren una interior o exterior?
Tú	*Say you prefer one facing the street, but you'd like to see it. Ask if it is possible.*
Recepcionista	Sí, por supuesto. Pasen por aquí, por favor.
Tú	*Say it's all right, you want to take the room, but you'd like to know what it costs.*
Recepcionista	Quince mil pesos con desayuno y veinte mil con media pensión.
Tú	*Say you want the room only. You prefer to eat out* (fuera).
Recepcionista	De acuerdo.

2 Can you make sense of these exchanges between customers and a waiter in a restaurant? Match each request with an appropriate question or statement.

    a Quiero pollo, por favor.
    b Para mí, patatas/papas (L.Am.).
    c Dos cafés, por favor.
    d Por favor, la cuenta.

    1 Un momento por favor, ahora mismo los traigo.
    2 ¿Con qué lo quiere?
    3 Aquí la tiene.
    4 ¿Cómo las quiere?

3 Complete the speech bubbles with a suitable phrase, according to the item being bought: **una muñeca** *a doll*, **un sombrero** *a hat*, **una chaqueta** *a jacket*, **unas gafas de sol** *sunglasses*. Two of the phrases are unsuitable.

a Prefiero el blanco.
b Quiero esta. La otra es demasiado pequeña.
c Prefiero esta, la más pequeña.
d Quiero unas más pequeñas. Estas son muy grandes.
e Quiero este, el más pequeño.
f Estos son demasiado pequeños. Prefiero unos más grandes.

TEST YOURSELF

1 *Fill in the gaps using the correct form of* **querer** *or* **preferir**.

a Yo __ (querer) viajar a la India, pero Elvira __ (preferir) ir a Egipto.

b Ramón lleva un año con Sofía. Él la __ (querer) mucho.

c Este coche es demasiado pequeño. (Nosotros) __ (preferir) uno más grande.

d ¿Qué __ (querer) hacer (vosotros) esta noche?

e – ¿Qué tipo de música __ (preferir) usted?

f Yo __ (preferir) la música clásica.

2 *Fill in the gaps with a suitable pronoun.*

a El té, ¿__ prefiere con leche o con limón?

b – Quería un agua mineral, por favor.
– __ quiere con gas o sin gas?

c Dos cervezas, por favor. __ quiero bien frías.

d Por favor, ¿puede enviar dos desayunos a la habitación 705? __ queremos ahora mismo.

e Llamo por el apartamento de la calle de Cervantes. Quisiera ver__ esta tarde.

Check your answers now; if you got them right, it means you are ready to request what you want and state your preferences in a number of contexts, whether ordering food in a restaurant, booking a hotel room or doing your shopping. All you need now is to expand your vocabulary related to these themes. And remember, you can always use **quiero** *I want* or **prefiero** *I prefer* to say what you want or prefer, followed by the neutral form **esto** *this* if you don't know the name of something.

13

Expressing likes and dislikes

In this unit, you will learn how to:
- *say whether you like or dislike something*
- *give similar information about other people*
- *ask questions about likes and dislikes*

Language points
- **gustar**
- *indirect object pronouns*
- *prepositional forms of pronouns*
- *position of indirect object pronouns*
- *other verbs expressing likes and dislikes*

Key sentences

In the grammar notes that follow, you will find information about how to express likes and dislikes using the verb **gustar** *to like*. You will also find an explanation of the pronouns which are normally used with this verb.

SAYING WHETHER YOU LIKE OR DISLIKE SOMETHING

Me/Nos *gusta* **el tenis/nadar.**
No me/nos *gusta* **esa música/ver la televisión.**

I/We like tennis/swimming.
We don't like that music/watching television.

SAYING WHETHER OTHERS LIKE OR DISLIKE SOMETHING

Le *gusta* **España/***gustan* **los españoles.**	*He/She likes Spain/Spaniards.*
Te *gusta/gustan,* **¿verdad?**	*You like it/them, don't you?*
A Sol y Paco/ellos les *gusta* **bailar.**	*Sol and Paco/They like dancing.*

ASKING QUESTIONS ABOUT LIKES AND DISLIKES

¿Te/le *gusta* **el español?**	*Do you like Spanish?* (fam./pol.)
¿Qué os/les *gusta* **hacer?**	*What do you like doing?* (fam./pol.)

Insight

Note that the *-ing* verb form in phrases like *I like listening to music*, *She likes singing*, etc. translates in Spanish with the infinitive: **Me gusta escuchar música, Le gusta cantar.**

Grammar summary

1 GUSTAR *TO LIKE*

To say whether you like or dislike something, you can use the verb **gustar**. It is a special kind of verb which is normally used in the third person singular or plural, depending on the number of the noun which follows. The verb must be preceded by an indirect object pronoun. These are words such as **me** (*me, to me*), **te** (*you, to you*), as in **me gusta** *I like it* or, literally, *it is pleasing to me*; **te gusta** *you like it* or, literally, *it is pleasing to you*. An explanation about indirect object pronouns is necessary before giving further examples of the use of **gustar**.

Insight

A more literal translation of this construction with **gustar** may help you to remember it: **Me gusta el cine** *To me is pleasing the cinema*, **Nos gusta viajar** *To us it is pleasing to travel*.

2 INDIRECT OBJECT PRONOUNS

In Unit 12, you learned the use of direct object pronouns, as in sentences like **Lo quiero** (*I want it*), **Los quiero** (*I want them*), **Me prefiere** (*He/She prefers me*). Here, we are dealing with another set of pronouns – indirect object pronouns – which, although mostly similar in form to the others, are used differently.

First and second person indirect object pronouns
Consider this sentence:

El recepcionista me cambia el dinero.	*The receptionist changes the money for me.*

Here, the subject of the sentence is **el recepcionista** *the receptionist*, the direct object is **el dinero** *the money* (the thing changed) and the indirect object is **me** *for me* (that is, the person for whom the money is changed). First and second person indirect object pronouns are no different in form from direct object pronouns (see Unit 12, **Grammar summary**). Here are their forms:

Subject pronouns		Indirect object pronouns	
yo	*I*	**me**	*me, to me, for me*
tú	*you* (fam. sing.)	**te**	*you, to you, for you*
nosotros/as	*we*	**nos**	*us, to us, for us*
vosotros/as	*you* (fam. pl.)	**os**	*you, to you, for you*

In sentences with **gustar**, indirect object pronouns will translate literally as *to me, to you, to us*.

me gusta	*I like it* (lit. *to me it is pleasing*)
te gusta	*you like it* (lit. *to you it is pleasing*)
nos gusta	*we like it* (lit. *to us it is pleasing*)
os gusta	*you like it* (lit. *to you it is pleasing*)

The verb itself may be in the plural.

me gustan	*I like them* (lit. *to me they are pleasing*)
te gustan	*you like them* (lit. *to you they are pleasing*)
no nos gustan	*we don't like them* (lit. *to us they are not pleasing*)

Notice that negative sentences are formed by placing **no** before the pronoun.

Here are some examples of the use of indirect object pronouns with verbs other than **gustar:**

¿Me/Nos da el dinero, por favor?	*Will you give me/us the money, please?*
¿Te traigo el periódico?	*Shall I bring you the newspaper?*
Él me/nos enseña español.	*He teaches me/us Spanish.*

··

Insight

Note that *Will you ...?* and *Shall I ...?* in requests and offers such as those above translate into Spanish with the present tense. Here are two further examples: *Will you bring us some more water, please?* **¿Nos trae más agua, por favor?**, *Shall I help you with the luggage?* **¿Te ayudo con el equipaje?**

··

Third person indirect object pronouns
In the third person, the indirect object pronoun is **le** for both masculine and feminine. The plural form is **les.**

Subject pronouns		*Indirect object pronouns*	
usted	*you* (pol.)	**le**	*you, to you, for you*
él	*he*	**le**	*him, to him, for him*
ella	*she*	**le**	*her, to her, for her*
ustedes	*you* (pol.)	**les**	*you, to you, for you*
ellos/as	*they*	**les**	*them, to them, for them*

Here are some examples with **gustar:**

Le gusta viajar.	*You like/He/She/likes to travel.*
Les gusta España.	*You/They like Spain.*
¿Le gusta el vino español?	*Do you/Does he/she like Spanish wine?*

Here are some examples with verbs other than **gustar**:

¿Le doy el pasaporte?	*Shall I give you/him/her the passport?*
Ella le prepara la cena.	*She prepares dinner for you/him/her.*
Él les repara el coche.	*He repairs the car for you/them.*

Insight

The following simple rule should help you to remember third person indirect object pronouns: for **él**, **ella**, **Vd.**, use **le**; for **ellos**, **ellas**, **ustedes**, use **les**. The indirect forms for **yo**, **tú**, **nosotros** and **vosotros** are the same as for direct object pronouns: **me, te, nos, os.**

3 PREPOSITIONAL FORMS OF PRONOUNS

Consider this sentence from the previous examples: **Le gusta viajar.** This sentence translates into English in three different ways: *You like to travel, He likes to travel, She likes to travel.* To avoid this kind of ambiguity, and also to add emphasis, we use another set of pronouns preceded by the preposition **a.** These are known technically as *prepositional pronouns* and, except for the first and second person singular, they are the same as subject pronouns: **mí** (for **yo**), **ti** (for **tú**), **él, ella, usted, nosotros, vosotros, ellos, ellas, ustedes.**

A usted le **gusta viajar.**	*You like to travel.*
A él **le gusta viajar.**	*He likes to travel.*
A ella **le gusta viajar.**	*She likes to travel.*
A ustedes **les gusta España.**	*You like Spain.*
A ellos **les gusta Madrid.**	*They like Madrid. (masc.)*
A ellas **les gusta Sevilla.**	*They like Seville. (fem.)*

The preposition **a** is also used before someone's name.

A Alfonso **no le gusta fumar.**	*Alfonso doesn't like to smoke.*
A Cristina **no le gusta beber.**	*Cristina doesn't like to drink.*
A Luis y Juan **no les gusta esto.**	*Luis and Juan don't like this.*
A Miguel **y a mí nos gustan los deportes.**	*Miguel and I like sports.*

Emphatic use of prepositional pronouns
Sometimes the function of prepositional pronouns is purely emphatic.

A mí **me gusta.**	I like it.
A ti **te gusta.**	You like it.
A nosotros **nos gusta.**	We like it.
A vosotros **os gusta.**	You like it.

To avoid repetition of **gustar**, use the construction **a** + prepositional pronoun.

Me gusta **muchísimo.**	I like it very much.
¿Y a ti**?**	Do you?
A mí **también.**	I do too.

The same construction may be used in negative sentences with **tampoco**.

No me gusta **Madrid.**	I don't like Madrid.
¿Y a usted**?**	Do you?
A mí **tampoco.**	I don't either.

4 POSITION OF INDIRECT OBJECT PRONOUNS

The position of indirect object pronouns is the same as that of direct object pronouns, that is, normally before the main verb. But when there are two object pronouns in a sentence (which may happen with verbs other than **gustar**), one indirect and one direct, the indirect object pronoun must come first. Consider these sentences:

Él me cambia el dinero.	He changes the money for me.
Él me lo cambia.	He changes it for me.

When the indirect object **le** or **les** precedes **lo, la, los** or **las**, the indirect object becomes **se**.

Yo *le* **cambio el dinero.**	*I change the money for you.*
Yo *lo* **cambio.**	*I change it.*
Yo *se lo* **cambio.**	*I change it for you.*

Insight

This use of **se** in place of **le, les,** etc. is another one to add to those you already know: **Se levantan** (reflexive), **¿Se puede entrar?** (impersonal), **Se produce en España** (passive).

5 OTHER VERBS EXPRESSING LIKES AND DISLIKES

Verbs such as **encantar, fascinar** *to like very much, to love* and **agradar** *to like* function in the same way as **gustar.**

Nos *encanta* **hablar español.**	*We love to speak Spanish.*
Me *fascina* **Sevilla.**	*I love Seville.*
No le *agradan* **las fiestas.**	*He/She doesn't like parties.*

Agradar is less frequent and less colloquial than **gustar.**

To say you don't like something at all, use the word **nada** *nothing* in a double negative construction: **No me gusta(n) nada** *I don't like it/them at all.* You can express even stronger dislike with **detestar** *to hate, detest* or **odiar** *to hate,* followed by an infinitive. These two verbs follow the pattern of ordinary verbs like **hablar, trabajar,** etc.

| *Detesto* **planchar.** | *I hate ironing.* |
| *Odio tener que* **hacerlo.** | *I hate having to do it.* |

Insight

There are a number of other verbs which, not related to liking and dislike, function in the same way as **gustar: apetecer** *to fancy,* **hacer ilusión** *to look forward to,* **importar** *to matter,* **interesar** *to interest,* **parecer** *to seem,* **preocupar** *to worry,* etc.

| **No me importa nada.** | *It doesn't matter at all to me.* |
| **Nos preocupa su salud.** | *We are worried about his/her health.* |

In context

1 In Seville for the first time.

> **Ella** ¿Te gusta Sevilla?
> **Él** Sí, me gusta muchísimo. ¿Y a ti?
> **Ella** A mí también, pero hace mucho calor, ¿verdad?
> **Él** Sí, yo prefiero el clima de Galicia.
> **Ella** A mí no me gusta nada la lluvia. En Galicia llueve demasiado.

la lluvia *rain*
Llueve demasiado. *It rains too much.*

2 An interview about Madrid.

> **Periodista** Señor, ¿le gusta a Vd. Madrid?
> **Señor** Sí y no.
> **Periodista** ¿Qué es lo que le gusta de Madrid?
> **Señor** Me gustan sus museos, sus espectáculos, sus restaurantes, que son estupendos …
> **Periodista** ¿Y qué es lo que no le gusta?
> **Señor** Bueno, no me gusta el tráfico excesivo que tiene Madrid. Es una ciudad muy ruidosa y a mí me gusta la tranquilidad.

Practice

1 Fill in the gaps in these sentences with a suitable pronoun.
  a A Juan no __ gusta el fútbol.
  b A nosotros __ gusta hacer deportes.
  c A Carmen y Antonio __ gusta mucho viajar.
  d A __ me gustan los idiomas.
  e A __ también te gustan, ¿verdad?
  f A ella __ encanta el cine.
  g Y a vosotros, ¿qué __ gusta hacer en las vacaciones?
  h A mí y a mi familia __ encantan los españoles.

2 You are thinking of sharing your flat with a Spanish-speaking person, so you want to know what he/she likes or dislikes. How would you ask him/her the following?

a Whether he/she likes the room.
b Whether he/she likes to cook.
c What music he/she likes.
d What programmes he/she likes (**programas de televisión**).
e Whether he/she likes animals (**los animales**).
f What he/she likes to do at weekends (**los fines de semana**).

3 Can you say what these people like to do on their holidays? Match the pictures with the phrases below and write full sentences using **gustar**.

Ejemplo: Enrique – leer y escuchar música
A Enrique le gusta leer y escuchar música.

1 Rafael y su novia – ir de camping
2 Juan – levantarse tarde
3 Andrés – montar en bicicleta
4 Ángeles – descansar y tomar el sol
5 Paco – nadar
6 María y su familia – ir de vacaciones a Nueva York

TEST YOURSELF

1 *Fill in the gaps with an appropriate pronoun, an indirect one or a prepositional one.*

    a A __ me gusta mucho hacer montañismo.

    b ¿Qué deportes te gustan a __?

    c A Enrique y Patricio __ encanta salir de excursión.

    d A Soledad no __ agrada su jefe. La verdad es que le odia.

    e A Pablo y a mí __ encanta Madrid. Y a mis hijos también __ gusta mucho.

2 *Put the following words and phrases in the right order.*

    a fascina – a – bailar salsa – le – Rebeca

    b también – gusta – vosotros – ¿verdad? – os – a

    c mucho – gustan – las novelas – me – de García Márquez

    d nada – me – esos – gustan – programas de televisión – no

    e Ricardo y Cristina – las películas – a – de Almodóvar – encantan – les

Words like **me, te, le, lo, la,** etc. are important, so if you are still uncertain about their use or the use of verbs like **gustar,** go back through the relevant points in the **Grammar summary** of this unit again or, for pronouns, study paragraph 5 of the **Grammar reference.** Don't be discouraged if you still make a few mistakes, as that is quite normal. As you progress in the course, you will gain more confidence and will probably be able to handle them.

14

Asking for and giving opinions

In this unit, you will learn how to:
- *ask opinions*
- *give opinions*

Language points
- **parecer**
- *relative pronoun* **que**
- *other verbs used in expressing opinions*
- *phrases expressing opinions*

Key sentences

As in English, opinions in Spanish can be expressed in a variety of ways using verbs like **parecer** *to seem*, **pensar**, **creer**, **opinar** *to think*, or expressions such as **a mi parecer, en mi opinión** *in my opinion*.

ASKING SOMEONE'S OPINION

¿Qué te parece el hotel/la gente?	*What do you think of the hotel/ the people?*
¿Qué opinas/piensas de él?	*What do you think about him?*
¿No crees que tengo razón?	*Don't you think I'm right?*

GIVING OPINIONS

Me parecen guapos/ simpáticos.	*I think they are good-looking/ nice.*
Lo considero difícil/imposible.	*I believe it's difficult/impossible.*
Creo/Pienso que es una buena idea.	*I think it's a good idea.*

Grammar summary

1 PARECER *TO THINK, SEEM*

To ask and give opinions, you can use **parecer** in a construction like that with **gustar** (Unit 13), with an indirect object pronoun (**me, te, le,** etc.) preceding the third person of the verb: **parece** (if followed by a singular form), **parecen** (when followed by a plural form).

Asking someone's opinion

¿Qué *te parece* **la gente?**	*What do you think of the people?*
¿Qué *le parecen* **las playas?**	*What do you think of the beaches?*
¿Qué *os parece* **si la invito?**	*What if I invite/about inviting her?*
Y a ti, ¿qué *te parece?*	*What do you think?*
Vamos al cine, ¿te *parece?*	*What do you say we go to the cinema?*
Podríamos ir a la piscina si *te parece.*	*We could go to the swimming pool if you like.*
¿Les parece bien este?	*Is this one all right with you?*

> ## Insight
> A more literal translation of the sentences starting with **que** would be *What does/do ... seem to you?*, while the last sentence is closer to the English *Does this seem all right with you?* Note that **te, le, os, les** *you* come right before **parecer.**

Giving your opinion

Me parece(n) **simpático(s).**	*I think he is/they are nice. (lit. To me he seems/they seem nice.)*
Nos parece(n) **difícil(es).**	*I think it's/they're difficult.*
Me parece **que es una buena idea.**	*I think it's a good idea.*
A mí *me parece* **bien.**	*I think it's all right./It's all right with me.*
Me parece **que sí/no.**	*I think so/don't think so.*

Reporting someone else's opinion

Le parece **una buena idea.**	*He/She thinks it's a good idea. (lit. To him/her it seems a good idea.)*
A Eva *le parece* **extraño.**	*Eva thinks it is strange.*
A Javier también.	*So does Javier.*

> **Insight**
>
> You will note that the constructions above are the same as those you encountered with **gustar** in Unit 13, with the preposition **a** followed by a prepositional pronoun (**mí, ti, él, ella,** etc.) or a name. The phrase **a mí** in **A mí me parece** is emphatic.

In statements, **parecer** can also be used without an indirect object pronoun, but its omission makes it impersonal, neutralizing the fact that it is *your* opinion, or someone else's, that you are expressing or reporting. The translation in English in this case would be *It seems ...*, *It doesn't seem ...*, etc. rather than *I think ..., you think ...*, etc.

Parece **difícil.**	*It seems difficult.*
No *parece* **apropiado.**	*It doesn't seem appropriate.*

> **Insight**
>
> In all the previous examples, **parecer** appears in the present tense, but its past tense forms (see Unit 18) are equally frequent. To say what you thought of something or someone, use **pareció** (sing.) or **parecieron** (pl.).

El concierto *nos pareció* excelente.	*We thought the concert was excellent. (lit. The concert to us seemed excellent.)*
Tus amigos *me parecieron* muy guapos.	*I thought your friends were very good looking. (lit. Your friends to me seemed very good-looking).*

2 QUE *THAT, WHICH, WHO*

The word *that*, as in *I think that it's a good idea*, translates into Spanish as **que**. In English, the word can sometimes be omitted, but not, however, in Spanish. Consider the use of **que** and its English equivalent in the following examples.

Creo *que* ella tiene razón.	*I think (that) she's right.*
El último libro *que* escribió es muy bueno.	*The last book (which) he/she wrote is very good.*
La persona *que* llamó me pareció muy agradable.	*The person who phoned seemed very pleasant.*

Insight

The main points to remember with regard to **que** is that it cannot be omitted and that it can stand for that, which and who: **Me parece que ...** *It seems (to me) that ...*, **La casa que ...** *The house which/that ...*, **La persona que ...** *The person who/that ...* For more information on this, see Relative pronouns in the **Grammar reference**.

3 *OTHER VERBS USED IN THE EXPRESSION OF OPINIONS*

Here are some other verbs used in the expression of opinions.

pensar (e > ie) to think
¿Qué *piensa* Vd. de mí?	*What do you think of me?*
Pienso que es Vd. muy amable.	*I think you're very kind.*

Pensamos **que es una idea excelente.**	*We think it's an excellent idea.*
Pienso **que sí/no.**	*I think so/don't think so.*

creer to think

¿Qué *cree* **Vd. que puede pasar?**	*What do you think can happen?*
Creo **que no hay que preocuparse.**	*I don't think one needs to worry.*
Creo **que sí/no.**	*I think so/don't think so.*
¿**No** *crees* **tú**/*cree* **Vd.**?	*Don't you think so?*

opinar to think

¿Qué *opinan* **Vds. de lo que digo?**	*What do you think of what I'm saying?*
Yo *opino* **que Vd. tiene razón.**	*I think you're right.*

considerar to consider, think

Considero **que debemos hablar con él.**	*I think we should speak to him.*
Ella *considera* **que es suficiente.**	*She thinks it's enough.*

Insight

Pensar and **opinar** are extremely common in questions: **¿Qué piensas/opinas tú?** *What do you think?* In statements, **creer** and **pensar** seem to be the most frequent: **Creo/Pienso que ...** *I think that ...*

4 PHRASES EXPRESSING OPINIONS

Personal opinions may also be expressed using phrases such as **a mi parecer, a mi juicio, en mi opinión,** all of which mean *in my opinion*.

A mi parecer, **no debemos aceptar.**	*In my opinion, we mustn't accept.*
A mi juicio, **ella es la persona más apropiada.**	*In my opinion, she is the most suitable person.*
En mi opinión, **debemos decírselo.**	*In my opinion, we must tell him/her.*

In context

Javier and Eva have just met at the lounge of their hotel in Spain. They discuss the place where they're staying.

Javier	¿Qué te parece el hotel?
Eva	Creo que no está nada mal, aunque la comida no me parece muy buena.
Javier	Las habitaciones son estupendas, ¿no crees tú?
Eva	Bueno, sí, la mía tiene unas vistas fantásticas, pero es un poco ruidosa. ¿Y la ciudad te gusta?
Javier	Sí, pienso que está bien, pero hay demasiada gente. Prefiero los sitios pequeños.
Eva	Sí, yo también.
Javier	¿Estás libre ahora?
Eva	Sí. No tengo nada que hacer.
Javier	¿Qué te parece si vamos a tomar un café?
Eva	De acuerdo. Vamos.

No está nada mal. *It's not bad at all.*
el sitio *place*
¿Qué te parece si vamos ...? *What about going ...?*
Vamos. *Let's go.*

Practice

1 A Spanish-speaking friend is visiting you at home for the first time, so you want to know what he/she thinks of the place and the people. Ask his/her opinion about the following using the expressions in brackets.

    a La ciudad (parecer)
    b Los museos (parecer)
    c Los parques (opinar)

d La gente (pensar)

e Mis amigos (opinar)

f La vida en la ciudad (pensar)

2 Antonio, from Spain, is spending some time with his relatives in Buenos Aires, the capital of Argentina. In a letter to you, he gives his opinion about the place. Fill in the gaps with an appropriate expression from the list, without repeating any.

a mi parecer	**en mi opinión**	**parecer**
considerar	**creer**	**pensar**

No te imaginas lo que es esta ciudad. A mí me (1) __ fantástica y (2) __ que los argentinos son muy simpáticos. (3) __, lo mejor de esta ciudad es la vida nocturna y la vida cultural. La vida cultural, especialmente, la (4) __ excelente. Hay mucho que ver. La ciudad es agradable, aunque, (5) __, la vida aquí no es fácil. (6) __ que es una ciudad cara.

3 You are on holiday in a Spanish-speaking country. A Spanish-speaking friend phones you at your hotel. Follow the guidelines and fill in your part of the conversation.

Tu amigo/a	¿Qué te parece el hotel?
Tú	*Say you think the hotel is very good, but you think the people are a bit noisy.*
Tu amigo/a	Y la playa, ¿qué tal?
Tú	*Say you think the beach is excellent.*
Tu amigo/a	Sí, es una playa muy buena. ¿Estás libre esta noche?
Tú	*Say yes, you are free, and ask your friend what he/she thinks about going to a club (una disco).*
Tu amigo/a	De acuerdo, vamos. Podemos ir a la disco que está cerca del hotel. ¿No te parece?

TEST YOURSELF

1 *Fill in the gaps with the correct forms of the verbs in brackets, using* **que** *where appropriate.*

   a ¿Qué te __ Isabel García? (parecer)
   b (Yo) __ es la persona ideal para el puesto. (pensar)
   c Pues, yo __ tiene poca experiencia. (creer)
   d Pero tiene muy buenas referencias, ¿no __ tú? (creer)
   e Y tú Miguel, ¿qué __? (opinar)
   f Pues, yo __ es la mejor candidata para el puesto. Los otros no me __ tan buenos. (opinar, parecer)

2 *Translate the following into Spanish using the verbs in brackets and the familiar form where appropriate.*

   a What do you think of the apartment? (**parecer**)
   b It's nice, but I think it is a bit small. (**pensar**)
   c The views are wonderful, don't you think? (**creer**)
   d Yes, I think so. (**creer**)
   e But I think it is expensive. (**considerar**)
   f What if we see the apartment on Molina Street? (**parecer**)

Expressing simple opinions such as those above is the first step towards being able to give more elaborate opinions later on in the course. If you got your answers right and you feel confident that you can handle all the key verbs, especially **parecer** and **creer**, which are the two most frequent ones, go on to Unit 15, in which you will learn to talk about the future.

15

Referring to future plans and events

In this unit, you will learn how to:
- *ask and answer questions about future plans*
- *ask and answer questions about future events*

Language points
- **ir a** + *infinitive*
- *future tense*
- *present tense with future meaning*
- **pensar** *to refer to plans and intentions*
- *the future of probability*

Key sentences

As in English, future plans and future events can be expressed in Spanish in a number of ways, the future tense being only one of them.

ASKING AND ANSWERING QUESTIONS ABOUT FUTURE PLANS

¿Vas/Vais a hacerlo/comprarlo?	*Are you going to do/buy it?*
Voy/Vamos a hacerlo/comprarlo.	*I'm/We're going to do/buy it.*
¿Qué piensas hacer?	*What do you intend to do?*
Pienso decírselo.	*I'm thinking of telling him/her.*

ASKING AND ANSWERING QUESTIONS ABOUT FUTURE EVENTS

¿A qué hora será/empezará la reunión?	*What time will the meeting be/ begin?*
No tendremos/haremos la reunión.	*We won't have/hold the meeting.*

Grammar summary

1 IR A + *INFINITIVE*

Future plans and intentions are normally expressed with the present tense of **ir** (**voy, vas, va, vamos, vais, van**) followed by the preposition **a** and an infinitive. This construction is equivalent to the English *to be going to* + infinitive. It is popular in Spanish and it is often used to replace the future tense.

¿Qué *vas a* **hacer esta noche?**	*What are you going to do tonight?*
Voy a **salir a cenar.**	*I'm going out for dinner.*
¿Cuándo *vais a* **volver?**	*When are you going to return?*
Vamos a **volver el sábado.**	*We're going to return on Saturday.*

Insight

This construction with **ir** + **a** + infinitive is far more frequent than the future tense, especially in the spoken language. It is a very useful construction to know, as it will allow you to refer to the future even where English uses the *will* form.

2 *FUTURE TENSE*

Uses

The future tense has become less common in the spoken language where it is being gradually replaced by the **ir a** construction explained above. Nowadays, its use is restricted more to certain contexts. In formal written language, such as that of the press for instance, the future tense is very frequent. In spoken language, it is often used in sentences expressing promises, commands, a certain degree of uncertainty and probability.

Formation

To form the future tense, you use the infinitive followed by the ending, which is the same for all three conjugations. Here are the future forms of three regular verbs, representing each of the three conjugations.

estar to be		**ver** to see	
estaré	I will be	veré	I will see
estarás	you will be (fam.)	verás	you will see (fam.)
estará	you/he/she will be	verá	you/he/she will see
estaremos	we will be	veremos	we will see
estaréis	you will be (fam.)	veréis	you will see (fam.)
estarán	you/they will be	verán	you/they will see

ir to go			
iré	I will go	iremos	we will go
irás	you will go (fam.)	iréis	you will go (fam.)
irá	you/he/she will go	irán	you/they will go

Press language

El presidente de Venezuela llegará a Barajas a las 7:30 horas, donde será recibido por el presidente del gobierno español.

The president of Venezuela will arrive at Barajas at 7.30, where he will be received by the president of the Spanish government.

La nueva fábrica de automóviles que se instalará en Zaragoza iniciará su producción el 30 de junio próximo.

The new car factory which will be installed in Zaragoza will start production on 30 June.

Expressing promises

Te lo daré mañana.	*I'll give it to you tomorrow.*
No se lo contaré.	*I won't tell him.*

Expressing commands

Os quedaréis aquí.	*You'll stay here.*
Lo terminarás inmediatemente.	*You'll finish it immediately.*

Expressing a degree of uncertainty

Irás a Francia, ¿verdad?	*You'll go to France, won't you?*
Me ayudarás, ¿no?	*You will help me, won't you?*

For the future of probability, see paragraph 5 below.

Insight

Some uses of *will* in English translate in Spanish with the present tense: *Will you pass me the salt, please?* **¿Me pasa la sal, por favor?**, *Will you sit down?* **¿Quiere sentarse?**, *He won't listen* **No quiere escuchar.**

Irregular future forms
Some verbs have an irregular stem in the future tense, but the endings are the same as those of regular verbs. Here is a list of the most important ones.

decir *to say, tell*	diré, dirás, dirá, diremos, diréis, dirán
haber *to have* (auxiliary)	habré, habrás, habrá habremos, habréis, habrán
hacer *to do, make*	haré, harás, hará, haremos, haréis, harán
obtener *to obtain*	obtendré, obtendrás, obtendrá, obtendremos, obtendréis, obtendrán
poder *can, be able to*	podré, podrás, podrá, podremos, podréis, podrán

(Contd)

poner *to put*	pondré, pondrás, pondrá,
	pondremos, pondréis, pondrán
querer *to want*	querré, querrás, querrá,
	querremos, querréis, querrán
saber *to know*	sabré, sabrás, sabrá,
	sabremos, sabréis, sabrán
salir *to go out*	saldré, saldrás, saldrá,
	saldremos, saldréis, saldrán
tener *to have*	tendré, tendrás, tendrá,
	tendremos, tendréis, tendrán
venir *to come*	vendré, vendrás, vendrá,
	vendremos, vendréis, vendrán

Insight

Verbs derived from those above have similar forms: **rehacer** *to redo, do again*, **desdecirse** *to retract*, **abstenerse** *to abstain*, **contener** *to contain*, **detener** *to detain*, **imponer** *to impose*, **proponer** *to propose*.

For a list of the most common irregular verbs, see the **Irregular verbs** section.

¿Qué harás mañana?	*What will you do tomorrow?*
Saldré con Ana.	*I'll go out with Ana.*
Tendrás que decírmelo.	*You'll have to tell me.*
No te lo diré.	*I won't tell you.*
Podrá Vd. venir el lunes,	*You'll be able to come on*
¿verdad?	*Monday, won't you?*
Creo que no podré.	*I don't think I'll be able to.*

3 PRESENT TENSE WITH FUTURE MEANING

As in English, Spanish also uses the present tense to refer to the future, particularly to the immediate future and with verbs which indicate movement, for example **ir** *to go*, **salir** *to go out*, **venir** *to come*, etc., but also with a few other verbs, such as **hacer** *to do*, **trabajar** *to work*, etc. Time phrases such as **mañana** *tomorrow*, pasado mañana *the day after tomorrow*, **la semana que viene** *next week*, **el mes que viene** *next month*, **la semana próxima** *next week*, **el mes próximo** *next month*, etc., will make it clear that the time reference is the future and not the present.

¿Qué haces *mañana***?**	*What are you doing tomorrow?*
Voy **a la piscina.**	*I'm going to the swimming pool.*
Salimos *pasado mañana.*	*We leave the day after tomorrow.*
Él llega *la semana que viene.*	*He is arriving next week.*
¿Trabajas *mañana***?**	*Are you working tomorrow?*

4 PENSAR (TO THINK, INTEND) TO REFER TO PLANS AND INTENTIONS

Pensar + infinitive corresponds to the English *to intend to* + infinitive, *plan to* + infinitive, *propose to* + infinitive, but a more literal translation would be *to be thinking of* + *-ing*.

¿Qué *piensas* **hacer este verano?**	*What are you planning to do this summer?*
Pienso **ir a Nueva York.**	*I'm thinking of going to New York.*
Pensamos **casarnos.**	*We intend/plan to get married.*

5 THE FUTURE OF PROBABILITY

The future tense is often used to express probability or conjecture.

¿Qué hora *será***?**	*I wonder what time it is?/What time can it be?*
Serán **las dos.**	*It must be two o'clock.*
¿Dónde *estará* **María?**	*I wonder where María is./Where can María be?*

Insight

The use of the future tense to express the idea of *I wonder* is extremely common in spoken Spanish, much more so than the alternative with **preguntarse** *to wonder* (lit. *to ask oneself*): **Me pregunto qué dirán,** *I wonder what they'll say,* **Me pregunto si todavía está/estará allí** *I wonder whether he/she is still there.*

In context

1 Víctor and Mercedes talk about their summer holiday.

Víctor	¿Qué vais a hacer tú y Pablo este verano?
Mercedes	Vamos a ir a Buenos Aires a visitar a unos parientes.
Víctor	¿Vais con los chicos?
Mercedes	No, ellos van a quedarse con los abuelos en Madrid.
Víctor	¿Cuánto tiempo vais a estar allí?
Mercedes	Un mes solamente. Vamos a volver a finales de agosto. Y tú, ¿qué planes tienes? ¿Irás otra vez a Málaga?
Víctor	No, esta vez iré a casa de unos amigos en Ibiza.
Mercedes	Ibiza te gustará mucho. Es un lugar precioso. ¿Vas a quedarte mucho tiempo?
Víctor	Un par de semanas. Tendré que volver antes del quince pues viene Marta a pasar unos días conmigo …

Insight

Note the position of the reflexive pronoun **se** in **Van a quedarse** *They are going to stay*, and **¿Vas a quedarte ...?** *Are you going to stay?* This follows the general rule that pronouns can be either attached to the end of the infinitive or can precede the main verb: **Se van a quedar, ¿Te vas a quedar?**

a finales de *at the end of*
otra vez *again*
esta vez *this time*
un par de semanas *a couple of weeks*
a pasar unos días *to spend a few days*

2 Read this paragraph from a newspaper:

El 1 de abril próximo llegará a nuestro país en visita oficial el ministro de asuntos exteriores británico Sir John Perkins, quien se entrevistará con el jefe del gobierno español. El ministro permanecerá en Madrid por espacio de tres días y en las conversaciones que sostendrá con las autoridades de gobierno se tratará el tema de Gibraltar …

el ministro de asuntos exteriors *minister of foreign affairs*
entrevistarse *to meet*
por espacio de *for, during*
permanecer *to remain*
sostener *to hold*
tratar *to deal with*

Practice

1 Here are Miguel's and María and Alberto's plans for this summer.

Miguel
Hacer un curso de inglés en Inglaterra

María and Alberto
Viajar a la India

  a How would you ask Miguel what he's going to do this summer, and how would you ask María and Alberto the same question?
  b How would Miguel reply? And María and Alberto?
  c How would you tell someone else about their plans?
  d How would you tell someone what you are going to do?

2 Sara sent an e-mail to Ana announcing her travel plans. Change the infinitives in brackets into the appropriate form of the future tense.

Querida Ana

Te escribo para confirmarte mi viaje a Madrid, que (1) (ser) el sábado 15 de septiembre. (2) (Salir, yo) de aquí a las 9:00 de la mañana y (3) (llegar) al aeropuerto de Barajas a las 12:00. (4) (Quedarse) en el hotel Victoria, y te (5) (llamar) inmediatamente. No (6) (poder) estar más de dos días en Madrid, porque (7) (tener) que viajar a Andalucía, pero en esos dos días (8) (poder, nosotras) salir juntas. (9) (Venir, tú) conmigo a Toledo, ¿verdad? (10) (Tener, tú) que acompañarme.

3 What will Ana do next year? Match the drawings with the phrases below and write full sentences using the correct form of the future tense.

    a (Ir) de vacaciones a Londres.
    b (Hacer) un curso de inglés.
    c (Practicar) deportes.
    d (Estudiar) enfermería.

TEST YOURSELF

1 *Change the verbs in brackets into the correct form of the future tense.*

   a Creo que Victoria (llegar) esta tarde, pero Pepe y Paco no (venir) hasta mañana.

   b Los pasajeros del vuelo AB506 (deber) embarcar por la puerta número doce.

   c (llamar, yo) por teléfono a Roberto y le (decir) lo que pasa.

   d Hoy (haber) una fiesta en casa de Paloma. ¿(Venir) tú también?

   e Llueve demasiado. (quedarse, nosotros) en casa y (mirar) la televisión.

   f ¿Qué (hacer) vosotros en las vacaciones? ¿(Ir) a Mallorca otra vez?

2 *Translate the following into Spanish.*

   a Diego is arriving tomorrow. He's going to stay for a week.

   b We are planning to go to Cuenca. I wonder whether he'll like it.

   c Will you come with us? You're not working tomorrow, are you?

   d I'm sorry, but I can't. I'm going to take the children to the dentist.

   e I'm going to have a coffee. Will you have one too?

   f Yes, thank you, but I'll have to go soon. I'm going out with Anita.

Question 1 assessed your correct handling of the future tense, while question 2 focused on the different alternative ways of referring to the future. The constructions in question 2 are very important, as these are the ones you are more likely to need when expressing yourself orally in Spanish. Check the **Grammar summary** again if necessary before you go on to Unit 16.

16

Making requests and offers

In this unit, you will learn how to:
- *make requests*
- *reply to a request*
- *make offers*
- *reply to offers*

Language points
- *present tense in requests and offers*
- poder *and* querer *in requests and offers*
- podría *in requests*

Key sentences

We can make requests and offers in English in a number of ways. Consider for instance the following sentences: *Will you help me, please?*, *Can you show me the way?*, *Shall I carry your suitcase?*, *Can I make you some coffee?* and *Do you want some biscuits?* Spanish, too, has several ways of expressing these ideas. The examples and notes that follow will teach you how to construct sentences of this type using some of the grammar you learned in previous units.

MAKING REQUESTS

¿Me/Nos trae más pan, por favor? *Will you bring me/us some more bread, please?*

¿Puedes ayudarme/nos? *Can you help me/us?*

REPLYING TO A REQUEST

Sí, claro. *Yes, certainly.*

Por supuesto./Desde luego. *Of course./Certainly.*

Naturalmente./Con mucho gusto. *Certainly./With pleasure.*

MAKING OFFERS

¿Le/Te llevo la maleta? *Shall I carry your suitcase?*

¿Quieres/Desea un café? *Do you want/Would you like a coffee?*

REPLYING TO OFFERS

Sí,/Bueno,/De acuerdo, (muchas) gracias. *Yes,/All right, thank you (very much).*

Vale, gracias. *OK, thank you.*

(Es Vd.) muy amable. *That's very kind (of you).*

No, muchas gracias. *No, thank you very much.*

Insight

Sí *yes* and **no** *no*, are often repeated twice or even three times in Spanish as a way of stressing the affirmation or negation: **sí, sí, claro** or **no, no, muchas gracias.** Each of the expressions above may be followed or preceded by others of a similar or different nature: **Sí, un momento/momentito** (diminutive), **por favor; Sí, sí, ahora mismo (se lo traigo); No, no es necesario, gracias; ¡Hombre!, gracias,** etc.

Grammar summary

1 PRESENT TENSE IN REQUESTS AND OFFERS

Requests
A frequent way of making requests is by using the present tense
preceded by an object pronoun.

¿Me despierta(s) a las 7:00, por favor?	*Will you wake me at 7.00, please?*
¿Me pasa(s) la sal?	*Will you pass the salt?*
¿Nos llama(s) un taxi?	*Will you call a taxi for us?*
¿Le dice(s) a Gloria que estoy aquí, por favor?	*Will you tell Gloria I'm here, please?*

> **Insight**
> This way of making requests is very common in the spoken
> language and is simple to use, as all you need is the present
> tense form (for **tú** or **usted**, or the plural forms for **vosotros**
> or **ustedes**) preceded by an object pronoun. This can be
> indirect, as in **¿Le dice(s) a Gloria ...?** *Will you tell Gloria ...?*;
> direct, as in **¿Lo deja(s) aquí, por favor?** *Will you leave it here,
> please?*; or an indirect object pronoun followed by a direct
> one: **¿Me lo deja aquí?** *Will you leave it here for me?*

Offers
The same construction – present tense preceded by an object
pronoun – may be used in making offers.

¿Le doy un poco más?	*Shall I give you some more?*
¿Les reservo una habitación?	*Shall I book a room for you?*
¿Te ayudo?	*Shall I help you?*
¿Os llamo a las 6:00?	*Shall I call you at 6.00?*

> **Insight**
> As in requests, the object pronoun in offers can be indirect,
> direct or an indirect one followed by a direct one: **¿Les**

reservo la habitación? (indirect) *Shall I book the room for you?;*
¿La reservo? (direct) *Shall I book it?;* **¿Se la reservo?** (indirect +
direct) *Shall I book it for you?.*

2 PODER *(CAN)* IN REQUESTS AND OFFERS

Requests
Poder *can, be able to* is used in requests.

¿Puede(s) **llamar al Sr. Martínez, por favor?**	*Can you call señor Martínez, please?*
¿Puede(s) **pasarme el azúcar?**	*Can you pass me the sugar?*
¿Pueden **darnos otra mesa, por favor?**	*Can you give us another table, please?*
¿Puede **Vd. cambiarme este dinero?**	*Can you change this money for me?*
¿Puede **Vd. ayudarnos?**	*Can you help us?*

Notice that the object pronoun may also be placed before the main
verb, **poder**.

¿Nos **pueden dar otra mesa, por favor?**	*Can you give us another table, please?*
¿Me **puede Vd. cambiar este dinero?**	*Can you change this money for me?*

Requests made with **poder** are slightly more formal and polite than
those made with the present tense.

Offers
Poder may also be used in making offers.

¿Puedo **llevarla a su hotel?**	*May I take you to your hotel?*
¿Puedo **hacer algo por Vd.?**	*Can I do something for you?*
¿Podemos **ayudarle?**	*Can we help you?*

3 QUERER *USED IN REQUESTS AND OFFERS*

Requests
Querer *to want* is also used in requests.

¿Quiere **dejarlo/ponerlo aquí, por favor?**	*Would you leave/put it here, please?*
¿Quiere **esperar/volver a llamar, por favor?**	*Would you wait/call again, please?*
Quería **una cerveza.**	*I'd like a beer.*
Quisiera **probarme estos zapatos.**	*I'd like to try on these shoes.*

Offers

¿Quieres/quiere **Vd. una copa?**	*Would you like a drink?*
¿Quiere **Vd. que le ayude/llame?**	*Do you want me to help/call you?*

The last sentence contains a main clause, **¿quiere Vd.?**, and a subordinate clause, **que le ayude/llame.** **Ayude** (from **ayudar** *to help*) and **llame** (from **llamar** *to call*) are in the present subjunctive tense. For an explanation of the subjunctive, see Unit 21.

> **Insight**
>
> An alternative and more formal way of making requests and offers is by using the conditional form (see Unit 22) **querría: ¿Querría Vd. esperar un momentito?** *Would you wait a moment?*, **¿Querría Vd. un café mientras espera?** *Would you like a coffee while you wait?*

4 ¿PODRÍA ...? *(COULD YOU ...?) USED IN REQUESTS*

¿Podría(n) ...? *Could you...?* (singular/plural), a form of the conditional tense (see Unit 22), is often used in making more polite and formal requests.

¿Podría(n) **venir un momento?**	*Would you come a moment?* (pol.)
¿Podría(n) **pasar, por favor?**	*Would you come in, please?* (pol.)
¿Podrías **hablar más despacio?**	*Could you speak more slowly?*

Insight

Podría is a useful word to know when making requests related to your Spanish: **¿Podría repetir, por favor? No entiendo** *Could you repeat, please? I don't understand*, **¿Podría deletrearlo, por favor?** *Could you spell it, please?*, **¿Podría decirme qué significa ... /cómo se pronuncia esta palabra?** *Could you tell me what ... means?/how you pronounce this word?*

In context

1 At the hotel reception.

Viajera	Buenas noches. Me marcho mañana a las 8:00. ¿Puede Vd. llamarme a las 7:00, por favor?
Recepcionista	Sí, por supuesto. ¿Le envío el desayuno a la habitación?
Viajera	Sí, por favor. Y me da la factura también. Quiero pagarla ahora mismo.
Recepcionista	De acuerdo, señora.
Viajera	Ah, necesito un taxi para mañana. ¿Puede Vd. llamarme uno para las 8:00 si es tan amable?
Recepcionista	Por supuesto. Es para ir al aeropuerto, ¿verdad?
Viajera	Sí, tengo que estar allí a las 8:45.
Recepcionista	Muy bien, señora. Yo mismo le llamaré uno. No se preocupe Vd.
Viajera	Muchas gracias.

¿le envío el desayuno ...? *shall I send your breakfast ...?*
si es tan amable *if you are kind enough*
yo mismo *I myself*
no se preocupe *don't worry*

QUICK VOCAB

2 A request note.

Raúl
¿Puedes pasar por mi despacho antes de irte a casa? Necesito hablar
urgentemente contigo. Es importante.
Alfonso

QV

pasar por *to drop in*
urgentemente *urgently*

Practice

1 You are in a hotel in a Spanish-speaking country. Can you make the following requests slightly more informal?

Ejemplo: ¿Podría darme la llave de mi habitación?
        Por favor, ¿me da la llave de mi habitación?

  a ¿Podría traernos dos cafés?
  b ¿Podría pasarme el azúcar?
  c ¿Podría despertarnos a las 7:00?
  d ¿Podría enviarnos el desayuno a la habitación?
  e ¿Podría darnos la cuenta?
  f ¿Podría llamarme un taxi?

2 Marta Díaz is visiting your company and you are looking after her. How would you make the following offers to her? Use the formal form.

  a Shall I help you?
  b Shall I bring you a cup of coffee?
  c Shall I take you to your hotel?
  d Shall I call you tomorrow at 9.00?
  e Shall I show you the city?
  f Shall I introduce you to the manager?

3 Which of the following phrases would be suitable as a caption for the picture below?

    a Tráeme un café.
    b ¿Le traigo un café?
    c Traiga un café.
    d ¿Podría traerme un café?
    e ¿Puedo traerle un café?

TEST YOURSELF

1 *Rephrase the following requests with* **poder** *using the construction object pronoun + present tense.*

   a ¿Puede darme la llave de la habitación 317?
   b ¿Puedes llevarme a la oficina en tu coche?
   c ¿Puede decirme la hora, por favor?
   d ¿Podéis ayudarnos con esto?
   e ¿Pueden reservarnos una mesa para las 9:00, por favor?

2 *Translate these requests into Spanish.*

   a Shall I help you? (fam.)
   b Will you give us the menu (**la carta**), please? (formal)
   c Could you tell me where it is? (formal)
   d Shall I give you some more coffee? (fam.)
   e Will you bring us another bottle of wine (**otra botella de vino**), please? (formal)

The present tense and object pronouns in requests and offers are the main focus of these tests. For a revision of object pronouns, go back to Unit 13 and to paragraph 5 of the **Grammar reference**. It may help you to remember that when you request something for yourself, or for you and someone else, the forms to use are **me** and **nos** respectively. If you are offering something to someone, use **te** or **os** (fam., sing./pl.) or **le** or **les** (formal, sing./pl.).

17

Referring to the recent past

In this unit, you will learn how to:
- *refer to past events which relate to the present*
- *refer to events which have taken place over a period of time, including the present*
- *refer to the recent past*

Language points
- *perfect tense*
- acabar de + *infinitive*
- *Latin-American usage*

Key sentences

REFERRING TO PAST EVENTS WHICH RELATE TO THE PRESENT

Ha recibido/tenido una buena noticia.	*He/She has received/had some good news.*
¿Quién ha llamado/llegado?	*Who's called/arrived?*

REFERRING TO EVENTS WHICH HAVE TAKEN PLACE OVER A PERIOD OF TIME WHICH INCLUDES THE PRESENT

Han estado/trabajado aquí todo el día.	*They've been/worked here all day.*
Lo he visto/hecho varias veces.	*I've seen/done it several times.*

REFERRING TO THE RECENT PAST

He visto/llamado a Nicolás
  hace un momento.

I saw/called Nicolás a moment
  ago.

Se han marchado/ido hoy.

They left today.

> **Insight**
>
> Note the ending of past participle forms: **-ido** for **-er** and **-ir** verbs (**recib**ido, **ten**ido, **ido**); -**ado** for **-ar** verbs (**llam**ado, **lleg**ado, **trabaj**ado). With the exception of a few irregular forms, like **visto**, all past participles are formed in the same way: remove the **-er, -ir** or **-ar**, and add the appropriate ending, the same for all persons of the verb.

Grammar summary

1 *PERFECT TENSE*

Usage

Past events related to the present, for example *She's happy because she's had some good news,* and events which have taken place over a period of time, including the present, as in *They've been here all day,* are normally expressed in English through the perfect tense. Spanish also uses the perfect tense to express the same ideas. Usage differs, however, when referring to the recent past, as in *I saw Peter a while ago,* where Peninsular Spanish favours the use of the perfect tense instead of the simple past.

> **Insight**
>
> The perfect tense is not normally used for referring to actions which took place and ended in the past. For this, you need the preterite tense (see Unit 18): **Vivieron diez años en Barcelona** *They lived for ten years in Barcelona* (but they no longer live there). The perfect tense is used as follows: **Han vivido en Barcelona por muchos años** *They have lived in Barcelona for many years* (they are still living there).

Formation

To form the perfect tense, we use the present tense of **haber** *to have* followed by a past participle, which is invariable. Remember that the past participle of **-ar** verbs ends in **-ado**, while **-er** and **-ir** verbs form the past participle by adding **-ido** to the stem. (For irregular past participles, see the **Irregular verbs** section.)

estudiar	to study
he estudiado	*I have studied*
has estudiado	*you have studied* (fam.)
ha estudiado	*you have studied, he/she has studied*
hemos estudiado	*we have studied*
habéis estudiado	*you have studied* (fam.)
han estudiado	*you/they have studied*

comer	to eat
he comido	*I have eaten*
has comido	*you have eaten* (fam.)
ha comido	*you have eaten, he/she/it has eaten*
hemos comido	*we have eaten*
habéis comido	*you have eaten* (fam.)
han comido	*you/they have eaten*

The following examples include regular and irregular forms.

He estudiado/vivido en España.	*I have studied/lived in Spain.*
Ha comido/bebido demasiado.	*He/She has eaten/drunk too much.*
Han salido/regresado hace unos minutos.	*They went out/came back a few minutes ago.*
¿Qué ha dicho/hecho Pedro?	*What did Pedro say/do?*

The perfect tense is often found with words and phrases like the following, which can also be used with the present tense or the simple past: **hace unos minutos/un momento** *a few minutes/a moment ago*, **ahora** *now*, **hoy** *today*, **esta mañana/tarde** *this morning/afternoon*, **esta semana/este año** *this week/year*, **aún/todavía** *still, yet*, **ya** *already*, etc.

2 ACABAR DE *(TO HAVE JUST)* + INFINITIVE

To express what you have just done, use the verb **acabar** (lit.,
to finish) in the present tense followed by the preposition **de** and
an infinitive.

Ella *acaba de* **salir.**	*She has just gone out.*
Acabo de **llegar.**	*I've just arrived.*
Acabamos de **verlo.**	*We've just seen him.*
Acaban de **marcharse.**	*They've just left.*

3 *LATIN-AMERICAN USAGE*

The perfect tense is used much less frequently in Latin America
than in Peninsular Spanish. To refer to recent events and to events
which are linked to the present, Latin Americans prefer to use the
simple past (see Unit 18), for example **terminé** *I finished* instead
of **he terminado** *I have finished*, ¿**Viste esta película?** *Did you see
this film?* instead of ¿**Has visto esta película?** *Have you seen this
film?* When reference is to events which have occurred over a
period of time, including the present, for example **Todavía/Aún no
hemos terminado** *We still haven't finished*, the tendency is to use

the perfect tense. Bear in mind, however, that there are regional
variations.

Insight

Regional variations with regard to the use of the perfect tense
also occur in Spain, with some areas favouring the use of the
simple past. In other places, you may hear the perfect tense in
contexts where most people would use the simple past: **¿Dónde
has nacido?** *Where were you born?*, **He nacido en Zaragoza**
I was born in Zaragoza. This usage should be avoided.

In context

1 Isabel is looking for her friend Enrique.

Isabel	Buenas tardes. ¿Está Enrique?
Señora	Lo siento, pero Enrique no está. Acaba de salir. Ha ido a casa de José.
Isabel	Por favor, ¿puede Vd. decirle que le he venido a buscar para ir a la piscina? Le esperaré allí.
Señora	Bueno, se lo diré.

2 What have you done today?

Él	¿Qué has hecho hoy?
Ella	Esta mañana he estado en la biblioteca un rato y he terminado de escribir un artículo para la clase de mañana. Luego he ido a la peluquería. Acabo de regresar. Y tú, ¿qué has hecho?
Él	Hoy me he levantado muy tarde y me he quedado en casa leyendo. ¿Has comido ya?
Ella	No, todavía no. No he tenido tiempo de preparar nada.
Él	Entonces, ¿qué te parece si vamos a comer algo? Podemos ir al bar de Pepe.
Ella	De acuerdo, vamos.

Practice

1 Match the phrases on the left with an appropriate phrase from the right, and then give the infinitive corresponding to each verb.

a Le he escrito ...	**1** ... sus nuevas gafas
b Antonio nos ha dicho ...	**2** .... las tiendas
c Carmen ha roto ...	**3** .... una carta a Manuel
d José ha vuelto ...	**4** .... el dinero en el banco
e Todavía no han hecho ...	**5** .... la verdad
f Han abierto ...	**6** .... de sus vacaciones
g He puesto ...	**7** .... sus reservas.

2 You phone your friend Ana to make arrangements to go to the cinema. Use the following guidelines to fill in your part of the conversation with her.

Voz	¿Dígame?
Tú	*Say hello and who you are, and ask whether Ana is in.*
Voz	Sí, acaba de llegar. Un momento, por favor.
Ana	Hola, ¿qué tal?
Tú	*Say hello to Ana and ask her whether she's free tonight.*
Ana	Sí, ¿por qué?
Tú	*Ask her whether she's seen the new Almodóvar film. You've been told it's very good.*
Ana	No, todavía no la he visto, pero quisiera verla.
Tú	*Say you've phoned the cinema and they've told you that there's a show* (una sesión) *at 9.00. Ask her what she thinks.*
Ana	Sí, a las 9:00 me parece bien.

3 While on holiday, Sarah writes a letter to a Spanish-speaking friend. Fill in the blank spaces in the letter with a suitable verb from those accompanying the pictures. The first two have been done for you.

Hola Carlos:

¿Qué tal estás? Te escribo para contarte que Tom y yo (a) hemos venido de vacaciones a España y hasta ahora lo hemos pasado estupendamente bien. (b) ___ a la playa casi todos los días y el fin de semana pasado (c) ___ un coche/carro (L.Am.) para salir de paseo. Hoy por la mañana, (yo) (d) ___ un rato en el mar y después Tom y yo (e) ___ a caballo. Por la tarde (f) ___ vela.

a venir, pasar   **b** ir   **c** alquilar

d nadar   **e** montar   **f** hacer

TEST YOURSELF

1 *Change the verbs in brackets into the correct form of the perfect tense.*

    a ¿Dónde (poner, yo) mis gafas (*glasses*)? No las encuentro.

    b Esteban me (llamar) y me (decir) que vendrá esta noche.

    c Le (escribir, yo) un email a Raquel, pero todavía no me (contestar, ella).

    d (pedir, nosotros) una pizza, pero todavía no la (traer).

    e ¿Qué (hacer, vosotros) este verano? ¿(Volver) a la Costa Brava otra vez?

2 *Match the questions and the answers.*

    a ¿Está abierto el banco?   **1** Sí, acabamos de cenar.

    b ¿Le has enviado el email a   **2** Sí, acaba de llegar.
       Cecilia?   **3** Sí, acabo de terminar.

    c ¿Has visto a Marta?   **4** No, lo acaban de cerrar.

    d ¿Habéis comido algo?   **5** Sí, le acabo de escribir.

    e ¿Has hecho tus deberes (*homework*)?

This is an important step forward in your course. If your handling of the perfect tense was correct in this test, you'll now be able to express yourself in a number of situations related to the past and linked to the present. Take some time to practise this further before you move on to Unit 18, in which you will learn other ways of talking about the past.

18

Referring to past events

In this unit, you will learn how to:
- *refer to events which are past and complete*
- *refer to events which lasted over a definite period of time and ended in the past*

Language points
- *preterite tense*
- *adverbs of time associated with the preterite*
- *hace in time phrases*
- *historic present*

Key sentences

Actions which happened and were completed in the past, as in *They went to Cuba last year*, and events which lasted over a definite period of time and ended in the past, for example *She lived in Spain for seven years*, are expressed in Spanish through the preterite tense or simple past.

REFERRING TO EVENTS WHICH ARE PAST AND COMPLETE

¿Cuándo saliste/llegaste?	*When did you leave/arrive?*
Salí/Llegué hace una hora.	*I left/arrived an hour ago.*
El año pasado viajaron/fueron a Cuba.	*Last year, they travelled/went to Cuba.*

REFERRING TO EVENTS WHICH LASTED OVER A DEFINITE PERIOD OF TIME AND ENDED IN THE PAST

Vivió/Estuvo siete años en España.	*He/She lived/was in Spain for seven years.*
Trabajamos/Estudiamos juntos durante dos años.	*We worked/studied together for two years.*

Insight

In some regions, especially within Latin America, the preterite is often used in places where Peninsular Spanish would normally use the perfect tense, as for past events which are related to the present: **Se enfrió la comida** *The food got cold*, instead of **Se ha enfriado la comida** *The food has got cold* (see Unit 17).

Grammar summary

1 *PRETERITE TENSE*

Formation
There are two sets of endings for this tense, one for **-ar** verbs and another one for verbs ending in **-er** and **-ir**.

viajar	*to travel*
viajé	*I travelled*
viajaste	*you travelled* (fam.)
viajó	*you/he/she travelled*
viajamos	*we travelled*
viajasteis	*you travelled* (fam.)
viajaron	*you/they travelled*

Note that the first person plural, **viajamos**, is the same as for the present tense.

responder	to answer
respondí	I answered
respondiste	you answered (fam.)
respondió	you/he/she answered
respondimos	we answered
respondisteis	you answered (fam.)
respondieron	you/they answered

recibir	to receive
recibí	I received
recibiste	you received (fam.)
recibió	you/he/she received
recibimos	we received
recibisteis	you received (fam.)
recibieron	you/they received

Insight

The addition of an **-s** to the second person singular, for
example **viajastes** instead of **viajaste**, which you are likely to
hear among some people, is incorrect and should be avoided.

Note that the first person plural, **recibimos,** is the same as for the
present tense.

El año pasado viajé **a Perú.**	Last year, I travelled to Peru.
Él viajó **por más de una semana.**	He travelled for more than a week.
Ayer respondí **la carta de Esteban.**	I answered Esteban's letter yesterday.
Carlos no respondió **mi carta.**	Carlos didn't answer my letter.
¿Cuándo recibiste **el paquete?**	When did you receive the parcel?
Lo recibí **el martes pasado.**	I received it last Tuesday.

Insight

Using the proper stress and written accents in the preterite
tense is very important, as meaning can be affected: **viajo**

(Contd)

I travel, **viajó** *he/she/you travelled*, **viaje** *travel* (imperative form for Vd. (Unit 20) and also first and third person singular of the present subjunctive [Unit 21]), **viajé** *I travelled*.

Irregular preterite forms

Some verbs have an irregular preterite. Here is a list of the most important ones:

andar *to walk*	anduve, anduviste, anduvo, anduvimos, anduvisteis, anduvieron
dar *to give*	di, diste, dio, dimos, disteis, dieron
decir *to say*	dije, dijiste, dijo, dijimos, dijisteis, dijeron
estar *to be*	estuve, estuviste, estuvo, estuvimos, estuvisteis, estuvieron
haber *to have* (aux.)	hube, hubiste, hubo, hubimos, hubisteis, hubieron
hacer *to do, make*	hice, hiciste, hizo, hicimos, hicisteis, hicieron
ir *to go*	fui, fuiste, fue, fuimos, fuisteis, fueron
obtener *to get*	obtuve, obtuviste, obtuvo, obtuvimos, obtuvisteis, obtuvieron
poder *to be able*	pude, pudiste, pudo, pudimos, pudisteis, pudieron
poner *to put*	puse, pusiste, puso, pusimos, pusisteis, pusieron
querer *to want*	quise, quisiste, quiso, quisimos, quisisteis, quisieron
saber *to know*	supe, supiste, supo, supimos, supisteis, supieron
ser *to be*	fui, fuiste, fue, fuimos, fuisteis, fueron
tener *to have*	tuve, tuviste, tuvo, tuvimos, tuvisteis, tuvieron
traer *to bring*	traje, trajiste, trajo, trajimos, trajisteis, trajeron
venir *to come*	vine, viniste, vino, vinimos, vinisteis, vinieron

Insight

The preterite forms of **ir** and **ser** are exactly the same: **Fuimos a la Alhambra** *We went to the Alhambra*, **Fuimos muy felices** *We were very happy*.

For a list of the most common irregular verbs, see the **Irregular verbs** section.

¿Qué hiciste **ayer?**	*What did you do yesterday?*
Fui **a casa de Manolo.**	*I went to Manolo's house.*
¿Dónde estuvisteis **este verano?**	*Where were you this summer?*
Estuvimos **en San Francisco.**	*We were in San Francisco.*
¿Qué le diste **a Roberto para su cumpleaños?**	*What did you give Roberto for his birthday?*
Le di **una corbata.**	*I gave him a tie.*

Insight

To help you remember irregular preterite forms, group them and learn them according to the type of change that they undergo, for example those that change the vowel of the stem into **u**: **haber, poder, poner, saber**; verbs that take **i**: **decir, hacer, querer, venir**; verbs which add **uv** at the end of the stem: **andar, estar, tener**; verbs which take **j**: **decir, traer**, etc.

Spelling changes in the preterite tense
Some verbs need a change in the spelling in the first person singular, normally to enable the final consonant of the stem to keep the same sound as in the infinitive.

1 -gar changes into -gué

llegar	*to arrive*	llegué	*I arrived*
jugar	*to play*	jugué	*I played*
pagar	*to pay*	pagué	*I paid*

2 -car changes into -qué

buscar	*to look for*	busqué	*I looked for*
sacar	*to get, e.g. tickets*	saqué	*I got*
tocar	*to play an instrument*	toqué	*I played*

3 **-guar** changes into **-güé**

averiguar	*to find out*	averigüé	*I found out*

4 **-zar** changes into **-cé**

almorzar	*to have lunch*	almorcé	*I had lunch*
cruzar	*to cross*	crucé	*I crossed*
empezar	*to begin, start*	empecé	*I began, started*

A spelling change may also occur because of an accent in the infinitive or because there would otherwise be more than two vowels together:

caer *to fall*	caí, caíste, cayó, caímos, caísteis, cayeron
leer *to read*	leí, leíste, leyó, leímos, leísteis, leyeron
oír *to hear*	oí, oíste, oyó, oímos, oísteis, oyeron

Verbs ending in **-uir** follow the pattern of **oír**.

incluir *to include*   incluí, incluiste, incluyó, incluimos, incluisteis, incluyeron

Llegué hace dos semanas.	*I arrived two weeks ago.*
Pagué la cuenta anoche.	*I paid the bill last night.*
Saqué dos entradas para el cine.	*I got two tickets for the cinema.*
Ella no **leyó** la carta.	*She didn't read the letter.*
No nos **incluyeron**.	*They didn't include us.*

Verbs ending in **-ducir** change **-c** into **-j** in all persons.

conducir *to drive*   conduje, condujiste, condujo, condujimos, condujisteis, condujeron

Other verbs like **conducir** include **deducir** *to deduce*, **producir** *to produce, cause*, **reducir** *to reduce*, **reproducir** *to reproduce*, **traducir** *to translate*, etc.

Conduje **con mucho cuidado.**	*I drove with great care.*
Su ausencia *produjo* **un gran problema.**	*His/Her absence caused a big problem.*
Tradujeron **la carta al castellano.**	*They translated the letter into Spanish.*

Stem-changing verbs

A few verbs change the stem in the preterite tense, but only in the third person singular and plural.

1 e changes into i

pedir *to ask for*	pedí, pediste, pidió, pedimos, pedisteis, pidieron

Other verbs of this kind include **competir** *to compete*, **corregir** *to correct*, **divertirse** *to enjoy oneself*, **elegir** *to choose, elect*, **impedir** *to prevent*, **mentir** *to lie*, **preferir** *to prefer*, **repetir** *to repeat*, **seguir** *to continue, follow*, **sentir** *to feel*, **servir** *to serve*, **vestirse** *to get dressed*, etc.

Me *pidieron* **dinero.**	*They asked me for money.*
Luis *se divirtió* **mucho.**	*Luis enjoyed himself very much.*
Ella me *mintió.*	*She lied to me.*

2 o changes into u

dormir(se) *to sleep, go to sleep*	dormí, dormiste, durmió, dormimos, dormisteis, durmieron

Morir(se) *to die* changes in a similar way.

El niño *se durmió.*	*The child went to sleep.*
¿Durmieron **bien?**	*Did you sleep well?*
Murió **mi abuela.**	*My grandmother died.*

Using the preterite tense

The preterite tense is used:

a to refer to actions which took place and were completed at some point in the past.

Ocurrió **en 1989**.	*It occurred/took place in 1989.*
Nos *vimos* **ayer**.	*We saw each other yesterday.*

b to refer to actions which occurred over a prolonged period of time.

Vivieron **juntos durante cinco años**.	*They lived together for five years.*
Estuvieron **aquí mucho tiempo**.	*They were here for a long time.*

c to refer to an action which was completed before another one took place.

Nora *vivió* **con su madre hasta que se** *casó*.	*Nora lived with her mother until she got married.*
Después que *desayunó se fue* **a la universidad**.	*After he/she had breakfast, he/she left for the university.*

d generally, in narrative texts to relate a series of past events.

Ella *entró* **en la habitación,** *saludó* **a su padre y** *se sentó* **a cenar**.	*She came into the room, greeted her father and sat down to have dinner.*

> ### Insight
> In narrative contexts, the preterite tense is often found alongside a form of the verb which is known as imperfect, one of whose functions is to describe things with reference to the past: **Ella entró en la habitación, que estaba a oscuras ...** *She came into the room, which was dark ...* (see Unit 19).

2 ADVERBS OF TIME AND TIME PHRASES NORMALLY ASSOCIATED WITH THE PRETERITE TENSE

The following adverbs of time and time phrases often occur in sentences with a verb in the preterite tense.

ayer	*yesterday*
anteayer	*the day before yesterday*
anoche	*last night*
el lunes/martes pasado	*last Monday/Tuesday*
la semana pasada	*last week*
el mes/el año pasado	*last month/year*
en 1975/en 1999	*in 1975/in 1999*
hace dos meses/tres años	*two months/three years ago*

Some of these time phrases may also occur with other tenses, for example the imperfect tense (see Unit 19).

3 HACE *IN TIME PHRASES*

With a verb in the preterite tense, **hace** translates into English as *ago*.

Vivió aquí *hace* **dos años.**	*He/She lived here two years ago.*
Hace **seis meses que llegó.**	*He/She arrived six months ago.*
¿Cuánto tiempo *hace* **que pasó?**	*How long ago did it happen?*

Compare this construction with the one you learned in Unit 8, in which **hace** is used with a verb in the present tense.

Vive aquí desde *hace* **dos años.**	*He/She has been living here for two years.*

4 HISTORIC PRESENT

The present tense is frequently used in narrative contexts (e.g. literature, history) with a past meaning in order to lend more force to the actions or events being described. It is also present in colloquial language.

Written language

En noviembre de 1975 muere el general Francisco Franco
y el príncipe Juan Carlos pasa a ocupar el trono de España.
El país empieza a vivir una serie de cambios de orden político
y social ...

*General Francisco Franco died in November 1975, and Prince Juan
Carlos came to the Spanish throne. The country began to undergo
a series of political and social changes...*

Spoken language

Esta mañana en el metro he visto a Antonia. ¿Sabes qué?, se acerca
a mí y me dice que siente mucho lo ocurrido ...

*This morning, in the underground, I saw Antonia. You know, she
came up to me and told me that she was very sorry about what
happened ...*

In both of these examples, depending on the context, the present
tense could be used in the English translation.

In context

1 What did you do on your holiday?

Marisol	¿Qué hiciste en tus vacaciones?
Fernando	Estuve unos días en Inglaterra en casa de unos amigos.
Marisol	¿Fuiste solo?
Fernando	No, fui con Ángela.
Marisol	¿Y qué os pareció Londres?
Fernando	Nos gustó muchísimo. Lo pasamos estupendamente. Y tú, ¿has estado alguna vez en Inglaterra?
Marisol	Sí, estuve allí hace cuatro años. Hice un curso de inglés en Brighton y viví un mes con una familia inglesa. Lo pasé muy bien. Pienso volver el año que viene.

¿Qué os pareció Londres? *What did you think of London?*
Lo pasamos estupendamente. *We had a great time.*
alguna vez *ever*
Lo pasé muy bien. *I had a very good time.*

2 The manager has been away from the office for a few days. On his return, he talks to his secretary.

Gerente	¿Hay algún recado para mí?
Secretaria	Sí, el lunes llamó el señor Solís para pedir una cita con usted. Vendrá mañana a las 10:00. También hubo una llamada del señor Francisco Riquelme de México. Dice que llegará a Madrid el viernes a las 2:00 de la tarde.
Gerente	¿Han traído el nuevo ordenador?
Secretaria	Sí, lo trajeron ayer. Lo dejaron en su despacho. Aquí está la factura.

¿Hay algún recado? *Are there any messages?*
pedir una cita *to ask for an appointment*
Hubo una llamada. *There was a call.*

Insight

Observe the contrast between the perfect tense and the preterite tense in these two sentences.

Y tú, *¿has estado* **alguna**   *And have you ever been to*
  vez en **Inglaterra**?   *England?*
Estuve **allí hace cuatro años.**   *I was there four years ago.*

The two tenses are not interchangeable in these sentences. Words such as **alguna vez** *ever* and **nunca** *never* require the use of the perfect tense because they somehow establish a relationship with the present: **alguna vez** is equivalent in meaning to **hasta ahora** *so far*. In the second sentence, the preterite tense is obligatory because it refers to an event which is past and complete.

Practice

1 In a letter to a friend, Silvia writes about her holidays. Fill in the blanks with a suitable verb from the list using the preterite tense.

ser	estar
invitar	volver
pasar	parecer
ir	gustar
traer	conocer

Querido Ignacio

Hace sólo una semana (1) (yo) ___ de México, y no sabes lo bien que lo (2) ___. (3) ___ en casa de unos parientes de mi madre que viven en Guadalajara. Me (4) ___ mucho la ciudad. Y la gente me (5) ___ muy amable. En mi última semana allí (6) ___ con mis parientes a Puerto Vallarta. ¡Es una ciudad preciosa! Allí (7) (nosotros) ___ a unos mexicanos que me (8) ___ a pasar unos días en su casa en Guanajuato. Creo que éstas (9) ___ las mejores vacaciones de mi vida (10) (yo) ___ muchas fotos de México. Te las enseñaré ...

2 Your Spanish boss is checking on your progress. Answer his/her questions using the preterite tense and the time phrases in brackets.

Ejemplo ¿Ha enviado Vd. las cartas? (ayer)

    a Sí, las envié ayer.
    b ¿Ha escrito Vd. el informe? (anteayer)
    c ¿Ha hecho Vd. las reservas de hotel? (el lunes)
    d ¿Ha llamado Vd. a la señora Miranda? (ayer por la mañana)
    e ¿Ha comprado Vd. el material de oficina? (la semana pasada)
    f ¿Ha mandado Vd. el fax a Buenos Aires? (anoche)
    g ¿Ha respondido Vd. la carta del señor Lira? (anteanoche/ antenoche L.Am.)

3 Here are some of the things Carmen and Pablo did in the office yesterday. Look at the pictures and write an appropriate sentence for each picture, saying what each one did. Choose from the phrases below.

> **enviar faxes   servir café a los clientes   contestar el teléfono
> trabajar en el ordenador/la computadora** (L.Am.) **leer la
> correspondencia   atender al público**

Ejemplo: (llamar por teléfono a un cliente) Carmen llamó por
teléfono a un cliente.

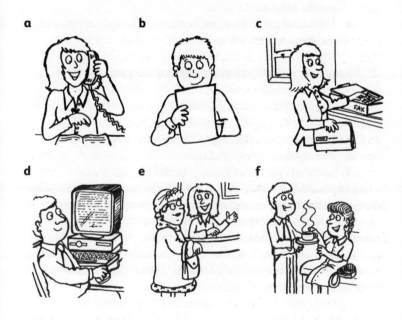

TEST YOURSELF

1 *Change the infinitives in brackets into the appropriate person of the preterite tense.*

   a Ayer (trabajar, yo) en casa todo el día, José (hacer) la compra, y Andrés y Laura (irse) de copas con unos amigos.

   b – ¿A qué hora (llegar) Mario anoche?
   – No sé, no le (oír, yo) llegar.

   c – ¿Qué (hacer, tú) en las vacaciones?
   – (irse, yo) a Londres a estudiar inglés. (Estar) un mes allí.

   d Rosa no (querer) venir a la fiesta, (quedarse, ella) en casa preparando un examen.

   e Este libro me lo (dar) mi hermano. Me (gustar) mucho, me (parecer) muy interesante.

2 *Change the infinitives into the appropriate persons of the preterite tense.*

   a buscar: (yo) __, (tú) __, (ellos) __
   b jugar: (yo) __, (él) __, (vosotros) __
   c llegar: (yo) __, (tú) __, (ellos) __
   d leer: (yo) __, (ella) __, (ellos) __
   f empezar: (yo) __, (Vd.) __, (vosotros) __

Most of the verbs in this test are extremely common, so it is important that you get their forms right. If after checking your answers you feel you need some further revision, go back through regular verbs first, then irregular ones, grouping them and learning them according to the similarity in their forms. See also the **Irregular verbs** section.

19

Describing the past

In this unit, you will learn how to:
- *describe things, places and people known in the past*
- *describe actions which were taking place when something else happened*
- *describe states or actions which were habitual in the past*
- *describe states or actions which occurred before some past event*

Language points
- *imperfect tense*
- *imperfect continuous*
- *pluperfect tense*
- soler *+ infinitive for past reference*
- acostumbrar *+ infinitive for past reference*

Key sentences

This unit introduces two new tenses, the imperfect tense and the pluperfect, both used with reference to the past. The imperfect, as found in sentences such as **Era bonito** *It was pretty*, **Estaba trabajando cuando ...** *I was working when ...*, **Nos visitaban siempre** *They always used to visit us*, has no direct correspondence in English. The pluperfect, as in **Ya habíamos salido** *We had already gone out*, is used in much the same way as the English pluperfect.

DESCRIBING THINGS, PLACES AND PEOPLE KNOWN IN THE PAST

Era/Eran caro(s).	*It was/They were expensive.*
Tenía/Había dos habitaciones.	*It had/There were two rooms.*

DESCRIBING ACTIONS WHICH WERE TAKING PLACE WHEN SOMETHING ELSE HAPPENED

¿Qué estabas haciendo/hacías cuando ocurrió?	*What were you doing when it happened?*
Estaba leyendo/Leía cuando él llamó.	*I/He/She was reading when he called.*

DESCRIBING STATES OR ACTIONS WHICH WERE HABITUAL IN THE PAST

Venían/Viajaban a Mallorca todos los años	*They used to come/travel to Mallorca every year.*
Nos levantábamos/marchábamos a las 7:00 todos los días.	*We used to get up/leave at 7.00 every day.*

DESCRIBING STATES OR ACTIONS WHICH OCCURRED BEFORE SOME PAST EVENT

La reunión había empezado/terminado cuando llegué.	*The meeting had begun/finished when I arrived.*
¿Habías estado/venido aquí antes?	*Had you been/come here before?*

Grammar summary

1 *IMPERFECT TENSE*

Uses

In general terms, the imperfect tense is used for actions which were taking place in the past and whose beginning or end are not specified. Unlike the preterite, which commonly indicates completed past events, the imperfect denotes actions which were incomplete. Consider these two sentences:

En aquel tiempo yo trabajaba en Barcelona.   *At that time, I used to work in Barcelona.*

Entre enero y junio de ese año trabajé en Barcelona.   *Between January and June of that year, I worked in Barcelona.*

In the first example, the beginning and end of the action are not specified. In the second, we are referring to a completed past event.

More specifically, the imperfect tense is used to describe things, places and people with reference to the past, to describe actions which were taking place when something else happened (the second action will normally be expressed in the preterite) and to describe states or actions which were habitual in the past (see examples in **Key sentences**).

The imperfect is also used instead of the present tense in direct address, as a more polite form:

Quería **ver esa camisa.**   *I'd like to see that shirt.*
(Instead of **Quiero** ...)

Queríamos **hablar con Vd.**   *We'd like to speak to you.*
(Instead of **Queremos** ...)

The imperfect usually stands in place of the present tense in indirect statements, when these are introduced by a verb in the past.

Quiero hablar contigo.   *I want to speak to you.*
(direct statement)

María me dijo que quería hablar conmigo.   *María told me she wanted to speak to me.* (indirect statement)

Formation

There are two sets of endings for the imperfect tense, one for **-ar**
verbs and another one for verbs ending in **-er** and **-ir**.

trabajar *to work*

trabajaba	*I worked/used to work*
trabajabas	*you worked/used to work* (fam.)
trabajaba	*you/he/she worked/used to work*
trabajábamos	*we worked/used to work*
trabajabais	*you worked/used to work* (fam.)
trabajaban	*you/they worked/used to work*

tener *to have*

tenía	*I had/used to have*
tenías	*you had/used to have* (fam.)
tenía	*you/he/she/it had/used to have*
teníamos	*we had/used to have*
teníais	*you had/used to have* (fam.)
tenían	*you/they had/used to have*

vivir *to live*

vivía	*I lived/used to live*
vivías	*you lived/used to live* (fam.)
vivía	*you/he/she lived/used to live*
vivíamos	*we lived/used to live*
vivíais	*you lived/used to live* (fam.)
vivían	*you/they lived/used to live*

Note that the first and third person singular share the same endings.

¿Dónde trabajabas **antes?**	*Where did you work/were you working before?*
Trabajaba **en una fábrica.**	*I worked/was working/used to work in a factory.*
¿Qué coche tenía **Vd. antes?**	*What car did you have before?*
Tenía **un Seat.**	*I had a Seat.*
¿Dónde vivíais **antes de llegar aquí?**	*Where did you live before arriving here?*
Vivíamos **en Toledo.**	*We lived/used to live in Toledo.*

Insight
Trabajabas/trabajaba and **vivíais/vivíamos** refer to ongoing past actions whose beginning or end or actual duration is not specified. Compare the previous sentences with **Trabajé cinco años allí** *I worked there for five years*, **Vivimos en Ávila entre 1980 y 2005** *We lived in Avila between 1980 and 2005.*

Irregular imperfect forms
There are only three irregular verbs in the imperfect tense: **ir** *to go*, **ser** *to be* and **ver** *to see*.

ir	ser	ver
iba	**era**	**veía**
ibas (fam.)	**eras** (fam.)	**veías** (fam.)
iba	**era**	**veía**
íbamos	**éramos**	**veíamos**
ibais (fam.)	**erais** (fam.)	**veíais**
iban	**eran**	**veían**

For a list of the most common irregular verbs in all tenses, see the **Irregular verbs** section.

Yo iba **al colegio cuando ocurrió el accidente.**	*I was going to school when the accident happened.*
¿Cómo era **la casa?**	*What was the house like?*

(Contd)

Era **una casa grande y moderna**   *It was a big modern house and it*
   y *tenía* **un gran jardín.**   *had a large garden.*
Francisca y yo nos *veíamos* **casi**   *Francisca and I used to see each*
   todos los días.   *other day.*

2 IMPERFECT CONTINUOUS

Usage
To make it clear we are referring to an action which was in
progress when something else happened, for example *I was eating
when he called me*, we can use the imperfect continuous as an
alternative to the imperfect tense.

Formation
The imperfect continuous is formed with the imperfect form of
estar followed by a gerund (for the gerund, see Unit 8).

Ella *estaba preparando* **el**   *She was preparing lunch when he*
   almuerzo cuando él entró.   *came in.*
Nosotros *estábamos durmiendo*   *We were sleeping when the theft*
   cuando ocurrió el robo.   *took place.*
¿Qué *estabas haciendo* **allí?**   *What were you doing there?*
Estaba hablando **con Marta.**   *I was talking to Marta.*

Insight
Many speakers tend to use the imperfect rather than the
imperfect continuous with common verbs such as **hacer,
hablar, ir, llover, venir: ¿Qué hacías allí?** *What were you
doing there?*, **¿Con quién hablabas?** *Who were you talking to?*,
Llovía a cántaros *It was raining cats and dogs.* Overall,
however, ongoing actions in the past are usually expressed
with the imperfect continuous.

3 PLUPERFECT TENSE

Usage
The Spanish pluperfect tense is equivalent to the English pluperfect
and it is normally used to describe states or actions which occurred

before some past event, as in *Her mother had died when John was born*.

Formation

The pluperfect tense is formed with the imperfect form of **haber** (**había, habías, había, habíamos, habíais, habían**) followed by a past participle which is invariable (for the formation of past participles, see Unit 11).

La fiesta ya *había empezado* **cuando nosotros entramos.**	*The party had already started when we went in.*
No aceptamos su invitación pues *ya habíamos visto* **la película.**	*We didn't accept their invitation because we had already seen the film.*
La carrera ya *había terminado* **cuando empezó a llover.**	*The race had already finished when it started to rain.*

4 SOLER + INFINITIVE (TO USUALLY DO SOMETHING) AND ACOSTUMBRAR + INFINITIVE (TO BE USED/ACCUSTOMED TO DOING SOMETHING) FOR PAST REFERENCE

Soler and **acostumbrar** (see Unit 9) may be used in the imperfect tense to refer to an action which was habitual in the past.

¿Qué *solías* **hacer?**	*What did you usually do?*
Solía **leer mucho.**	*I used to read a lot.*
Solíamos **vernos regularmente.**	*We used to see each other regularly.*
Acostumbraban **venir una vez por semana.**	*They used to come once a week.*
Acostumbrábamos **dar largos paseos.**	*We used to go for long walks.*

....

Insight

Overall, and especially in Spain, the construction **acostumbrar** + infinitive is considered more formal than **soler** + infinitive. **Acostumbrar**, to refer to an action which is

(Contd)

habitual or was habitual in the past, should not be followed
by a preposition, but many speakers, both in Spain and Latin
America, use it with the preposition **a: Acostumbraba a**
levantarme temprano I used to get up early.

In context

1 Remembering the past.

Ignacio	¿Cuánto tiempo hace que vives aquí?
Eliana	Hace dos años solamente.
Ignacio	¿Y dónde vivías antes?
Eliana	Vivía en Nueva York.
Ignacio	¡En Nueva York! ¿Y qué hacías allí?
Eliana	Trabajaba en un colegio como profesora de español, y al mismo tiempo estudiaba inglés en la universidad. Con lo que ganaba como profesora pagaba mis estudios y el alquiler de un apartamento.
Ignacio	¿Vivías sola?
Eliana	No, compartía el apartamento con dos colegas. Uno era español y el otro colombiano.
Ignacio	¿Hablabas ya inglés cuando llegaste allí?
Eliana	Lo hablaba bastante mal y entendía muy poco, pero conseguí aprender bastante.

QUICK VOCAB

al mismo tiempo at the same time
con lo que ganaba with what I earned
un/una colega colleague
conseguí aprender I managed to learn

2 Read this extract from a short story.

Eran ya las 9:00 de la noche cuando Lucía llegó a la casa de la
señora Velarde. Hacía frío y la lluvia empezaba a caer. Lucía llamó
a la puerta tres veces pero nadie respondió. La señora Rosario

Velarde era una mujer mayor, tenía unos ochenta años, y vivía sola
con su perro Damián. Lucía llamó otra vez, pero nadie respondió.
Dentro de la casa había luz y por la ventana se veía el pequeño
salón ...

La lluvia empezaba a caer. *The rain was starting to fall.*
Llamó a la puerta. *She knocked at the door.*
una mujer mayor *an old woman*
tenía unos ochenta años *she was about 80 years old*
había luz *there was a light*
por la ventana *through the window*
el salón *sitting room*

QUICK VOCAB

Insight

Notice the use of the imperfect and preterite tenses in the
second text.

Hacía frío.	*It was cold*
La lluvia empezaba a caer.	*The rain was starting to fall*
Lucía llamó a la puerta.	*Lucia knocked at the door.*
Nadie respondió.	*No one answered.*

Here, the imperfect tense is descriptive, while the preterite
serves to indicate a series of completed past events.

Practice

1 Tomás tells a friend about someone special he knew long ago.
Fill in the gaps in his description with the right form of the verb in
brackets.

(1) _____ (llamarse) Elena, (2) _____ (tener) 28 años,
(3) _____ (ser) alta, delgada y muy guapa y (4) _____ (vestir)
muy bien. Elena (5) _____ (ser) enfermera y cuando la conocí
(6)_____ (trabajar) en un hospital cerca de casa. Elena (7) _____
(compartir) un apartamento con una amiga. El apartamento

(8) _____ (ser) pequeño, pero (9) _____ (tener) unas vistas
maravillosas. En aquel tiempo Elena (10) _____ (estudiar) piano y
(11) _____ (tocar) muy bien. A mí me (12) _____ (gustar) mucho
oírla tocar.

Now use this passage as a model to describe someone you knew.

2 Victoria used to live and work in England. Read this account of
her life there and choose the correct tense.

(1) Llegué/Llegaba a Londres en el año 1986. En aquel tiempo
(2) tuve/tenía 22 años e/y* (3) hizo/hacía sólo seis meses que
(4) terminaba/había terminado mis estudios de Derecho. Al llegar
a Inglaterra (5) supe/sabía muy poco inglés y lo primero que
(6) hice/hacía al llegar a Londres (7) fue/era tomar clases de inglés.

El primer mes (8) me quedé/me quedaba en casa de unos amigos
españoles, hasta que (9) encontré/encontraba una habitación donde
vivir. Pero Londres (10) fue/era una ciudad muy cara y yo no
(11) tuve/tenía mucho dinero. Un amigo me (12) ayudó/ayudaba
a encontrar un trabajo donde (13) gané/ganaba lo suficiente para
vivir. Allí (14) trabajé/trabajaba durante seis meses ...

Try writing a brief passage about a period in your own life.

*y changes to e before i or hi (except for hie-).

3 This is the house where Ana and her family used to live. Fill in
the gaps in the description with an appropriate verb from the box.

> **haber gustar tener ser estar**

La casa de Ana era muy bonita, (1) _____ en medio del campo y
(2) _____ dos plantas. No (3) _____ una casa muy grande,
pero (4) _____ muy cómoda. Delante de la casa (5) _____ un
jardín y detrás de ella (6) _____ una colina. Sobre la colina

(7) _____ unos árboles. Los padres de Ana (8) _____ un coche y Ana (9)_____ una bicicleta. Ana (10) _____ un perro. Al perro le (11) _____ jugar en el jardín.

TEST YOURSELF

1 *Choose the correct tense, the imperfect or the preterite.*

   a La casa de Antonio <u>era/fue</u> construida en 1928. <u>Era/Fue</u> una casa muy bonita.

   b Mi abuelo, que <u>se llamaba/llamó</u> Manuel, <u>moría/murió</u> el año pasado.

   c El hotel donde nos <u>quedábamos/quedamos</u> este verano <u>estaba/estuvo</u> a cinco minutos de la playa.

   d – ¿Con quién <u>hablabas/hablaste</u> por teléfono?
      – <u>Estaba/Estuve</u> hablando con Cristóbal.

   e <u>Iba/Fui</u> al supermercado cuando <u>empezaba/empezó</u> a llover.

2 *Translate these sentences into Spanish.*

   a They used to go to Spain every year. They had many friends there.

   b We used to leave the house at 8.00 in the morning and didn't come back until 7.00 in the evening.

   c Her Spanish was very good. She had lived in Mexico for five years.

   d The class had already started when he arrived.

   e Agustín told me that he wanted to see me.

Most of the questions in this test focus on the use of the imperfect and the difference between this and the preterite. If the answer to any of the following questions is yes, then the verb should be in the imperfect tense: Does the verb refer to a repeated action with unspecified beginning or ending?, Does it refer to an action which continued over an indefinite period, or does it describe certain past conditions with no specific time limit?

20

Giving directions and instructions

In this unit, you will learn how to:
- *ask and give directions*
- *give commands and instructions*

Language points
- *imperative*
- *present tense used in directions*
- *infinitive used in directions*

Key sentences

We can give directions and instructions in a variety of ways in English, for example: *You have to/can turn left*, *Go straight on*, *Wait for the dialling tone*. Spanish also has a number of ways of giving directions and instructions. These involve some of the constructions you learned in previous units.

ASKING FOR DIRECTIONS

¿Dónde está el banco/correos?	*Where's the bank/post office?*
¿Puede decirme dónde está el museo/la catedral?	*Can you tell me where the museum/cathedral is?*
¿Sabe Vd./Sabes dónde está?	*Do you know where it is?*
¿Por dónde se va al aeropuerto/a la estación?	*Can you tell me the way to the airport/station? (Lit. Which way does one go …?)*

GIVING DIRECTIONS

Está en la esquina/al final de esta calle.	It's on the corner/at the end of this road.
Tiene que/Puede girar a la izquierda/derecha.	You have to/can turn left/right.
Siga todo recto/hasta el semáforo.	Go straight on/as far as the traffic lights.
Coja (*Spain*)/**Tome esta calle.**	Take this road.

GIVING COMMANDS AND INSTRUCTIONS

Abre/Abra (Vd.) la ventana.	Open the window.
No tardes/tarde (Vd.) mucho.	Don't take too long.
Espera/Espere (Vd.) el tono de marcar.	Wait for the dialling tone.
Toma Vd. el autobús número 10 y se baja en la plaza de San Juan.	You take the number 10 bus and get off at San Juan Square.

Insight

The word **coger** *to take*, *catch* is extremely common in Spain, but is a taboo word in some Latin American countries. You can avoid this by using the alternative verb **tomar**, which is acceptable in all Spanish-speaking countries: **Tome la segunda calle a la derecha** *Take the second street on the right*, **Tomen el tren** *Take the train*.

Grammar summary

1 *IMPERATIVE*

Uses

The imperative is the form most commonly associated with directions, commands and instructions. Study the formation of the imperative and look at the **Key sentences** again.

Formation: polite imperatives

In Spanish, we use different imperative forms depending on who we are talking to (polite or familiar) and whether we are speaking to one or more than one person (singular or plural). To form the imperative, use the stem of the first person singular of the present tense plus the appropriate ending. Here are the polite imperatives of three regular verbs – **girar** to *turn*, **responder** to *answer* and **subir** to *go up* – representing each of the three conjugations.

Present tense (first person)	Imperative	
giro	**gire**	*turn* (sing.)
	giren	*turn* (pl.)
respondo	**responda**	*answer* (sing.)
	respondan	*answer* (pl.)
subo	**suba**	*go up* (sing.)
	suban	*go up* (pl.)

The negative imperative is formed by placing **no** before the verb:
no gire *don't turn*, **no responda** *don't answer*, **no suba** *don't go up*.

The following examples contain only regular verbs:

-ar	girar	Gire(n) a la derecha.	*Turn right.*
	continuar	Continúe(n) por esta calle.	*Continue along this street.*
	cambiar	Cambie(n) este dinero.	*Change this money.*
-er	responder	Responda(n) estas cartas.	*Answer these letters.*
	leer	Lea(n) las instrucciones.	*Read the instructions.*
	correr	No corra(n).	*Do not run.*
-ir	subir	Suba(n) al segundo piso.	*Go up to the second floor.*
	escribir	Escriba(n) al señor García.	*Write to Mr García.*
	abrir	Abra(n) la puerta.	*Open the door.*

Observe that first conjugation verbs (-**ar**) acquire the endings of second conjugation verbs (-**er**), while second and third conjugation verbs (-**er** and -**ir**) acquire the endings of the first conjugation.

The pronoun **Vd.** or **Vds.** is often added after the verb in order to soften the command.

Gire Vd. a la izquierda.	*Turn left.*
Continúen Vds. por esta calle.	*Continue along this street.*

Insight
A simpler way of giving the directions above is with **tener que** followed by the infinitive: **Tiene(s) que girar a la derecha/ continuar por esta calle/subir al segundo piso**: *You have to turn right/continue along this street/go up to the second floor.*

Irregular polite imperatives
As the imperative is formed with the stem of the first person singular of the present tense, verbs which are irregular in the present are also irregular in the imperative. This rule also applies to stem-changing verbs.

Infinitive		Present	Imperative (sing./pl.)
seguir	*to follow*	**sigo**	siga(n)
cerrar	*to close*	**cierro**	cierre(n)
dar	*to give*	**doy**	dé/den
estar	*to be*	**estoy**	esté(n)
hacer	*to do, make*	**hago**	haga(n)
poner	*to put*	**pongo**	ponga(n)
traer	*to bring*	**traigo**	traiga(n)
volver	*to return*	**vuelvo**	vuelva(n)
conducir	*to drive*	**conduzco**	conduzca(n)
decir	*to say*	**digo**	diga(n)
oír	*to hear*	**oigo**	oiga(n)
salir	*to go out*	**salgo**	salga(n)
tener	*to have*	**tengo**	tenga(n)
venir	*to come*	**vengo**	venga(n)

Venga(n) **mañana.**	*Come tomorrow.*
Conduzca(n) **con cuidado.**	*Drive carefully.*
No haga(n) **eso.**	*Don't do that.*
Vuelva(n) **el martes.**	*Come back on Tuesday.*
Cierre(n) **la puerta.**	*Close the door.*

Ir, saber *and* **ser**

Ir *to go,* **saber** *to know* and **ser** *to be* form the imperative in a different way.

Infinitive		Present	Imperative (sing./pl.)
ir	to go	**voy**	vaya(n)
saber	to know	**sé**	sepa(n)
ser	to be	**soy**	sea(n)

Vaya a **la recepción.**	*Go to the reception.*
Sépase **que no lo haré otra vez.**	*Let it be known that I won't do it again.*
Sean **Vds. puntuales, por favor.**	*Be punctual, please.*

Insight

Observe the passive **se** attached to the imperative form **sepa**. The addition of a syllable to the word requires the use of an accent in the third syllable from the end (see **Pronouns with imperative** later in this **Grammar summary**).

Spelling changes

Note the following spelling changes in verbs ending in **-car, -gar** and **-ger.**

Infinitive		Present	Imperative (sing./pl.)
buscar	to look for	**busco**	busque(n)
tocar	to touch, play	**toco**	toque(n)
pagar	to pay	**pago**	pague(n)
llegar	to arrive	**llego**	llegue(n)
coger	to take, catch	**cojo**	coja(n)

Busque la llave.		*Look for the key.*	
Pague Vd. ahora.		*Pay now.*	
Por favor lleguen a la hora.		*Please arrive on time.*	

Familiar imperatives
Familiar imperatives have different positive and negative forms.

Infinitive		Present	Imperative (sing./pl.)
girar	*to turn*	**giro**	gira(d)
responder	*to answer*	**respondo**	responde(d)
subir	*to go up*	**subo**	sube/subid

Insight

The positive familiar imperative for **tú** is like the **tú** form of the present tense but without the **-s**: **cruzas** (present tense) – **cruza** (imperative), **sigues** (present tense) – **sigue** (imperative). Note, however, the different positions of pronouns, as for **bajarse** *to get off*: **te bajas** (present tense) – **bájate** (imperative).

Gira **a la izquierda.**	*Turn left.* (sing.)
Girad **a la derecha.**	*Turn right.* (pl.)
Responde **pronto.**	*Answer soon.* (sing.)
Responded **rápido.**	*Answer quickly.* (pl.)
Sube **al primer piso.**	*Go up to the first floor.* (sing.)
Subid **por esta calle.**	*Go up this road.* (pl.)

Insight

The positive familiar imperative for **vosotros** is like the infinitive, but with a final **-d** instead of an **-r**: **esperar** (infinitive) – **esperad** (imperative), **volver** (infinitive) – **volved** (imperative), **decir** (infinitive) – **decid** (imperative).

Some examples of negative familiar forms are:

Infinitive		Present	Imperative (sing./pl.)
girar	to turn	giro	no gires
			no giréis
responder	to answer	respondo	no respondas
			no respondáis
subir	to go up	subo	no subas
			no subáis

No *giréis* **aquí,** *girad* **en la esquina.**	*Do not turn here, turn at the corner.* (pl.)
No *respondas* **hoy,** *responde* **mañana.**	*Do not reply today, reply tomorrow.* (sing.)
No *subáis* **al primer piso,** *subid* **al segundo.**	*Don't go up to the first floor, go up to the second.* (pl.)

Irregular familiar imperatives
The following verbs form the singular positive familiar imperative in an irregular way.

decir	to say	di
hacer	to do, make	haz
ir	to go	ve
oír	to hear	oye
poner	to put	pon
salir	to go out	sal
ser	to be	sé
tener	to have	ten
venir	to come	ven

Haz **lo que digo.**	*Do what I say.*
Ve **inmediatamente.**	*Go immediately.*
¡Oye!	*Listen!*
¡Sal **de aquí!**	*Get out of here!*
Ven **aquí un momento.**	*Come here a moment.*

Plural forms are regular, for example ¡**Venid!** *Come!*

Pronouns with imperative
If the imperative includes a pronoun, this must go at the end of the positive form but before the negative one. Positive imperatives which carry a pronoun may need to add an accent.

Díga*le* **que necesito verla.**	*Tell her I need to see her.*
No *lo* **traiga hoy.**	*Do not bring it today.*
Tráiga*lo* **mañana.**	*Bring it tomorrow.*
No *lo* **haga así.**	*Don't do it like this.*
Hága*lo* **de esta manera.**	*Do it this way.*
Lláma*me* **a las 6:00.**	*Call me at 6.00.*

2 PRESENT TENSE USED IN DIRECTIONS

One simple and frequent way of giving directions is by using the present tense (for its forms, see Units 7 and 8) instead of the imperative.

Vd. *coge/toma* **la segunda calle a la izquierda.**	*You take the second turning on the left.*
Vd. *sube/baja* **hasta la tercera planta.**	*You go up/down to the third floor.*
Tomas **la línea 5 y** *te bajas* **en la segunda estación.**	*You take line 5 and get off at the next station.*
Vas **al supermercado y** *me traes* **cien gramos de queso.**	*Go to the supermarket and bring me 100g of cheese.*

3 INFINITIVE USED IN DIRECTIONS

Directions and instructions are sometimes given through the use of infinitives. This is particularly common in the written language, for example in notices, advertisements and traffic signals.

No fumar.	*Do not smoke.*
No adelantar/aparcar.	*Do not overtake/park.*
Tomar un comprimido con cada comida.	*Take one tablet with each meal.*

In context

1 Asking the way.

> **Turista** ¿La oficina de turismo, por favor?
> **Policía** Siga Vd. todo recto por esta calle hasta el final, allí gire Vd. a la izquierda y continúe por esa misma calle hasta el segundo semáforo. La oficina de turismo está en la esquina.

por esta calle *along this street*
esa misma calle *that same street*

2 Giving instructions in the office.

> **Jefe** Teresa, venga a mi despacho un momento, por favor.
> **Secretaria** Sí, ¿dígame?
> **Jefe** Mire, vaya al banco e ingrese estos cheques en mi cuenta corriente y después vaya a correos y eche estas cartas. Antes de volver pase por la papelería y tráigame el material de oficina que pedimos ayer. Ah, y pregunte en la agencia de viajes si está lista mi reserva para Buenos Aires …

mire *look*
ingrese (ingresar) *deposit (to deposit, pay in)*
pase por (pasar) *stop by (to stop by)*
pedimos (pedir) *we ordered (to order)*
si está listo/a *if it's ready*

Practice

1 In a familiar context, you need to use the informal imperative.
Practise changing the formal imperatives in dialogues 1 and 2
above into the familiar form, as if talking to a friend.

2 A Spanish-speaking friend is moving house and you are helping
him/her. Complete your friend's instructions by changing the
infinitives in brackets into the familiar imperative form.

Ejemplo: No (abrir) esta habitación ahora. (Abrir) la después.
No abras esta habitación ahora. Ábrela después.

    a No (poner) esa caja en el comedor. (Poner) la en el salón.
    b No (dejar) esas cosas aquí. (Llevar) las a la cocina.
    c No (traer) las maletas al salón. (Dejar) las en el dormitorio.
    d No (cerrar) esa ventana. (Cerrar) la otra.
    e No (limpiar) la cocina todavía. (Hacer) lo después.
    f No (ir) al supermercado ahora. (Ir) más tarde.
    g No (hacer) la limpieza todavía. (Hacer) la en otro
      momento.
    h No (tirar) esa caja todavía. (Esperar) un momento.

3 A Spanish-speaking friend who is visiting your home town needs
to get to the station. Follow the arrows in the picture and tell
your friend how to get there.

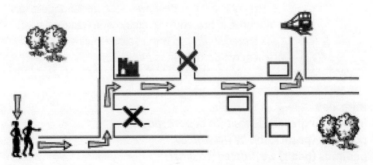

TEST YOURSELF

1 *Rephrase these sentences using the formal imperative.*
  a Tiene que estar aquí antes de las 5:00.
  b Tiene que conducir con cuidado. Hay mucho tráfico en la carretera.
  c Tienen que seguir por esta calle hasta el final.
  d Tiene que esperar un momentito. El doctor está ocupado.
  e Tienen que tomar el autobús número 10 y tienen que bajarse en la calle de la Rosa.

2 *Give the familiar imperative for each of these instructions.*
  a No se lo digan a nadie.
  b Póngalo en la cocina, por favor.
  c No hagan ruido. El niño está durmiendo.
  d Hágalo ahora mismo. Es urgente.
  e Por favor, lleguen a la hora.

Did you get most of the forms right? If so, you will now be able to use your knowledge in a number of contexts requiring the imperative, especially directions. If you are still uncertain about the forms, go back to paragraph 1 of the **Grammar summary** or see paragraph 12 of the **Grammar reference**. Don't forget that the present tense is just as common as the imperative when giving directions. And, as a beginner, you are much more likely to be asking for and understanding directions than actually giving them.

21

···

Expressing emotional reactions, possibility and doubt

In this unit, you will learn how to:
- *express emotional reactions: hope, fear, regret, satisfaction*
- *express possibility*
- *express doubt or uncertainty*
- *express emotional reactions, possibility and doubt with reference to the recent past*

Language points
- *subjunctive*
- *present subjunctive*
- *verbs and phrases denoting emotion*
- *subjunctive or indicative*
- *perfect subjunctive*

Key sentences

In English, emotional reactions such as hope, regret and satisfaction may be expressed through sentences such as *She hopes he answers soon*, *I'm sorry they can't come*, *I'm glad she's here*. These sentences contain two clauses: a main clause with a verb in the present tense (e.g. *She hopes ...*), followed by another clause with a verb which is also in the present tense (e.g. *... (that) he answers soon*).

Sentences which express possibility and doubt have a similar structure, for example: *It's possible that they may get married, I doubt that he has the money*.

Spanish differs somewhat from English in the way it expresses these ideas. In the main clause, there is no variation. As in English, the main verb may be in the present, the past or the future, but the linking word **que** (*that* in English), which introduces the second clause, known as the subordinate clause, may not be omitted. If the subject of the subordinate clause is different from that of the main clause (e.g. *She hopes that he answers*), then the verb in the subordinate clause must be in the subjunctive. This is an alternative form of the verb, not a tense.

The subjunctive covers a range of tenses – present, imperfect, perfect and pluperfect subjunctive – which are different from the tenses you have learned so far in this book, and which grammar books refer to as tenses of the *indicative*.

EXPRESSING EMOTIONAL REACTIONS

Ella espera que él responda/ escriba pronto.	*She hopes he answers/writes soon.* (hope)
Siento que no vengan/viajen.	*I'm sorry they can't come/travel.* (regret)
Me alegro de que ella esté/ trabaje aquí.	*I'm glad she is/works here.* (gladness)
Le molesta que le interrumpan.	*It bothers him to be interrupted.* (bother)

EXPRESSING POSSIBILITY

Es posible que se casen/ divorcien.	*It's possible that they may get married/divorced.*
Es probable que llueva/nieve.	*It'll probably rain/snow.*
Puede que hayan salido.	*They may have gone out.*

EXPRESSING DOUBT OR UNCERTAINTY

No creo que lo compren/vendan.	*I don't think they'll buy/sell it.*
Dudo que él tenga/consiga el dinero.	*I doubt that he has/he'll get the money.*

Grammar summary

1 *THE SUBJUNCTIVE*

General usage

a The subjunctive is generally associated with a subordinate clause introduced by **que**, which is dependent on a main clause. The main clause usually carries the type of verb which calls for the use of the subjunctive in the subordinate clause, for example, verbs expressing emotion, possibility and doubt (see earlier examples).

b The subjunctive may also occur in clauses introduced by **que**, for example when the antecedent is not known.

Buscamos una secretaria *que* **hable inglés.**	*We're looking for a secretary who speaks English.*
Queremos una persona *que conozca* **el oficio.**	*We want a person who knows the trade.*

c The subjunctive is always used after certain subordinators.

para que	*so that*
La invitaré para que la *veas.*	*I'll invite her so that you may see her.*
en caso de que	*in case*
En caso de que *llegue* **dile que me espere.**	*In case he/she arrives, tell him/her to wait.*
con tal de que	*as long as*
Te lo contaré con tal de que no se lo *digas.*	*I'll tell you as long as you don't tell him/her.*

In clauses introduced by **aunque** *even though*, *although*, *even if*, use the indicative if the action expressed by the verb is a fact, and the subjunctive if this refers to a possibility.

Aunque *llueve*, **iré.**	*Even though it's raining, I'll go.*
Aunque *llueva*, **iré.**	*Even if it rains, I'll go.*

d The subjunctive is found in main clauses containing commands or instructions (imperative form).

Venga **aquí un momento, por favor.**	*Come here a moment, please.*
No se lo *diga.*	*Don't tell him/her.*

e The idea of unreality or something which has not yet taken place is a common feature of many subjunctive clauses.

Se lo diré cuando *llegue.*	*I'll tell him/her when he/she arrives*
Trabajaré hasta que *termine.*	*I'll work until I finish.*

Insight

If the action referred to by the verb is a reality, use the indicative and not the subjunctive. Compare these two sentences:

Cuando *voy* **a su casa le llevo chocolates.**	*When I go to his/her house I (always) take him/her chocolates.*
Cuando *vaya* **a su casa le llevaré chocolates.**	*When I go to his/her house I'll take him/her chocolates.*

For other uses of the subjunctive, see Units 22 and 23.

2 PRESENT SUBJUNCTIVE

Uses

The uses of the present subjunctive are no different from those of the subjunctive in general, as outlined earlier. The decision whether to use the present rather than some other subjunctive tense will depend largely on tense agreement and time reference. Although there is no strict rule about it, the present subjunctive normally occurs in sentences which carry a main clause in the present indicative, future perfect indicative or imperative.

Present indicative > present subjunctive

No creo que él esté allí.   *I don't think he's there.*

Future > present subjunctive

Será imposible que ellos nos   *It'll be impossible for them to*
visiten.   *visit us.*

Imperative > present subjunctive

Alégrate de que no sea nada   *You should be glad it's nothing*
serio.   *serious.* (lit. *be glad ...*)

Perfect indicative > present subjunctive

Luis me ha pedido que le ayude.   *Luis has asked me to help him.*

Formation
Like the imperative (see Unit 20), the present subjunctive is formed from the first person singular of the present indicative, e.g. **hablo** (**hablar** *to speak*), **respondo** (**responder** *to reply, answer*), **escribo** (**escribir** *to write*). Drop the -o and add the corresponding endings: one set of endings for first conjugation verbs and another for second and third conjugation. The first and third person singular of the present subjunctive correspond in form to formal imperatives (see Unit 20).

hablar *to speak*	**responder** *to reply*	**escribir** *to write*
hable	responda	escriba
hables	respondas	escribas
hable	responda	escriba

hablar *to speak*	responder *to reply*	escribir *to write*
hablemos	respondamos	escribamos
habléis	respondáis	escribáis
hablen	respondan	escriban

Study the use of the present subjunctive in the following sentences:

1 With verbs expressing some kind of emotion:

Espero que ellos *hablen* **español.**   *I hope they speak Spanish.* (hope)

Insight

The use of the subjunctive above is determined not just by the verb **esperar**, but also by the fact that this is followed by a subordinate clause introduced by **que** in which the verb is in a different person from that in the main clause: **Yo espero que ellos hablen ...** (subjunctive) *I hope that they speak ...* Compare this with: **Yo espero hablar ...** (infinitive) *I hope to speak ...*

Ojalá (que) *vuelvan* **pronto.**   *I hope they come back soon.* (hope)
Ojalá (que) tu madre no se   *Let's hope your mother doesn't find*
entere.   *out.* (hope)

Insight

Ojalá is a word derived from the Arabic *Inshallah*!, which has come to mean *I hope so, Let's hope so*. It can be used in full sentences such as those above, where **que** is often omitted, or on its own: **Seguro que te llamarán. ¡Ojalá!** *I'm sure they'll call you. Let's hope so!*

Me alegro de que ellos *trabajen*   *I'm glad they work so well*
tan bien juntos.   *together.* (gladness)
A mi abuela le gusta/encanta   *My grandmother likes/loves to be*
que la *visiten.*   *visited.* (gladness)
Temo que ella no *comprenda.*   *I'm afraid she may not*
  understand. (fear)

Siento mucho que no *puedas*   *I'm very sorry you can't come to*
venir a mi fiesta.   *my party.* (regret)

2 With phrases indicating possibility:

Es posible que ellos no respondan.	*It's possible that they may not answer.*
Es probable que él nos *escriba*.	*He'll probably write to us.*

Insight

Impersonal phrases such as *Is it possible to do it?*, *It's impossible to understand him*, *It's important to be there on time*, etc. take the infinitive and not the present subjunctive: **¿Es posible hacerlo?, Es imposible entenderle, Es importante estar allí a la hora.**

Puede (ser) que regresen en avión. *They may return by plane.*

3 With verbs indicating doubt or uncertainty:

Dudamos que él nos *responda*.	*We doubt that he will reply to us.*
No creo que Carlos me *escriba*.	*I don't think Carlos will write to me.*

4 In independent clauses with words indicating doubt and possibility:

Quizá(s) John *hable* **con él mañana.**	*Perhaps John will speak to him tomorrow.*
Tal vez ella *viaje* **a Inglaterra.**	*Perhaps she may travel to England.*
Posiblemente se *queden* **allí.**	*They may stay there.*
Probablemente lo *vendan*.	*They'll probably sell it.*

Posiblemente and **probablemente** can take the indicative if the action expressed by the verb is thought as being more likely to happen: **Posiblemente se quedarán allí, Probablemente lo venderán.**

If the clause with **creer** is in the affirmative, the verb in the subordinate clause will be an indicative verb. Compare these two sentences:

No creo que él me llame.	*I don't think he'll call me.*
Creo que él me llamará.	*I think he'll call me.*

Irregular forms of the present subjunctive
As with imperatives, verbs which are irregular in the first person singular of the present indicative are also irregular in the present subjunctive.

Infinitive	Present indicative first person	Present subjunctive
decir *to say, tell*	**digo**	**diga**
		digas
		diga
		digamos
		digáis
		digan

Verbs which change their stem in the present indicative – for example **cerrar** *to close*, **volver** *to come back*, **jugar** *to play* – change in a similar way in the present subjunctive: **cierro, vuelvo, juego** (present indicative); **cierre, vuelva, juegue** (present subjunctive).

For other examples of irregular forms, refer to irregular imperatives in Unit 20.

As was the case with imperatives, some verbs are irregular in a different way.

dar *to give*	dé, des, dé
	demos, deis, den
estar *to be*	esté, estés, esté,
	estemos, estéis, estén
haber *to have* (aux.)	haya, hayas, haya,
	hayamos, hayáis, hayan
ir *to go*	vaya, vayas, vaya,
	vayamos, vayáis, vayan
saber *to know*	sepa, sepas, sepa,
	sepamos, sepáis, sepan
ser *to be*	sea, seas, sea,
	seamos, seáis, sean

The first and third person singular of **dar** must carry an accent in order to distinguish them from the preposition **de**. The accents in the present subjunctive of **estar** are the same as in the present indicative: **está, está, estáis, están**.

Me alegro de que me lo *digas*.	*I'm glad you're telling me.*
Temo que él no lo *haga* **bien**.	*I'm afraid he may not do it well.*
Esperamos que ella lo *tenga*.	*We hope she has it.*
Dudo que Pedro *esté* **allí**.	*I doubt that Pedro is there.*
No creo que Enrique *vaya* **a Granada**.	*I don't think Enrique will go to Granada.*
Es posible que Elena *sepa* **dónde está Carlos**.	*It's possible that Elena may know where Carlos is.*
Espero que *sea* **posible**.	*I hope it's possible.*

3 VERBS AND PHRASES DENOTING EMOTION

Here is a list of verbs and phrases denoting emotion, which require the use of the subjunctive in the subordinate clause.

alegrarse	*to be glad*
encantar	*to love/like very much*
esperar	*to hope*
gustar	*to like*
importar	*to mind*
molestarse	*to be annoyed*
sentir (e→ie)	*to be sorry*
sorprenderse	*to be surprised*
temer	*to fear*
Es una lástima ...	*It's a pity ...*
Es una pena ...	*It's a pity ...*
Es una vergüenza ...	*It's a shame ...*
¡Qué pena ...!	*What a pity!*
¡Qué lástima ...!	*What a pity!*
¡Qué vergüenza ...!	*What a shame!*
¡Qué rabia ...!	*What a nuisance!*

Me *sorprende* **que digas eso.**	*I'm surprised you say that.*
No me *importa* **que él se marche.**	*I don't mind if he leaves.*
Es una vergüenza **que hagas eso.**	*It's a shame you did that.*
¡Qué rabia **que él no hable** **español!**	*What a nuisance that he* *doesn't speak Spanish!*

4 SUBJUNCTIVE OR INDICATIVE

Some words and phrases associated with the expression of possibility and doubt may be used equally with the indicative or the subjunctive.

Quizá(s) él habla/hable español.	*Perhaps he speaks Spanish.*
Tal vez ella sabe/sepa la verdad.	*Maybe she knows the truth.*

But note that when **quizá(s)** or **tal vez** come after the verb, this must be in the indicative form.

Él habla español *quizá(s)*.	*He speaks Spanish perhaps.*
Ella sabe la verdad *tal vez*.	*She knows the truth maybe.*

A lo mejor *perhaps* is always used with an indicative verb.

A lo mejor **vienen/nos invitan.**	*Perhaps they'll come/invite us.*

Posiblemente *possibly* is normally used with the subjunctive, but it also accepts the indicative.

Posiblemente **está/esté allí.**	*He's possibly there.*

5 EXPRESSING EMOTIONAL REACTIONS, POSSIBILITY AND DOUBT WITH REFERENCE TO THE RECENT PAST

To express ideas such as *I hope he has found it*, *I don't think they have seen me*, you need to use a present indicative verb in the main clause followed by a verb in the perfect subjunctive in the subordinate clause.

Perfect subjunctive

The perfect subjunctive is formed with the present subjunctive of **haber** *to have* (**haya, hayas, haya, hayamos, hayáis, hayan**), followed by a past participle.

Espero que él lo *haya encontrado.*	*I hope he has found it.*
No creo que me *hayan visto.*	*I don't think they have seen me.*
Ojalá no *se hayan perdido.*	*I hope they haven't got lost.*
Cuando *hayas terminado,* **llámame.**	*When you have finished, call me.*

Insight

The uses of the perfect subjunctive are the same as those covered in the previous pages. Its use in a sentence is determined by the time reference. Compare the first two examples above with **Espero que él lo encuentre** *I hope he finds it,* **No creo que me vean** *I don't think they'll see me.*

In context

1 An invitation to a birthday party.

Felipe	Hola José Luis. Quiero invitarte a casa esta noche. Es el cumpleaños de Paloma.
José Luis	Lo siento, Felipe, pero no creo que pueda ir. Hoy llegan mis padres de Tenerife y tendré que ir al aeropuerto a recogerles.
Felipe	Es una lástima que no puedas venir. Posiblemente venga Francisco. Está en Madrid.
José Luis	Me alegro de que esté otra vez aquí. Espero verle otro día. Dile que me llame.
Felipe	Se lo diré. ¿Estarás en casa mañana?
José Luis	Tal vez salga un par de horas por la mañana, pero volveré antes del mediodía.
Felipe	Vale. Le diré a Francisco que te llame por la tarde.
José Luis	De acuerdo. Gracias.

Es una lástima. *It's a pity.*
otro día *another day*
un par de horas *a couple of hours*

2 Read this extract from a letter.

Querida Jane

Hemos recibido tu carta y nos alegramos de que estés bien y tengas tanto éxito en tus estudios. Sentimos mucho que no puedas venir a Barcelona el próximo verano, pero esperamos que vengas para las Navidades. Es posible que Gonzalo también pase las Navidades con nosotros. ¿Te acuerdas de él? Es aquel chico guapo que conocimos en Blanes ...

tanto éxito *so much success*
¿Te acuerdas de él? *Do you remember him?*
que conocimos (conocer) *that we met (to meet, get to know)*

Practice

1 Read this letter sent to Paul by a Spanish-speaking friend and change the infinitives in brackets into the appropriate form.

Querido Paul

¡Hace tanto tiempo que no sé nada de ti! Espero que (1) (recibir, tú) la carta que te envié hace dos meses, en la que te decía que es muy probable que este verano (2) (ir, yo) a verte. No creo que (3) (quedarse, yo) mucho tiempo, pero creo que (4) (estar, yo) contigo por lo menos dos semanas. ¿Qué te parece?
Lola me contó que habías encontrado trabajo en un colegio. Me alegro mucho de que (5) (conseguir, tú) lo que buscabas, y espero que (6) (estar, tú) contento allí y que el colegio te (7) (pagar) bien. A mí no me gusta mucho lo que hago, pero dudo que (8) (encontrar, yo) algo mejor. No es nada fácil ...

2 You and a Spanish-speaking friend are exchanging news about people you have not seen for a long time. Use the phrases in brackets to express your feelings about the news you hear.

Ejemplo: ¿Sabes que Antonio se casa? (alegrarse)
Me alegro de que se case.

- **a** ¿Sabes que Cristina se divorcia? (es una lástima)
- **b** Alfredo vuelve a España. (alegrarse)
- **c** Laura no seguirá estudiando. (¡qué pena!)
- **d** Pepe y Paca van a comprar una casa. (alegrarse)
- **e** Mario está enfermo. (sentir)
- **f** Cristóbal espera ir a Nueva York. (esperar)
- **g** Mariana deja su trabajo. (sorprenderse)
- **h** María y Lola se van de Madrid. (¡qué lástima!)

3 Choose a caption for each picture from the phrases below.
- **a** Me encanta que me regalen flores.
- **b** Es probable que la reparación sea un poco cara. Está en muy malas condiciones.
- **c** Espero que hoy esté Vd. mejor.
- **d** Espero que con esto me deje tranquilo.

TEST YOURSELF

Put the infinitives in brackets in the appropriate tense.

a Creo que Carlos y Paca (llegar) el domingo próximo. Ojalá nos (confirmar, ellos) la hora de su llegada.

b Es posible que (hacer) mal tiempo, pero aunque (llover) iremos.

c Cuando (ir, tú) al supermercado, quiero que me (traer) jabón.

d Mañana vendré con mi novio para que Vd. le (conocer). Espero que le (gustar).

e Este verano Ricardo y yo quizá (viajar) a Londres. Ojalá (encontrar, nosotros) un hotel que no (ser) muy caro.

f Siento mucho que tú no nos (poder) acompañar. Es una pena que (estar, tú) tan ocupada.

g Me alegro mucho de que (encontrar, vosotros) un piso tan bueno. En caso de que (necesitar, vosotros) ayuda, me lo decís.

h No creo que Antonio (saber) lo que pasó. Cuando se lo (decir, yo) se alegrará mucho.

i – ¿Sabes dónde (estar) Raúl?
– No lo sé, es posible que (salir, él) con Cristina. Querían ir al cine.

j Dudo que Alfonso (hablar) inglés. Nunca le gustaron los idiomas.

Did you manage to get most answers right? **¡Enhorabuena!** (*Congratulations!*), as the language covered in this unit can be a little tricky. Don't be discouraged if you made a few mistakes. Time and practice will help you to achieve the accuracy that you are aiming at. Go back through the unit again if necessary or see paragraph 11 of the **Grammar reference**. In Units 22 and 23 you will find more information on the subjunctive, which may help you to consolidate what you have learned.

22

Expressing wishes and indirect commands, requests and advice

In this unit, you will learn how to:
- *express wishes and preferences involving others*
- *report commands, requests and advice*

Language points
- *imperfect subjunctive*
- *verbs and phrases denoting wishes and preferences*
- *verbs used for reporting commands, requests and advice*
- *direct and indirect speech*
- *conditional tense*

Key sentences

In this unit, you will learn a new tense of the subjunctive, the imperfect subjunctive, in the expression of wishes and preferences involving other people and in the reporting of commands, requests and advice. The use of the imperfect rather than the present subjunctive in the following **Key sentences** is determined by the tense of the main verb.

EXPRESSING WISHES AND PREFERENCES INVOLVING OTHERS

Emilio quería que le llamara/
escribiera.

*Emilio wanted me to call him/
write to him.*

¿Qué querías que
hiciera/dijera?

*What did you want me to
do/say?*

Preferiría que Vd. esperara/
volviera mañana.

*I'd prefer you to wait/come back
tomorrow.*

¡Cómo desearía que Marta
estuviera aquí!

How I wish Marta were here!

Me gustaría que me
acompañaras.

I'd like you to accompany me.

REPORTING COMMANDS, REQUESTS AND ADVICE

Nos ordenó que saliéramos/lo
hiciéramos.

He/She ordered us to leave/do it.

Amalia me dijo que te invitara.

Amalia told me to invite you.

Os pedí que llegarais/
estuvierais aquí a las 6:00.

*I asked you to arrive/be here
at 6.00.*

Me aconsejaron que guardara
silencio.

They advised me to keep quiet.

Le sugerí a mi madre que
llamara a un médico.

*I suggested to my mother that
she called a doctor.*

Insight

Compare some of the previous sentences with these ones in which the main verb is in the present indicative, the future, the imperative or the perfect indicative: **Emilio quiere que le llame** *Emilio wants me to call him*, **Le ordenaré que salga** *I'll order him to leave*, **Pídeles que estén aquí a las 6:00** *Ask them to be here at 6.00*, **Me han aconsejado que guarde silencio** *They have advised me to keep quiet*. In all of these examples, the verb in the subordinate clause is in the present subjunctive (see Unit 21).

Grammar summary

1 IMPERFECT SUBJUNCTIVE

Uses
The imperfect subjunctive normally occurs in sentences which carry a main clause in the imperfect, preterite or pluperfect, or else in the conditional (see paragraph 5 of the **Grammar summary**) or the conditional perfect (see Unit 23).

Imperfect indicative > imperfect subjunctive

Yo no quería que él se **marchara**.   *I didn't want him to leave.*

Preterite > imperfect subjunctive

Él no quiso que yo lo **llevara**.   *He didn't want me to take him.*

Pluperfect indicative > imperfect subjunctive

Ella nos había pedido que la   *She had asked us to call her.*
  llamáramos.

Conditional > imperfect subjunctive

Yo preferiría que os **quedarais**.   *I'd prefer you to stay.*

Conditional perfect > imperfect subjunctive

Yo habría preferido que os   *I'd have preferred you to stay.*
  quedarais.

Insight
Compare some of the previous sentences with: **No quiero que él se marche** *I don't want him to leave*, **Él no querrá que lo lleve** *He won't want me to take him*, **Ella nos ha pedido que**

la llamemos *She has asked us to call her.* Tense agreement
requires that in these sentences, the verb in the subordinate
clause be in the present and not the imperfect subjunctive,
just as in the examples in the previous **Insight.**

Formation

The imperfect subjunctive can be formed in two ways. The first
is directly derived from the third person plural of the preterite
(see Unit 18). Here are some examples with regular verbs.

Infinitive	Preterite (3rd person pl.)	Imperfect subjunctive (1st and 3rd person sing.)
llegar *to arrive*	llegaron	llegara
beber *to drink*	bebieron	bebiera
subir *to go up*	subieron	subiera

The same derivation occurs with irregular and stem-changing
verbs.

poder *to be able to*	pudieron	pudiera
estar *to be*	estuvieron	estuviera
decir *to say*	dijeron	dijera
ir/ser *to go/to be*	fueron	fuera
traer *to bring*	trajeron	trajera

Here is the imperfect subjunctive of three regular verbs representing
each of the three conjugations: **llegar** *to arrive*, **beber** *to drink* and
subir *to go up*. Note that **-er** and **-ir** verbs share the same endings.

llegar	**beber**	**subir**
llegara	bebiera	subiera
llegaras	bebieras	subieras
llegara	bebiera	subiera

llegáramos	bebiéramos	subiéramos
llegarais	bebierais	subierais
llegaran	bebieran	subieran

Insight

Note that the imperfect subjunctive forms **llegara** (for **yo, él, ella, Vd.**) and **llegaras** (for **tú**), in which the stress falls on the second syllable (**-ga**), have no written accents. Compare these with the future forms **llegará** *he/she/you* (formal) *will arrive* and **llegarás** *you will arrive* (fam.), in which the stress falls on the last syllable. The **nosotros** form is the only one that has a written accent: **llegáramos**.

The imperfect subjunctive has a second set of endings which appear to be less frequent than the first. The two forms are generally interchangeable. Again, -**er** and -**ir** verbs share the same endings.

llegar	**beber**	**subir**
llegase	bebiese	subiese
llegases	bebieses	subieses
llegase	bebiese	subiese
llegásemos	bebiésemos	subiésemos
llegaseis	bebieseis	subieseis
llegasen	bebiesen	subiesen

Insight

If in doubt about the forms of the imperfect subjunctive, simply take the corresponding form of the third person plural of the preterite, remove the ending **-ron** and add **-ra** or **-se** for the first and third person singular. There are no special irregular verbs in the imperfect subjunctive, so any verb which is irregular or stem-changing in the preterite will follow the same pattern in the imperfect subjunctive (see examples above).

Here are some further examples showing you the use of the imperfect subjunctive:

Wishes and preferences involving others

Él quería que yo *llegara/llegase*   *He wanted me to arrive on time.*
a la hora.

Ella prefería que yo no   *She preferred me not to drink.*
bebiera/bebiese.

Roberto no deseaba que tú   *Roberto didn't want you to go.*
fueras/fueses.

Yo preferiría que nos   *I'd prefer us to stay.*
quedáramos/quedásemos.

Reporting commands, requests and advice

La gerente me ordenó que lo   *The manager ordered me to finish*
terminara **hoy.**   *it today.*

El jefe me exigió que *trabajara/*   *The boss ordered me to work*
trabajase **hasta las 6:00.**   *until 6.00.*

Nos pidió que le *devolviéramos*   *He asked us to return his money.*
su dinero.

Él me rogó que no le *dejara.*   *He begged me not to leave him.*

Insight

The use of the **-ra** or the **-se** form is generally a matter of
personal choice, but the second form tends to be more
common in formal written language. Spanish Americans
show preference for the **-ra** form. Note, however, the
following two uses in which the **-se** form is not acceptable:
Quisiera (for **quería** or **querría**) **hablar con Vd.** *I'd like to
speak to you* and **Debieras** (for **deberías**) **decírselo** *You should
tell him/her.*

2 VERBS AND PHRASES DENOTING WISHES
AND PREFERENCES

The verbs most commonly associated with the expression of
wishes and preferences are **querer** *to want*, **gustar** *to like*, **preferir**
to prefer. Other less frequent words and expressions are the
following: **agradar** *to like*, **desear** *to wish*, **encantar** *to like very
much, love*, **sería bueno/estupendo/magnífico** *it would be
good/great*.

Agradar and **desear** are used in more formal contexts, especially in the written language.

Me *agradaría* **mucho que nos visitara.**	*I'd very much like you to visit us.*
Desearía **que me respondiera lo antes posible.**	*I should like you to answer me as soon as possible.*
Me *encantaría* **que pasaras tus vacaciones conmigo.**	*I'd very much like you to spend your holidays with me.*
Sería estupendo **que nevara.**	*It would be great if it snowed.*

Note that **agradar** and **encantar** are conjugated like **gustar**.

3 VERBS USED FOR REPORTING COMMANDS, REQUESTS AND ADVICE

The following are the main verbs associated with the reporting of commands, requests and advice: **decir** *to say*, **ordenar** *to order*, **exigir** *to beg, plead, demand*, **pedir** (e > i in the preterite tense) *to ask*, **rogar** *to beg, plead*, **aconsejar** *to advise*, **sugerir** (e > i in the preterite tense) *to suggest*, **recomendar** *to recommend*.

Les *ordené* **que se marchasen.**	*I ordered them to leave.*
Te *dije* **que no bebieras tanto.**	*I told you not to drink so much.*
Me *exigió* **que se lo contara.**	*He/She begged me to tell him/her.*
Yo le *pediría* **que renunciase.**	*I'd ask him/her to resign.*
Nos *rogó* **que le prestáramos el dinero.**	*He/She pleaded with us to lend him/her the money.*
Me *recomendaron* **que lo leyera.**	*They recommended that I should read it.*

Insight

Rogar is often used in formal letter writing to express requests: **Le ruego que nos envíe el pedido lo antes posible** *Please send us the order as soon as possible*. Note that **rogar** is in the present tense indicative and **enviar** in the present subjunctive.

4 DIRECT AND INDIRECT SPEECH

Each of the previous sentences represents an indirect statement conveying the original command, request or advice in an indirect way. In direct speech, you reproduce the exact words said by the speaker, for example **La gerente me dijo: "Termínelo hoy"** *The manager told me: 'Finish it today'*. In indirect speech, you convey what someone said in an indirect way, not using the exact words said by the original speaker, as in the sentence above. The transformation from direct into indirect speech normally involves a number of changes, among them the following ones:

a The original words will constitute a subordinate clause introduced by **que** (... **que lo terminara**).

b The time reference usually calls for a change in verb forms, including tenses: **Termínelo ...** (imperative) > **Me ordenó que lo terminara ...** (imperfect subjunctive). In the examples given above for reporting commands, requests and advice, all the main verbs are in the preterite tense, while those in the subordinate clause introduced by **que** are in the imperfect subjunctive.

c Pronouns and other grammatical words such as demonstratives and possessives may also change: **Por favor, no me dejes** > **Él me rogó que no *le* dejara, Devolvedme *mi* dinero** > **Nos pidió que le devolviéramos *su* dinero**.

The changes affecting indirect speech go much further than this and are determined by factors such as the nature of the original words (a statement, a command, a question, etc.), by the tense of the original verb (present, past, future, etc.), the actual time reference which may have been mentioned by the speaker (**hoy** *today*, **mañana** *tomorrow*, **la semana que viene** *next week*, etc.) and place references (**aquí** *here*, **allí** *there*). It is beyond the scope of this book to cover all the transformations that may occur, but a few examples will help you to become aware of what they involve. Many of these changes are similar to those that may occur in English.

Direct speech	Indirect speech
¿Vendrás a mi fiesta?	**Carlos me preguntó si iría a su fiesta.**
Will you come to my party?	*Carlos asked me whether I'd come to his party.*
¿Lo hiciste tú?	**Ana me preguntó si lo había hecho yo.**
Did you do it yourself?	*Ana asked me if I had done it myself.*
No creo que lo hayan vendido.	**Él dijo que no creía que lo hubieran vendido.**
I don't think they have sold it.	*He said he didn't think they had sold it.*
Nos quedaremos aquí hasta mañana.	**Dijeron que se quedarían allí hasta el día siguiente.**
We'll stay here until tomorrow.	*They said they'd stay there until the following day.*

5 CONDITIONAL TENSE

Uses

a The conditional tense is often used in sentences which express a wish or preference of some sort.

Me *gustaría* **que me escribieras/ escribieses.**	*I'd like you to write to me.*
Yo *preferiría* **que él no viniera/ viniese.**	*I'd prefer him not to come.*

b It is also generally used with verbs which express emotion (see Unit 21).

Sentiría **que ella no viniera/ viniese.**	*I'd be sorry if she didn't come.*

| Me alegraría **de que lo hicieras/** **hicieses.** | I'd be glad if you did it. |
| Sería **una lástima que no la** **encontráramos/encontrásemos.** | It would be a pity if we didn't find her. |

c Uses of the conditional, without the imperfect subjunctive, include polite requests, advice, approximation in relation to the past, indirect speech (see also **Conditional sentences** in Unit 23).

¿Podría **ayudarme?**	Could you help me?
Deberías **trabajar más.**	You should work more.
En aquel tiempo yo tendría treinta **años.**	At that time, I must have been 30 years old.
Juan me dijo que me llamaría.	Juan said he would call me.

Formation
Like the future tense, the conditional is formed with the infinitive, to which the endings are added. The endings of the three conjugations are the same as those of the imperfect tense of **-er** and **-ir** verbs (see Unit 19). Here is the conditional tense of a regular verb.

preferir	*to prefer*
preferiría	*I'd prefer*
preferirías	*you'd prefer* (fam.)
preferiría	*you/he/she would prefer*
preferiríamos	*we would prefer*
preferiríais	*you would prefer* (fam.)
preferirían	*you/they would prefer*

The endings are exactly the same for **-ar** and **-er** verbs.

| Preferiría **que no fueras/fueses** **a Bogotá.** | I'd prefer you not to go to Bogota. |
| Me gustaría **que nos** **encontráramos/encontrásemos** **en España.** | I'd like us to meet in Spain. |

| *Nos gustaría* **que tú nos acompañaras/acompañases.** | *We'd like you to accompany us.* |

Note that all forms of the conditional, including regular and irregular verbs, carry a written accent.

Irregular conditional forms

Verbs which have irregular stems in the future tense (see Unit 15) also have them in the conditional. The endings are the same as those of regular verbs. Here are some of the most common.

decir *to say*	diría, dirías, diría, diríamos, diríais, dirían
haber *to have* (aux.)	habría, habrías, habría, habríamos, habríais, habrían
hacer *to do, make*	haría, harías, haría, haríamos, haríais, harían
poder *can, to be able*	podría, podrías, podría, podríamos, podríais, podrían
poner *to put*	pondría, pondrías, pondría, pondríamos, pondríais, pondrían
querer *to want*	querría, querrías, querría, querríamos, querríais, querrían
saber *to know*	sabría, sabrías, sabría, sabríamos, sabríais, sabrían
salir *to go out*	saldría, saldrías, saldría, saldríamos, saldríais, saldrían
tener *to have*	tendría, tendrías, tendría, tendríamos, tendríais, tendrían
venir *to come*	vendría, vendrías, vendría, vendríamos, vendríais, vendrían

For a list of the most common irregular verbs in all tenses, see the **Irregular verbs** section.

Yo no *querría* **que él se marchara/ marchase.**	*I wouldn't want him to leave.*
Yo no *sabría* **qué hacer.**	*I wouldn't know what to do.*
Tú *tendrías* **que trabajar más.**	*You'd have to work more.*
¿Qué *haríamos* **sin ti?**	*What would we do without you?*

Because of the meaning of these irregular verbs, some of the examples do not correspond to the expression of wishes and indirect orders.

In context

1 An invitation to the cinema.

Antonio	Sara, me gustaría que me acompañaras al cine esta noche. Hay una película estupenda en el cine Capri.
Sara	Me encantaría ir contigo, pero desgraciadamente no puedo. Javier me pidió que fuera a su casa esta noche. Si no te importa, preferiría que lo dejáramos para mañana.
Antonio	De acuerdo. Hasta mañana, entonces.

me encantaría *I'd love to*
si no te importa *if you don't mind*
preferiría que lo dejáramos *I'd prefer to leave it*

QV

2 Read this extract from an e-mail:

Querida Soledad

Cristóbal me pidió que te escribiera para reiterarte nuestra invitación para este verano. Nos gustaría mucho que pasaras estas vacaciones con nosotros. Podríamos ir a Viña del Mar, como lo hicimos la última vez que estuviste en Chile. ¿Te gustaría?
Mi jefe me ha dicho que tome mis vacaciones a partir del 15 de enero, de manera que si estás libre entonces puedes venirte de inmediato. Preferiría que me lo confirmaras lo antes posible para hacer las reservas de hotel. ¿Qué te parece?

como lo hicimos *as we did*
la última vez *the last time*
a partir de *starting on*
lo antes possible *as soon as possible*

QUICK VOCAB

Practice

1 Simón and Lola never seem to agree in their wishes and preferences. Use the phrases in brackets to complete Lola's replies to Simón's statements.

Ejemplo: Me gustaría que pasáramos las vacaciones en Italia.
(Prefiero que … en Francia)
Prefiero que las pasemos en Francia.

   a Me gustaría que fuéramos en avión. (Prefiero que … en el coche)
   b Quiero que nos quedemos en un camping. (Me gustaría que … en un hotel)
   c Prefiero que salgamos el viernes. (Preferiría que … el sábado)
   d Quiero que invitemos a mi madre. (Preferiría que no la…)
   e Me encantaría que Paco viniera con nosotros. (Prefiero que … Julio)
   f Sería mejor que tú hicieras la reserva. (Prefiero que … tú mismo)

2 Felipe has been away from the office for a couple of days. On his return, he found the following note from a colleague. Change the infinitives in brackets into the appropriate form.

Felipe

Ayer llamó el señor Parker de Inglaterra y me pidió que te (1) (informar, yo) que no podrá viajar el día 30 como tenía planeado. Quiere que tú lo/le (2) (llamar) esta tarde para fijar una nueva fecha. También llamaron de la empresa Grasco y me pidieron que te (3) (recordar, yo) que todavía no han recibido el pedido. Quieren que se lo (4) (enviar, tú) lo antes posible. El gerente quiere que (5) (pasar, tú) por su despacho y le (6) (llevar, tú) el informe que te pidió.

Isabel

3 Match each picture with a suitable caption from the sentences below.

    a Me gustaría que Luis aprendiera a tocar la guitarra.
    b No me gustaría que mi novio hiciera el servicio militar.
    c Preferiría que no condujera tan rápido.
    d Creo que sería mejor que viajáramos en avión.
    e Nos gustaría mucho que nuestro hijo fuera médico.
    f Me encantaría que me escribieras un poema.

TEST YOURSELF

1 *Put the infinitives in brackets into the appropriate form.*

   a Me gustaría que este año tú y yo (ir) a Nueva York.

   b Le pedí a Raúl que me (ayudar), pero me dijo que no tenía tiempo.

   c Alba quería que yo lo (ver) para que (yo) le (dar) mi opinión.

   d Preferiría que vosotros me (acompañar). No quiero ir sola.

   e Nos gustaría mucho que Vds. (venir) a nuestra fiesta de aniversario.

2 *Translate these sentences into Spanish.*

   a She didn't want him to know the truth.

   b They ordered us to leave.

   c Roberto had asked me to call him.

   d I'd like you to be here on time.

   e He pleaded with us not to say anything.

Don't forget that the imperfect subjunctive derives from the third person plural of the preterite, so if you had difficulty with any of the verbs in the test, practise converting forms like **fueron, ayudaron, supieron**, etc. into the corresponding forms of the imperfect subjunctive. You have now covered most of the essentials of the Spanish verb, so if you did well in the test, go on to Unit 23, the last unit in this course.

23

Expressing conditions

In this unit, you will learn how to:
- *express open conditions*
- *express remote conditions*
- *express unfulfilled conditions*

Language points
- **si** *in conditional sentences*
- *pluperfect subjunctive*
- *conditional perfect*
- *pluperfect subjunctive for conditional perfect in unfulfilled conditions*
- *phrases expressing conditions*

Key sentences

Conditions may be expressed in English through the word *if*, in constructions such as the following: *If I have time I'll go, If I had time I'd go, If I'd had time I'd have gone.* Look at the following sentences and their translations and then read the **Grammar summary** which follows for an explanation of how these ideas are expressed in Spanish.

EXPRESSING OPEN CONDITIONS

Si tengo tiempo, iré.	*If I have time, I'll go.*
Si ella viene/me lo pregunta, se lo diré/contaré.	*If she comes/asks me, I'll tell her.*

EXPRESSING REMOTE CONDITIONS

Si tuviera/tuviese tiempo, iría.   *If I had time, I'd go.*
Si me llamara/llamase, la invitaría.   *If she called me, I'd invite her.*

EXPRESSING UNFULFILLED CONDITIONS

Si yo hubiera/hubiese tenido   *If I'd had time, I'd have gone.*
  tiempo, habría ido.
Si hubiéramos/hubiésemos   *If we'd known, we'd have come.*
  sabido, habríamos venido.

Insight

Note that unlike **sí** *yes*, **si** *if* does not have a written accent. The written accent is used to differentiate meanings between certain pairs of words whose form and pronunciation are the same. Other such words include **mí** *me* **mi** *my*, **tú** *you* **tu** *your*, **él** *he* **el** *the*, **dé** *give* **de** *of, from*, **sé** *I know* **se** *pronoun*.

Grammar summary

1 SI *(IF) IN CONDITIONAL SENTENCES*

In open conditions
Si is the word most frequently used in Spanish when we want to express conditions. In open conditions – that is, conditions which may or may not be fulfilled, **si** is always followed by an indicative tense, with a tense pattern which is no different from English. Consider these examples and, again, the ones under **Key sentences**:

Si es como él dice, es mejor no   *If it is as he says, it's better not*
  hacerlo.   *to do it.*
(**si** + present + present)
Si ella me escribe, le responderé de   *If she writes to me, I'll answer*
  inmediato.   *her right away.*
(**si** + present + future)

Si tienes tiempo, llámame.	*If you have time, call me.*
(**si** + present tense + imperative)	
Si has hecho tus deberes, podrás salir.	*If you've done your homework, you'll be able to go out.*
(**si** + perfect tense + future)	
Si salieron a las 6:00, ya deben de estar en Caracas.	*If they left at 6.00, they must already be in Caracas.*
(**si** + preterite + present)	

Insight

Si has the same meaning as **cuando/siempre que/cada vez que** *every time* (every time the condition was fulfilled) in: **Si necesitaba dinero, me llamaba** *If he/she needed money, he/she used to call me*, **Si tenían tiempo, nos visitaban** *If they had time, they used to visit us*. The verb in the **si** clause (the subordinate clause) and that in the main clause are both in the imperfect indicative.

In remote conditions

In remote conditions such as **Si lloviera/lloviese, no saldríamos** *If it rained, we wouldn't go out*, the si clause carries a verb in the imperfect subjunctive (see Unit 22) followed by a clause with a verb in the conditional.

Imperfect subjunctive + conditional

Si fueras/fueses allí, la verías.	*If you went there, you'd see her.*
Si tomáramos/tomásemos un taxi, llegaríamos a tiempo.	*If we took a taxi, we'd arrive on time.*

The two examples above correspond to conditions which may be fulfilled. There is little difference between these conditions and the ones expressed in:

Si vas allí, la verás.	*If you go there, you'll see her.*
Si tomamos un taxi, llegaremos a tiempo.	*If we take a taxi, we'll arrive on time.*

Now consider these examples:

Si ella hablara/hablase inglés, la contrataríamos	*If she spoke English, we'd hire her.*
Si él estuviera/estuviese aquí, te lo presentaría.	*If he were here, I'd introduce him to you.*

The two examples above correspond to conditions which are contrary to fact.

Ella no habla inglés.	*She doesn't speak English.*
Él no está aquí.	*He's not here.*

The verb in the **si** clause here must necessarily be in the subjunctive.

Unfulfilled conditions
In unfulfilled conditions such as **Si hubiera/hubiese llovido, no habríamos salido** *If it had rained, we wouldn't have gone out*, the **si** clause carries a verb in the pluperfect subjunctive followed by a clause with a verb in the perfect conditional.

Si ellos se hubieran/hubiesen casado, habrían sido felices.	*If they had married, they'd have been happy.*
Si Miguel me hubiera/hubiese invitado, yo habría aceptado.	*If Miguel had invited me, I'd have accepted.*

For the formation of the pluperfect subjunctive and the conditional perfect and further examples of conditional sentences, see paragraphs 2 and 3 below.

2 PLUPERFECT SUBJUNCTIVE

Usage

Apart from its specific use in unfulfilled conditions, the uses of the pluperfect subjunctive are, generally speaking, those of the subjunctive as a whole. It is normally found in subordinate clauses preceded by a main clause with a verb in the past, but also in independent clauses.

¡Ojalá me lo hubieras dicho!	*I wish you had told me!*
Me dijo que una vez que/cuando hubiera terminado, me podría marchar.	*He/She told me that once/when I had finished, I could leave.*
No creí que él hubiera tenido éxito.	*I didn't think he had succeeded.*

But note further:

Creí que él había tenido éxito.	*I thought he had succeeded.*

Formation

The pluperfect subjunctive is formed with the imperfect subjunctive of **haber** plus a past participle.

Si		If	
	hubiera/hubiese ido		*I had gone*
	hubieras/hubieses ido		*you had gone* (fam.)
	hubiera/hubiese ido		*you/he/she had gone*
	hubiéramos/hubiésemos ido		*we had gone*
	hubierais/hubieseis ido		*you had gone* (fam.)
	hubieran/hubiesen ido		*you/they had gone*

The two endings are interchangeable.

Si hubieras/hubieses ido a Sevilla, te habría gustado.	*If you had gone to Seville, you'd have liked it.*
Si ellos hubieran/hubiesen tenido dinero, habrían viajado.	*If they had had money, they'd have travelled.*

3 CONDITIONAL PERFECT

Usage
The most common use of the conditional perfect is in sentences which refer to actions which could have taken place under certain conditions, as in *If I had known he was here, I wouldn't have come.*

Formation
The conditional perfect is formed with the conditional of **haber** followed by a past participle.

habría estudiado	*I would have studied*
habrías estudiado	*you would have studied* (fam.)
habría estudiado	*you/he/she would have studied*
habríamos estudiado	*we would have studied*
habríais estudiado	*you would have studied* (fam.)
habrían estudiado	*you/they would have studied*

Si yo hubiera/hubiese tenido el libro, habría estudiado.	*If I had had the book, I would have studied.*
Si ella hubiera/hubiese visto la película, le habría gustado.	*If she had seen the film, she would have liked it.*
Si hubiéramos/hubiésemos podido, te habríamos ayudado.	*If we had been able to, we would have helped you.*

4 PLUPERFECT SUBJUNCTIVE FOR CONDITIONAL PERFECT IN UNFULFILLED CONDITIONS

In colloquial speech, the conditional perfect is sometimes replaced by the pluperfect subjunctive (the **-ra** form).

The result is that you get the same tense in the **si** clause and in the main clause.

Si yo no hubiera/hubiese comido *If I hadn't eaten that fish, I*
ese pescado, no me hubiera *wouldn't have become ill.*
(habría) enfermado.
Si Juan hubiera/hubiese sabido, *If Juan had known what happened*
lo que pasó se hubiera (habría) *he would have got angry.*
enfadado.

5 PHRASES EXPRESSING CONDITIONS

a menos que, a no ser que *unless*:

No vendré mañana, *a menos* *I won't come tomorrow unless you*
que/a no ser que **tú me lo pidas.** *ask me to.*

a condición de que, con tal (de) que *as long as*:

Te lo contaré *a condición de que/* *I'll tell you as long as you don't*
con tal (de) que **no se lo digas a** *tell anybody.*
nadie.

....
Insight
A menos que, a no ser que, a condición de que, con tal (de) que are all followed by a subjunctive verb. When reference is to the past, the subjunctive verb must also be in the past: **Me lo contó** *a condición de que* **no se lo dijera a nadie** *He told me on condition that I didn't tell anyone.*
....

por si *in case*, **por si acaso** *just in case*:

He comprado más carne *por si* *I've bought more meat in case*
José viene a cenar. *José comes to dinner.*
Cambiaré más dinero *por si* *I'll change some more money just*
acaso. *in case.*

In context

1 If I had known …

> **Ricardo** ¿Sabes que Julia estuvo aquí ayer?
>
> **Gonzalo** ¡Qué lástima! Si lo hubiera sabido, habría venido yo también. Hace mucho tiempo que no la veo.
>
> **Ricardo** Ahora está en casa de sus padres. Si quieres podemos llamarla.
>
> **Gonzalo** De acuerdo.

2 If I had money …

> **Edgardo** Alba ha decidido vender su piso. ¿Lo sabías?
>
> **Mónica** ¡No me digas! Es un piso estupendo. Si tuviera dinero, lo compraría. ¿Sabes en cuánto lo vende?
>
> **Edgardo** No lo sé, pero si te interesa puedo preguntárselo.
>
> **Mónica** Sí, me interesa mucho. Es un piso muy bonito y es bastante grande.
>
> **Edgardo** Se lo preguntaré.

QV

ha decidido (decidir) *she has decided*
¡No me digas! *You're kidding!*

Practice

1 Match each phrase (**a–f**) with a suitable phrase (**1–6**).

 a Si hubiera tenido dinero, …
 b Si tuviera tiempo, …
 c Si veo a Ángeles, …
 d Si lloviera, …
 e Si hubiese sabido que vendrían, …
 f Si hablara mejor español, …

1 la invitaré a la fiesta.
2 le darían el puesto.
3 los hubiera esperado.
4 te lo habría prestado.
5 te ayudaría.
6 nos quedaríamos en casa.

2 Your friend Helen has received an invitation from someone in Spain, and as her Spanish is not very good, she has asked you to translate the following reply for her.

Dear Mari Carmen,

Thanks for your e-mail and your invitation to visit you in Spain. Unfortunately, I have to work all summer, but if I were free, I'd certainly visit you. I'd love to see you again. Perhaps at Christmas, if I can, unless you want to come and stay with me then? It would be great! I'm glad you've found a job. I know it's not what you wanted, but it's a job. I'd have taken it too. I hope you like it.

3 A group of people were asked what they would do if they won a big lottery prize. What were their answers? Match the pictures with the phrases and put the verbs in the correct form.

Ejemplo: Si (ganar) la lotería, (yo) (dejar) mi trabajo y (dedicarse) a viajar.
Si ganara la lotería, dejaría mi trabajo y me dedicaría a viajar.

Si ganara la lotería...
  1 ... (construir, yo) una gran casa junto al mar.
  2 ... mi familia y yo (comprar) un yate y (dar) la vuelta al mundo.
  3 ... mi mujer y yo (cambiar) nuestros coches/carros (L.Am.).
  4 ... mi novio y yo (ir) de vacaciones a la montaña y (aprender) a esquiar.
  5 ... mi familia y yo (hacer) una gran fiesta e (invitar) a todos nuestros amigos.
  6 ... mi vida no (cambiar) mucho y (seguir) trabajando igual.

TEST YOURSELF

1 *Translate these sentences into Spanish.*
  a If Alfonso calls me, please tell him I'll be back at 5.00.
  b If they come for lunch, I'll prepare a paella.
  c If I could, I would do it.
  d If she spoke Spanish, she would earn more.
  e If I were rich, I would buy that house.

2 *Use the verbs in brackets to complete these unfulfilled conditions.*
  a Si (tener, yo) dinero, lo habría comprado.
  b Si (decírnoslo, tú), te hubiéramos ayudado.
  c Si (llegar, ellos) quince minutos antes, no habrían perdido el vuelo a Londres.
  d Si Carmen hubiese podido, seguro que (venir, ella).
  e Si vosotros lo hubierais visto, os (encantar).

Are you satisfied with your performance in the test? If so, **¡enhorabuena!** You are now familiar with all the essentials of Spanish grammar and are ready to move on to a more advanced stage. If you had difficulty with any of the verb forms in the test, perhaps you need to revise the notes on the subjunctive again (Units 21, 22, 23) or study paragraph 11 of the **Grammar reference**. Remember that language learning implies constant reinforcement, so go back to your book as often as you think necessary and try to find ways in which to practise what you have learned.

Congratulations

Congratulations on completing *Essential Spanish Grammar!*

We hope you have enjoyed working your way through the course. We are always keen to receive feedback from people who have used our course, so why not contact us and let us know your reactions? We'll be particularly pleased to receive your praise, but we should also like to know if things could be improved. We always welcome comments and suggestions, and we do our best to incorporate constructive suggestions into later editions.

You can contact us through the publishers at:

Teach Yourself Books, Hodder Headline Ltd, 338 Euston Road, London NW1 3BH, UK.

We hope you will want to build on your knowledge of Spanish and we have made a few suggestions to help you do this in the section entitled **Taking it further**.

¡Buena suerte!

Juan Kattán-Ibarra

Glossary of grammatical terms

adjectives Adjectives are words used to describe nouns, e.g. The house is very *comfortable* **La casa es muy cómoda**.

adverbs Adverbs provide more information about verbs, adjectives or other adverbs, e.g. She spoke *slowly* **Habló pausadamente**, It's *absolutely* necessary **Es absolutamente necesario**, They behaved *incredibly* well **Se comportaron increíblemente bien**.

articles There are two types of articles, *definite* and *indefinite*. Definite articles are **el, la, los** and **las** (*the* in English). Indefinite articles are **un** and **una** (*a* in English) and **unos, unas** *some*.

clause In a sentence such as *I hope that they come* **Espero que vengan**, there are two clauses: a main clause *I hope* **Espero** and a subordinate clause *that they come* **que vengan**.

demonstratives Demonstratives are words like *this* **este, esta**, *that* **ese, esa**, *these* **estos, estas**, *those* **esos, esas**.

gender There are two genders in Spanish, masculine and feminine. All nouns are, therefore, either masculine or feminine, e.g. **la casa** *house*, feminine, **el coche** *car*, masculine.

gerund Words such as *speaking* **hablando** and *drinking* **bebiendo** are known as gerunds.

imperative The imperative is the form of the verb that is used to give directions, instructions, orders or commands, e.g. *Go straight on* **Siga todo recto**, *Put it here* **Póngalo aquí**.

....

infinitive This is the basic form of the verb, as found in the dictionary, e.g. *to speak* **hablar,** *to answer* **responder.**

....

nouns Nouns are words like *book* **libro,** *difficulty* **dificultad.**

....

number This word is used to indicate whether something is *singular* or *plural.*

....

object This is that part of the sentence which undergoes the action expressed by the verb. In a sentence such as *He sold the car to Maria* **Vendió el coche a María,** *the car* **el coche** is said to be the *direct object,* because the car is what was sold. María, the recipient, is the *indirect object.*

....

past participle A past participle is that part of the verb which is used in compound tenses, e.g. *I have finished* **He terminado,** *They had returned* **Habían vuelto.** *Finished* **terminado** and *returned* **vuelto** are the past participles.

....

personal pronouns These are words such as *I* **yo,** *he* **él,** *she* **ella,** *we* **nosotros/as.**

....

possessives Words like *my* **mi,** *mine* **mío,** *your* **tu, su,** *yours* **tuyo, suyo** are called possessives.

....

prepositions These are words such as *with* **con,** *in, on, at* **en,** *for* **para, por,** *from* **de, desde.**

....

pronouns Pronouns are words which stand in place of nouns or noun phrases which have already been mentioned, e.g. *My friend Gloria* (noun) *is Spanish. She* (pronoun) *lives in Madrid* **Mi amiga Gloria es española. Ella vive en Madrid.**

....

reflexive In a sentence such as *He washed himself* **Se lavó,** the verb is said to be reflexive because the subject and object are one and the same. Words such as *myself* **me,** *himself, herself* **se,** *ourselves* **nos** are called reflexive pronouns.

subject In a sentence such as *Patricia bought the house* **Patricia compró la casa,** Patricia is the subject of the verb *to buy* **comprar,** because it was she who bought the house.

subjunctive mood In a sentence such as *If I were you* **Yo en tu lugar,** the verb *to be* is said to be in the subjunctive mood. The subjunctive is not used much in English nowadays, but it is common in Spanish.

tense Tenses are forms of the verb which indicate aspects of time, e.g. past, present, futurecw.

verbs Words such as *to go* **ir,** *to arrive* **llegar,** *to eat* **comer** are called verbs.

Grammar reference

This grammar reference section brings together the main grammatical points studied in the units and expands on some of them. It also deals with others which have not been covered.

1 ARTICLES

Definite and indefinite articles (the, a/an)
  a The word for *the* for singular nouns is **el** for masculine and **la** for feminine, e.g. **el hotel, la habitación**. The plural forms are **los** and **las**, e.g. **los hoteles, las habitaciones**.
  b **A** + **el** becomes **al**, e.g. **Voy** *al* **cine**, and **de** + **el** becomes **del**, e.g. **Vengo** *del* **supermercado**.
  c The word for *a/an* is **un** for masculine and **una** for feminine, e.g. **un** señor, **una** señora. The plural forms **unos, unas** mean *some*.

Use of the definite article
  a Before nouns used in a general sense, e.g. *los* animales.
  b Before an abstract noun, e.g. *la* dificultad.
  c Before people's names when they are preceded by a noun or an adjective, e.g. *la* señora García, *el* pobre Carlos.
  d Before names of languages, unless they are preceded by the verb **hablar** or the preposition **en**, e.g. **Me gusta** *el* **español**.
  e Before the names of certain countries, although the general tendency nowadays is to omit it, e.g. *la* Argentina, *el* Brasil, *el* Perú, *los* Estados Unidos.
  f Before names of substances and food, e.g. *el* pescado.
  g Before subjects, sports, arts, sciences and illnesses, e.g. *las* matemáticas, *el* tenis, *la* literatura, *la* física, *el* cáncer.
  h Before names of drinks and meals, e.g. *el* café, *la* cena.
  i Before colours, e.g. *el* negro.
  j Before parts of the body, e.g. *las* manos.

k Before days of the week and other expressions of time, e.g. *el* sábado, *el* 23 de julio, *la* semana pasada.

l Before words indicating measure and weight, e.g. diez euros *el* kilo.

m As a substitute for a noun, e.g. *La casa* de María es grande y *la* de José también.

Omission of the indefinite article

a Before words for occupations and professions, nationality, religion, e.g. Soy *estudiante/americano*.

b Before nouns used in a general sense, e.g. No tengo *coche/teléfono*. But Tengo *un* coche Japonés.

c Before words like cien, mil, otro, e.g. Tengo *cien/mil* euros, ¿Tienes *otro*?

d In exclamations after words like qué what a ... and tal *such a* ..., e.g. ¡*Qué* lástima!, ¡Hicieron *tal* ruido!

The neuter article lo
This is used only with certain adjectives, adverbs and whole sentences, *never* with a noun.

¡No sabes *lo* bonito que es!	*You don't know how beautiful it is!*
Lo mejor es no decir nada.	*The best thing is not to say anything.*
¿Recuerdas *lo* que te dije ayer?	*Do you remember what I told you yesterday?*

2 NOUNS

Masculine and feminine
In Spanish, all nouns are either masculine or feminine. It is not always possible to recognize the gender of nouns, but the following simple rules may help you to do so.

Masculine nouns
The following endings correspond normally to masculine nouns, but there are many exceptions.

-o	el trabaj**o**	*work*
-e	el beb**é**	*baby*
-l	el so**l**	*sun*
-r	el amo**r**	*love*
-n	el tre**n**	*train*
-s	el me**s**	*month*

The following nouns are also masculine:

▶ *nouns referring to males, e.g.* **el señor**
▶ *mountains, rivers and seas, e.g.* **el Pacífico**
▶ *days and seasons, e.g.* **el verano**
▶ *colours, e.g.* **el violeta**
▶ *substances, e.g.* **el metal**
▶ *languages, e.g.* **el español**

Feminine nouns
The following endings usually correspond to feminine nouns, but there are exceptions.

-a	la vid**a**	*life*
-ad	la ciud**ad**	*city*
-z	la pa**z**	*peace*
-ción	la na**ción**	*nation*
-sión	la pa**sión**	*passion*
-ud	la juvent**ud**	*youth*

Special rules
a To form the feminine of nouns which refer to people, you normally change the -o into -a or add an -a to the final consonant, e.g. **el arquitecto, la arquitecta; un inglés, una inglesa**.

b Nouns endings in -ista do not change for masculine or feminine, e.g. **el/la dent*ista***.

c Most nouns which end in -ente or -ante are also invariable, e.g. **el/la estudi*ante***.

d Some nouns have different forms for each sex, e.g. *el* **padre** *father,* *la* **madre** *mother,* *el* **hombre** *man,* *la* **mujer** *woman*.

e Some nouns change meaning according to gender, e.g. *el* **policía** *policeman*, *la* **policía** *police*; *el* **capital** *capital, money*, *la* **capital** *capital city*.

Plural of nouns

a Most nouns form the plural by adding -s, e.g. **la casa, las casas**.

b Nouns which end in a consonant normally add -es, e.g. **el profesor, los profesores**.

c Nouns which end in -z change -z to -c and add -es, e.g. **una vez, dos** *veces*.

d The masculine plural of some nouns may be used to refer to members of both sexes, e.g. **el padre** *father*, *los* **padres** *parents*; **el hermano** *brother*, *los* **hermanos** *brothers and sisters*.

e Some nouns lose their accent in the plural, e.g. **un inglés** an Englishman, **unos ingl*es*es** *some English people*.

f Some nouns gain an accent in the plural, e.g. **el joven** *young man*, **los jóvenes** *the young people*.

3 ADJECTIVES

Gender and number agreement
Adjectives must agree in gender and number with the noun they describe.

a Adjectives ending in -o change -o to -a with feminine nouns, e.g. **un hotel pequeño, una habitación pequeñ*a***.

b Adjectives that end in a vowel other than -o or -a do not change for feminine, e.g. **una mujer/un hombre inteligente** *an intelligent woman/man*.

c Adjectives that end in a consonant do not normally change for masculine and feminine, e.g. **un vestido azul** *a blue dress*, **una camisa azul** *a blue shirt*.

d Adjectives indicating nationality form the feminine by changing -o into -a or adding -a to the consonant, e.g. **un periódico español** *a Spanish newspaper*, **una revista española** *a Spanish magazine*.

To form the plural of adjectives, follow the same rules as for nouns (see paragraph 2).

Position of adjectives
  a The great majority of adjectives come after the noun, e.g. **una persona inteligente**.
  b Adjectives are sometimes used before nouns for emphasis or to convey some kind of emotion, e.g. **un *excelente* profesor**.
  c Certain adjectives – among them **grande, pequeño, bueno, malo** – usually precede the adjective, e.g. **un *pequeño* problema**.
  d **Grande** normally follows the noun when its meaning is *big* or *large*, but it goes before it when it means *great*. Before the noun, **grande** becomes **gran**, e.g. **una persona *grande*, una *gran* persona**.
  e Like **grande, bueno** *good* and **malo** *bad* have a different form when they come before a noun, e.g. **un libro *bueno*** or **un *buen* libro** *a good book*; **un día *malo*** or **un *mal* día** *a bad day*.

Comparative form of adjectives
Superiority
Madrid es *más grande* **que Barcelona.**   *Madrid is bigger than Barcelona.*

Inferiority
Mi coche es *menos potente* **que el tuyo.**   *My car is less powerful than yours.*

Equality
Mi casa es *tan bonita* **como la de ella.**   *My house is as pretty as hers.*

Irregular forms

bueno	good	mejor	better
malo	bad	peor	worse
grande	big	mayor/más grande	bigger
pequeño	small	menor/más pequeño	smaller

Superlative form
To express ideas such as *the fastest* or *the most expensive*, use the construction definite article (**el, la, los** or **las**) followed by **más** and the appropriate adjective.

Mi coche es *el más rápido.*   *My car is the fastest.*
Esta tienda es *la más cara.*   *This shop is the most expensive.*

To say *the best* or *the worst*, use the definite article followed by the appropriate word, **mejor** or **peor**.

Esa es *la mejor* **solución.**   *That is the best solution.*
Estos son *los peores.*   *These are the worst.*

4 ADVERBS

a To form an adverb from an adjective, add **-mente** to the singular form of the adjective, e.g. **amable** > *amablemente.*
b If the adjective ends in **-o**, change the **-o** to **-a** and then add **-mente**, e.g. **rápido** > *rápidamente.*
c Many adverbs are not derived from adjectives, e.g. **ahora, mañana, aquí, bien.**

5 PRONOUNS

Subject pronouns

Singular		Plural	
yo	*I*	**nosotros/as**	*we*
tú	*you* (fam.)	**vosotros/as**	*you* (fam.)
usted	*you* (formal)	**ustedes**	*you* (pl.)
él, ella	*he, she*	**ellos, ellas**	*they* (masc./fem.)

1 **Vosotros** and all forms associated with it are not used in Latin America, where **ustedes** is used in formal and informal address.

2 Subject pronouns are usually omitted in Spanish, unless you want to add emphasis or to avoid ambiguity.

3 In some Latin-American countries, among them Argentina, Uruguay and Paraguay (River Plate region), you will hear **vos** instead of **tú** in informal address. The verb forms used with **vos** are not the same in all countries. While in the River Plate countries **vos** is the norm, in other places its use is less extensive and may be considered as uneducated (Chile, for example).

Direct and indirect object pronouns: first and second persons

Object pronouns can be direct, e.g. **La invité** *I invited her*, or indirect, as in **Le dije** *I said to her/him/you* (formal).

In the first and second person singular and plural, there is no distinction between direct and indirect object pronouns, e.g. *Me* **invitó** *He/She invited me*, *Me* **dijo** *He/She said to me*.

Singular		Plural	
me	*me, to me*	**nos**	*us, to us*
te	*you, to you* (fam.)	**os**	*you, to you* (fam.)

In the third person, direct and indirect object pronouns differ, e.g. **Lo** (or **Le**) **invité** (direct) *I invited him*; **Le dije** (indirect) *I said to him/her*.

Direct object pronouns: third person

Singular		Plural	
lo/le	*you* (formal)/*him/it* (m.)	**los/les**	*you* (formal)/*them* (m.)
la	*you* (formal)/*her/it* (f.)	**las**	*you* (formal)/*them* (f.)

Le(s), as a direct object, is used by most people in central and northern Spain when talking about human males, e.g. **Le(s) llamé** *I called him/them*, with **lo(s)** referring to masculine objects, e.g. **Lo(s) compré** *I bought it/them*. In other parts of Spain and in Latin America as a whole, most people use **lo(s)** for both human males and masculine objects, e.g. **Lo llamé** I *called him*, **Lo compré** I *bought it*. In the feminine, there are generally no regional differences. The **lo** form may be easier for you to remember.

Indirect object pronouns: third person

Singular	Plural
le *(to) you* (formal)/*him/her/it*	**les** *(to) you* (formal)/*them*

Le and **les** become **se** before **lo, la, los, las**: *Se* **lo daré** I'll *give it to you* (formal)/*him/her/it*.

Position of object pronouns

a Object pronouns normally precede the verb: **¿Me trae un café?**

b In sentences with two object pronouns, the indirect one comes first: **Te las daré** I'll *give them to you*.

c With imperatives, they follow positive forms but come before negative ones: e.g. **Dígale, No le diga**.

d In constructions with a main verb followed by an infinitive (e.g. **llevar**) or a gerund (e.g. **haciendo**), the object pronoun can either precede the main verb or be attached to the infinitive or gerund: **Voy a llevarlo** or **Lo voy a llevar** I'm *going to take it*, **Estoy escribiéndola** or **La estoy escribiendo** I'm *writing it*.

Pronouns with prepositions

With prepositions, use **mí, ti** for the first and second person singular, and subject pronouns **él, ella, usted**, etc. for the remaining persons.

Para mí un café.	*Coffee for me.*
No iré sin ti.	*I won't go without you.* (fam.)
Lo hice por él/ella.	*I did it for him/her.*

Note the special use of the preposition **con** in:

conmigo	*with me*
contigo	*with you* (fam.)

But note: **con él/ella/usted**.

In the River Plate area, the prepositional pronoun **ti** is replaced by **vos**: **Esto es para vos** *This is for you*. **Contigo** becomes **con vos**.

Reflexive pronouns
These are **me, te, se, nos, os** and **se**. And they accompany reflexive verbs such as **levantarse**, e.g. **me levanto** *I get up*.

Relative pronouns
Que *who, that, which*
Que is the most common relative pronoun and it is used to refer to people or things.

El chico *que* **está allí es mi amigo.**	*The boy who's there is my friend.*
El tren *que* **va a Madrid es ese.**	*The train that/which is going to Madrid is that one.*

Quien, quienes *who*
Quien can only be used for people and it is used after a preposition.

La persona con *quien* **me viste es mi hermana.**	*The person with whom you saw me is my sister.*

El que
El (or **la, los, las**) **que** can refer to people or things and, like **quien**, it is used after a preposition.

Ése *es el* **señor con** *el que* **debes hablar.**	*That's the gentleman you must speak with.*
La empresa para *la que* **trabajábamos cerró.**	*The company we worked for closed down.*

Lo que *what*
No sé *lo que* **pasa.**   *I don't know what happens.*

Cuyo/a, cuyos/as *whose*
Andrés Pérez, *cuya* **boda tuvo lugar ayer, es famoso.**	*Andrés Pérez, whose wedding took place yesterday, is famous.*

6 DEMONSTRATIVES

	Masculine	Feminine	
singular	**este**	**esta**	this, this one
plural	**estos**	**estas**	these, these ones
singular	**ese**	**esa**	that, that one
plural	**esos**	**esas**	those, those ones
singular	**aquel**	**aquella**	that, that one
plural	**aquellos**	**aquellas**	those, those ones

1 Neuter forms are: **esto** *this*, **eso** *that*, **aquello** *that*, e.g. ¿Qué es esto/eso? *What's this/that?*
2 **Aquel, aquella**, etc. are used to refer to something or someone that is far from you.
3 When demonstratives are used as pronouns, meaning *this one, that one*, etc., they are sometimes written with an accent, e.g. **Me gusta éste** *I like this one*. The accent is optional, except when there is ambiguity, which is rarely the case. In this book, they have been used without the accent.

7 POSSESSIVES

Short forms

	Singular	Plural	
	mi	**mis**	my
	tu	**tus**	your (fam.)
	su	**sus**	your (formal) his, her, its
masc./fem.		**nuestro/a nuestros/as**	our
masc./fem.		**vuestro/a vuestros/as**	your (fam.)
	su	**sus**	your (formal) their

The short forms of possessives function as adjectives and they agree with the noun referred to, not with the owner, e.g. **nuestra casa** *our house*; **nuestros amigos** *our friends*.

Long forms

	Singular	*Plural*	
masc./fem.	**mío/a**	**míos/as**	*mine*
masc./fem.	**tuyo/a**	**tuyos/as**	*yours* (fam.)
masc./fem.	**suyo/a**	**suyos/as**	*yours* (formal) *his, hers, its*
masc./fem.	**nuestro/a**	**nuestros/as**	*ours*
masc./fem.	**vuestro/a**	**vuestros/as**	*yours* (fam.)
masc./fem.	**suyo/a**	**suyos/as**	*yours* (formal) *theirs*

1 Like the short forms, the long forms agree with the thing possessed, not with the owner, e.g. **un pariente mío** *a relative of mine*, **Esas cartas son tuyas** *Those letters are yours*.
2 Note that Latin Americans do not use the **vuestro** form of possessives, which is replaced by the phrase **de ustedes** or the possessive **suyo**, e.g. **Este apartamento es de ustedes/suyo, ¿verdad?** *This apartment is yours, isn't it?*

8 PREPOSITIONS

Only the most common prepositions and meanings are given here.

a *at* **a las 4:00** *at 4.00*
   on **a la derecha/izquierda** *on the right/left*
   a **una vez a la semana** *once a week*

Personal **a** used before the direct object when this is a person:
Invité a Manuel *I invited Manuel.*

con	*with*	**café con leche** *coffee with milk*
de	*from*	**Julio es de Granada.** *Julio is from Granada.*
	made of	**de lana** *woollen*
	in	**la ciudad más grande de México** *the biggest city in Mexico*
desde	*from*	**desde las 2:00 de la tarde** *from 2.00 in the afternoon*
	for	**desde hace cinco años** *for five years*

en	in	**Viven en Salamanca.** *They live in Salamanca.*
	on	**Las llaves están en la cama.** *The keys are on the bed.*
	at	**Trabaja en la Universidad de Madrid.** *He works at Madrid University.*
hasta	until	**hasta las 5:00** *until 5.00*
	as far as	**hasta el semáforo** *as far as the traffic lights*

Para and por

Para and **por** tend to be confused by English speakers, as both can translate into English as *for*. Special treatment has been given to them here, with their main uses and meanings clearly defined.

para

▶ *length of time (for)*

Quiero una habitación *para* **dos noches.**	*I want a room for two nights.*

▶ *with time phrases (for, by)*

Lo necesito *para* **el jueves.**	*I need it for/by Thursday.*

▶ *direction (for)*

Salió *para* **Barcelona.**	*He/She left for Barcelona.*

▶ *purpose (so, in order to)*

Te prestaré el libro *para* **que lo leas.**	*I'll lend you the book so that you can read it.*
Llamaré *para* **confirmar.**	*I'll call to (in order to) confirm.*

▶ *before names and personal pronouns (for)*

Para **Ana es muy difícil.**	*For Ana, it's very difficult.*
Para **mí un té con limón.**	*Lemon tea for me.*

▶ *with words* such as **muy, suficiente, bastante, demasiado** *(to)*

No hay bastante dinero *para* **comprarlo.**	*There isn't enough money to buy it.*
Es demasiado tarde *para* **decírselo.**	*It's too late to tell him/her.*

por
   ▶ *in time phrases (in, at)*

Él saldrá *por* **la mañana.**	*He'll leave in the morning.*
Llegaremos *por* **la noche.**	*We'll arrive at night.*

   ▶ *means (by, over, through)*

Viajarán *por* **avión.**	*They'll travel by plane.*
Me lo dijeron *por* **teléfono.**	*They told me over the phone.*
Lo supe *por* **Carmen.**	*I found out through Carmen.*

   ▶ *movement (through, along)*

Pasaremos *por* **Madrid.**	*We'll go through Madrid.*
Continúe *por* **esta calle.**	*Continue along this street.*

   ▶ *cost, measure and number (for, a, per)*

Pagué dos mil euros *por* **él.**	*I paid two thousand euros for it.*
Cobran trescientos *por* **hora.**	*They charge 300 an/per hour.*
Subió un 10 *por* **cien/ciento.**	*It went up 10 per cent.*
Viajan a España tres veces *por/al* **año.**	*They travel to Spain three times a/per year.*

   ▶ *reason or cause (for, because of)*

Lo hice *por* **ti.**	*I did it for you.*

   ▶ *purpose or aim (for)*

Lo hizo *por* **el dinero.**	*He/She did it for the money.*
Fue *por/a* por (Spain) **pan.**	*He/She went for/to get some bread.*

▶ *indicating proximity (around, nearby)*

¿Hay un hotel por **aquí?** *Is there a hotel around here/nearby?*

▶ *introducing the agent in passive sentences with* ser *(by)*

Fue hecho por **ella.** *It was made by her.*

9 VERBS

Types of verb
a -ar, -er, -ir
According to the ending of the infinitive, Spanish verbs may be
grouped into three main categories: **-ar**, **-er** and **-ir**, e.g. **hablar**
to speak, **comer** *to eat,* **vivir** *to live.*

b Regular and irregular verbs
Most Spanish verbs are regular, that is, they follow a fixed pattern
in their conjugation, but some very common verbs are irregular.
A list of these can be found in the **Irregular verbs** section.

c Stem-changing verbs
There are certain verbs which undergo a change in the stem, for
example -e into **-ie** or -o into **-ue** when the vowel within the stem
or root is stressed, e.g. **querer** > **quiero** *I want,* **poder** > **puedo**
I can. (See Unit 8 **Grammar summary** paragraph 3.)

d Reflexive verbs
Verbs like **levantarse** *to get up,* **acostarse** *to go to bed,* **lavarse**
to wash, which carry the particle **se** attached to them, are called
reflexive. These are used with reflexive pronouns, for example **me**
levanto *I get up.* Reflexive verbs, if they are regular, are conjugated
in the normal way. (See **Reflexive pronouns** above and Unit 9
Grammar summary paragraph 1.)

10 THE INDICATIVE TENSES

The formation of each of the tenses is shown below through three
regular verbs, representing each of the three conjugations: **hablar**

to speak, **comer** *to eat*, **vivir** *to live*. Only the present tense is given here in full with the corresponding subject pronouns. For irregular verbs, see the **Irregular verbs** section.

Simple tenses

a Present indicative tense
FORMATION

yo	**habl**o	**com**o	**viv**o
tú	**habl**as	**com**es	**viv**es
Vd./él/ella	**habl**a	**com**e	**viv**e
nosotros/as	**habl**amos	**com**emos	**viv**imos
vosotros/as	**habl**áis	**com**éis	**viv**ís
Vds./ellos/ellas	**habl**an	**com**en	**viv**en

In the River Plate countries, notably Argentina and Uruguay, where **vos** instead of **tú** is the norm, the present tense forms for the second person singular are: **vos hablás, vos comés, vos vivís.**

For irregular verbs in the present, see the **Irregular verbs** section.

USES
a To refer to an action taking place at the moment of speaking:
¿Qué haces?   *What are you doing?*

b To refer to habitual actions:
Me levanto a las 8:00.   *I get up at 8.00.*

c To refer to something which is generally true:
En Brasil se habla portugués.   *In Brazil, they speak Portuguese.*

d To refer to future actions, especially with verbs of movement:
Salimos mañana a las 3:00.   *We leave tomorrow at 3.00.*

e To give directions and instructions:
Sigues por esta calle hasta el   *You go along this street as far as*
  semáforo.   *the traffic light.*

Subes a la tercera planta y me esperas allí.   *You go up to the third floor and wait for me there.*

f To refer to the past, in a historical context:

En 1939 termina la guerra.   *The war ends in 1939.*

b Preterite tense

FORMATION

Verbs in **-er** and **-ir** share the same endings.

habl- $\begin{cases} é \\ aste \\ ó \\ amos \\ asteis \\ aron \end{cases}$ *com-/viv-* $\begin{cases} í \\ iste \\ ió \\ imos \\ isteis \\ ieron \end{cases}$

For irregular preterite forms, see the **Irregular verbs** section.

USES

The preterite tense is used to refer to actions or events that were completed at a specific point in the past or which lasted over a definite period and ended in the past.

Ayer hablé con él.   *I spoke to him yesterday.*

c Imperfect tense

FORMATION

Verbs in **-er** and **-ir** share the same endings.

habl- $\begin{cases} aba \\ abas \\ aba \\ ábamos \\ abais \\ aban \end{cases}$ *com-/viv-* $\begin{cases} ía \\ ías \\ ía \\ íamos \\ íais \\ ían \end{cases}$

For irregular imperfect forms, see the **Irregular verbs** section.

a Generally, to talk about actions whose beginning or end are not specified.

En aquel tiempo vivía conmigo.   *At that time, he/she lived/was*
                                     living with me.

b To describe people, places and things known in the past.

La casa tenía dos dormitorios.   *The house had two bedrooms.*

c To say what people used to do.

Trabajaban en Buenos Aires.   *They used to work in Buenos Aires.*

d To refer to an action that was taking place when something else happened.

Cuando salíamos, empezó a   *When we were going out, it started*
  llover.   *to rain.*

d Future tense
FORMATION
The same endings, added to the whole infinitive, apply to **-ar**, **-er** and **-ir** verbs.

$$hablar\text{-}/comer\text{-}/vivir\text{-} \begin{cases} \text{é} \\ \text{ás} \\ \text{á} \\ \text{emos} \\ \text{éis} \\ \text{án} \end{cases}$$

For irregular verbs in the future, see the **Irregular verbs** section.

USES

a To refer to a future action.

Mañana hablaré con él.   *Tomorrow I'll speak to him.*

b To indicate probability and uncertainty.

Supongo que vivirá aquí.   *I suppose he/she lives here.*
¿Qué hora será?   *I wonder what time it is.*

c To express promises.

Prometo que te lo daré.   *I promise I'll give it to you.*

d To give commands.

Te lo comerás todo.   *You'll eat it all.*

Conditional tense
FORMATION
The same endings, added to the whole infinitive, apply to **-ar**, **-er** and **-ir** verbs.

$$
\textit{hablar-/comer-/vivir-} \left\{
\begin{array}{l}
\text{ía} \\
\text{ías} \\
\text{ía} \\
\text{íamos} \\
\text{íais} \\
\text{ían}
\end{array}
\right.
$$

For irregular conditional forms, see the **Irregular verbs** section.

USES

a To say what you would do or would like to do.

Yo hablaría con ella.   *I would speak to her.*
Nos gustaría ir.   *We'd like to go.*

b As a sign of politeness in requests.

¿Sería tan amable de venir aquí? *Would you be kind enough to come here?*

c In conditional sentences.

Si tuviera dinero, lo compraría. *If I had money, I would buy it.*

Compound tenses

a Perfect tense
FORMATION
The perfect tense is formed with the present tense of **haber** followed by a past participle. This ends in **-ado** for **-ar** verbs and **-ido** for **-er** and **-ir** verbs.

he	
has	habl*ado*
ha	com*ido*
hemos	viv*ido*
habéis	
han	

For irregular past participles, see the **Irregular verbs** section.

USES
a To talk about past events which relate to the present.

Ya has comido demasiado. *You've already eaten too much.*

b To talk about recent events.

Hoy he hablado con Pepe. *Today I have spoken with Pepe.*

c To refer to actions which have taken place over a period of time which has not yet ended.

Hemos vivido aquí largo tiempo. *We've lived here a long time.*

Note that, unlike the preterite, the perfect tense is not normally used when talking about actions which occurred at some specific point in the past such as *I spoke to her last week*.

b Pluperfect tense
FORMATION
The pluperfect tense is formed with the imperfect of **haber** and a past participle.

había	
habías	habl*ado*
había	com*ido*
habíamos	viv*ido*
habíais	
habían	

USE
The pluperfect tense is used for referring to actions which took place before some other past event.

La fiesta había terminado   *The party had finished when*
cuando llegué.   *I arrived.*

c Future perfect
FORMATION
The future perfect is formed with the future of **haber** followed by the past participle.

habré	
habrás	habl*ado*
habrá	com*ido*
habremos	viv*ido*
habréis	
habrán	

USES
a To express probability.

¿Habrá llegado el tren?   *Do you think the train will have arrived?*

b To say that something will happen before a moment in the future.

Para las 3:00 ya lo habré *By 3.00 I will have finished it.*
 terminado.

d Conditional perfect
FORMATION
The conditional perfect is formed with the conditional form of
haber followed by a past participle.

habría	
habrías	habl*ado*
habría	com*ido*
habríamos	viv*ido*
habríais	
habrían	

USES
a Generally, the conditional perfect is used for saying what one
would have done.

Yo habría ido. *I would have gone.*

It is also found in sentences expressing unfulfilled conditions.

Si hubiera sabido, la habría *If I had known, I would have called*
 llamado. *her.*

11 *THE SUBJUNCTIVE TENSES*

Uses of the subjunctive
The subjunctive is not normally used on its own, but is dependent
on another verb or phrase. Verbs which express hope, doubt,
emotions, preferences and orders are among those requiring the
use of the subjunctive in a subordinate clause introduced by **que**.
The subject of the main clause must be different from that of
the subordinate clause. (For more information on the use of the
subjunctive, see Units 21–23.)

a Present subjunctive

To form the present subjunctive, remove the **-o** of the first person of the present tense indicative and add the endings, one set for **-ar** verbs, another for verbs ending in **-er** and **-ir**. This rule applies also to stem-changing verbs and most irregular verbs.

habl-		*com-/viv-*	
	e		a
	es		as
	e		a
	emos		amos
	éis		áis
	en		an

For irregular forms in the present subjunctive, see the **Irregular verbs** section.

USES

The present subjunctive normally occurs in sentences which carry a main clause with a verb in the present indicative, but also sometimes in the future, the perfect or the imperative. Its uses are generally no different from those of the subjunctive as a whole, as you will see from the examples below. Only main uses are given here.

a hope

Espero que regreses pronto.   *I hope you come back soon.*

b doubt

No creo que hablen español.   *I don't think they speak Spanish.*

c emotions

Siento que no puedas venir.   *I'm sorry you can't come.*
Me alegro de que les escribas.   *I'm glad you're writing to them.*

d wishes and preferences

Quiero que me ayudes.   *I want you to help me.*
Prefiero que te lo comas tú.   *I'd prefer you to eat it.*

e requirements with regard to someone or something

Buscan a alguien que hable   *They're looking for someone who*
  español.   *speaks Spanish.*

f possibility

Es posible que lleguen hoy.   *It's possible that they may arrive*
        today.

g indirect commands

Les he dicho que me llamen.   *I've told them to call me.*
Le pediré que lo compre.   *I'll ask him/her to buy it.*
Dile que lo venda.   *Tell him/her to sell it.*

h with expressions such as **cuando** and **hasta que** when they refer to the future.

Comeremos cuando llegues.   *We'll eat when you arrive.*

i with the phrase **para que**, which indicates purpose.

He traído la carta para que la   *I've brought the letter so that you*
  leas.   *can read it.*

b Imperfect subjunctive
FORMATION
There are two alternative endings for the imperfect subjunctive, which are generally interchangeable. The first, which seems to be more common, is directly derived from the third person plural of the preterite.

Preterite (3rd person pl.)	Imperfect subjunctive (1st and 3rd person sing.)
hablaron they spoke	hablara
comieron they ate	comiera
vivieron they lived	viviera

Here are the full forms for the two alternative endings:

habl-
- ara/ase
- aras/ases
- ara/ase
- áramos/ásemos
- arais/aseis
- aran/asen

com-/viv-
- iera/iese
- ieras/ieses
- iera/iese
- iéramos/iésemos
- ierais/ieseis
- ieran/iesen

For irregular imperfect subjunctive forms, see the **Irregular verbs** section.

USES

The imperfect subjunctive occurs in sentences which carry a main clause with a verb in the past or conditional. Its uses are generally those of the subjunctive as a whole, but it also occurs in conditional sentences expressing ideas such as *if they called me...*, *if they spoke Spanish... .*

Yo esperaba que me ayudaras/ ayudases.	*I was hoping you would help me.*
Él no quiso que lo comprara/ comprase.	*He didn't want me to buy it.*
Nos pidió que esperáramos/ esperásemos.	*He/She asked us to wait.*
Me gustaría que volvieran/ volviesen.	*I'd like them to come back.*
Si me llamaran/llamasen, los invitaría.	*If they called me, I'd invite them.*

c Perfect subjunctive

FORMATION

The perfect subjunctive is formed with the present subjunctive of
haber followed by a past participle.

haya	
hayas	hablado
haya	comido
hayamos	vivido
hayáis	
hayan	

USES

The uses of this tense correspond to those of the subjunctive as a
whole. It usually occurs in subordinate clauses with the verb in the
main clause in the present tense indicative.

No creo que Luis haya llegado. *I don't think Luis has arrived.*
Espero que me hayas entendido. *I hope you have understood me.*

d Pluperfect subjunctive

FORMATION

This is formed with the imperfect subjunctive of **haber,** with its two
alternative endings **-ra** or **-se,** followed by a past participle.

hubiera/hubiese	
hubieras/hubieses	hablado
hubiera/hubiese	comido
hubiéramos/hubiésemos	vivido
hubierais/hubieseis	
hubieran/hubiesen	

USES

This tense is normally associated with the expression of unfulfilled
conditions.

Si hubiera/hubiese llovido, no *If it had rained, we wouldn't have*
  habríamos ido. *gone.*

Si hubieras/hubieses estudiado,   *If you had studied, you would have*
habrías aprobado.   *passed.*

The **-ra** form of the pluperfect subjunctive is often used in place of the conditional perfect.

Si lo hubiera/hubiese sabido, no   *If I had known, I wouldn't have*
hubiera/habría venido.   *come.*

12 *IMPERATIVE*

FORMATION
Spanish uses different imperative forms, depending on who you are talking to (formal or informal) and whether you are speaking to one or more than one person (singular or plural). Familiar imperatives have different positive and negative forms.

a Formal imperative
To form the imperative for **usted,** change the ending of the third person singular of the present tense indicative from -**a** to -**e** for -**ar** verbs, and from -**e** to -**a** for verbs ending in -**er** and -**ir**. For the plural, add an -**n**.

present tense	usted	ustedes
Vd. habla	hable	hablen
Vd. come	coma	coman
Vd. vive	viva	vivan

b Informal imperative
To form the imperative for **tú,** remove the -**s** from the second person singular of the present tense. For **vosotros,** remove the -**r** of the infinitive and replace it with -**d**.

infinitive	present tense	tú	vosotros
hablar	tú hablas	habla	hablad
comer	tú comes	come	comed
vivir	tú vives	vive	vivid

The familiar singular imperative forms in the River Plate area, where **vos** instead of **tú** is the norm, are: **hablá, comé, viví.**

c Negative imperatives
Negative imperatives are formed with the present subjunctive. All you need to do is put **no** before the corresponding verb form.

usted	ustedes	tú	vosotros
no hable	no hablen	no hables	no habléis
no coma	no coman	no comas	no comáis
no viva	no vivan	no vivas	no viváis

For irregular imperatives, see the **Irregular verbs** section.

USES
The imperative is used in instructions, directions and commands.

Lea las instrucciones cuidadosamente.	*Read the instructions carefully.*
Gire a la derecha en la esquina.	*Turn right at the corner.*
No hables con él.	*Don't speak to him.*

Pronouns with imperatives
Object and reflexive pronouns are attached to the ending of positive imperatives. With negative imperatives, they precede the verb.

¡Déjame solo!	*Leave me alone!*
¡No me dejes solo!	*Don't leave me alone!*
Siéntese allí.	*Sit down there.*
No se siente allí.	*Don't sit there.*

13 GOVERNMENT OF VERBS

Main verb + infinitive
As in English, the construction main verb + infinitive is very common in Spanish.

a With verbs denoting wants and likes, e.g. **querer** *to want*, **preferir** *to prefer*, **gustar** *to like*.

Quieren volver.	*They want to come back.*
Me gusta bailar.	*I like to dance.*

b With verbs denoting ability and capacity, e.g. **poder** *to be able to, can*, **saber** *to know how to*.

No puedo hacerlo.	*I can't do it.*
No sé nadar.	*I don't know how to swim.*

c With verbs of perception, e.g. **ver** *to see*, **oír** *to hear*.

La vimos salir.	*We saw her go out.*
No la oí entrar.	*I didn't hear her come in.*

d Certain verbs are always used with an infinitive, for example **acabar de** *to have just*, **acostumbrar** *to be in the habit* of, **deber** *must, have to*, **dejar de** *to give up, stop doing something*, **empezar** *to begin*, **soler** *to be in the habit of*.

Acaba de llegar.	*He/She has just arrived.*
No acostumbro hacer eso.	*I'm not in the habit of doing that.*
Debemos esperar.	*We must wait.*
Dejó de fumar.	*He/She gave up smoking.*
Empezó a llover.	*It started to rain.*
No suelen venir aquí.	*They don't usually come here.*

Main verb + gerund
The gerund is that form of the verb which in English ends in **-ing**, e.g. *working*. In Spanish, this is formed by adding **-ando** to the stem of **-ar** verbs and **-iendo** to that of **-er** and **-ir** verbs. There are a number of constructions with the gerund in Spanish.

a With **estar**, to indicate an action in progress.

Están trabajando.	*They're working.*

b With **llevar** followed by a time expression to denote *for*.

Llevamos un año viviendo aquí.   *We've been living here for a year.*

c With **seguir** and **continuar** *to continue, go on.*

Sigue viviendo allí.   *He/She continues living there.*
Continuaremos andando.   *We'll continue walking.*

Main verb + past participle
The past participle is formed by adding -**ado** to the stem of -**ar** verbs and -**ido** to that of verbs ending in -**er** and -**ir**. The two most important constructions with the past participle are:

a With **haber** (auxiliary verb) *to have*, to form compound tenses.

Hemos terminado.   *We have finished.*
Se han ido.   *They've left.*

b With **estar**, to denote a state which is the result of an action. Here, the past participle agrees in gender and number with the noun it refers to.

La habitación está reservada.   *The room is booked.*
Los museos están cerrados.   *The museums are closed.*

14 *USING* SE

Se is used with the third person of the verb:

a to form impersonal sentences, e.g. **¿Cómo se va al aeropuerto desde aquí?**
b to convey the idea that something '*is done*', e.g. **Aquí se habla español.**
c with reflexive verbs (e.g. **levantarse**), e.g. **Se levantaron a las 6:00.**

15 *USING* SER *AND* ESTAR

Ser is used:

a to give personal information such as who you are, nationality, where you are from, occupation, marital status (L.Am.), e.g. **Plácido Domingo es español** *Plácido Domingo is Spanish.*
b to describe people, places and things, e.g. **Barcelona es una ciudad preciosa** *Barcelona is a beautiful city.*
c with the time and certain time phrases, e.g. **Mañana es domingo** *Tomorrow is Sunday.*
d to refer to the material something is made of, e.g. **Esta camisa es de algodón** *This shirt is made of cotton.*
e to denote possession, e.g. **Este libro es mío** *This book is mine.*
f to ask and say how much something is, e.g. **¿Cuánto es?** *How much is it?*
g to indicate where an event will take place, e.g. **La fiesta es en casa de Isabel** *The party is in Isabel's house.*
h to denote characteristics which are considered universal or part of someone's nature, e.g. **La Tierra es redonda** *The Earth is round.*
i in passive constructions followed by a past participle, e.g. **El cuadro fue robado** *The picture was stolen.*
j with a noun complement, e.g. **Es un ordenador/computador/una computadora (L.Am.)** *It's a computer.*

In the River Plate area, where **vos** replaces **tú**, you will hear **vos sos** instead of **tú eres**.

Estar is used:

a to ask and say where something is, e.g. **La catedral está en la plaza** *The cathedral is in the square.*
b to express marital status, e.g. **Paco está soltero** *Paco is single.*
c to ask people how they are and respond, e.g. **¿Cómo estás? – Estoy bien** *How are you? – I'm well.*
d to denote a temporary state or condition, e.g. **Gloria está muy guapa hoy** *Gloria is looking very pretty today.*

e to refer to cost when prices fluctuate, e.g. **¿A cuánto está (el cambio de) la libra?** *How much is (What's the rate of exchange for) the pound?*
f with past participles, to denote a condition resulting from an action, e.g. **El restaurante está abierto** *The restaurant is open.*
g with gerunds, to talk about actions in progress, e.g. **Está bañándose** *He/She is having a bath.*

16 *VERBS WITH SPECIAL MEANINGS*

Certain common verbs are used with meanings which are not the usual ones. For reasons of space only a few of these verbs and their meanings are listed here.

dejar *to leave*

a to *give up, stop* (followed by **de**): **Ana dejó de fumar** *Ana gave up smoking*, **Dejaron de molestarnos** *They stopped bothering us*, **No ha dejado de llover** *It hasn't stopped raining.*
b *not to fail* (in negative sentences only): **No dejes de venir** *Don't fail to come.*

hacer *to do, make*

a weather expressions: **Hace/Hizo calor/frío** *It is/was hot/cold*, **Hace/Hizo sol/viento** *It is/was sunny/windy*, **¿Qué tiempo hace?** *What's the weather like?*, **Hace buen/mal tiempo** *The weather is good/bad.*
b to *order*: **Haré pintar la casa** *I'll have the house painted*, **Hizo reparar el coche** *He/She had the car repaired.*
c *to think*: **Te hacía en casa de Alfonso** *I thought you were in Alfonso's house*, **Le hacíamos más joven** *We thought he/she was younger.*
d *to behave*: **Haces bien en decírselo** *You are right to tell him/her*, **Hiciste mal en no ayudarles** *It was wrong of you not to help them.*
e *to fit, be good at*: **Esta llave no le hace a mi puerta** *This key doesn't fit my door*, **Carlos le hace a todo** *Carlos is good at everything.*

f *to play, work temporarily as* (followed by **de**): **En la obra Elena hizo de monja** *In the play, Elena played the part of a nun*, **Luis está haciendo de camarero** *Luis is working as a waiter*.

g with a time phrase: **Hace una hora que están aquí** *They've been here for an hour*, **Hace una hora que llegaron** *They arrived an hour ago*, **Patricia vive en España desde hace mucho tiempo** *Patricia has been living in Spain for a long time*.

llevar *to carry, take*

a Used with a time phrase and the gerund to refer to events or states which began in the past and which are still in progress: **Llevo un año trabajando en esta empresa** *I've been working in this company for a year*. The gerund may be omitted if the verb is understood: **Llevo un año en esta empresa** *I've been in this company for a year*.

b *to wear*: **Ana llevaba un vestido rojo** *Ana was wearing a red dress*.

c *to have*: **Este plato no lleva carne** *This dish doesn't have meat in it*, **No llevo dinero** *I have no money on me*, **Luis lleva el pelo largo** *Luis has long hair*.

quedar, quedarse *to stay, remain*

a *to be*: **¿Dónde queda?** *Where is it?*, **¿Queda muy lejos?** *Is it very far?*, **Queda al final de esta calle** *It's at the end of this street*.

b *to fit, suit*: **Esos pantalones te quedan bien** *Those trousers suit you*, **¿Qué tal me queda esta chaqueta?** *Does this jacket suit me/look all right?*, **Me queda grande/largo** *It's too big/long for me*.

c *to be left*: **No queda pan** *There's no bread left*, **¿Cuánto vino queda?** *How much wine is there?*, **¿Le quedan billetes para el tren de las 3:00?** *Do you have any tickets left for the 3.00 train?* **Queda sólo una semana para la Navidad** *Christmas is only a week away*.

d *result*: **El cuadro te quedó estupendo** *The painting (you did) looks great*, **Sofía quedó muy triste cuando nos fuimos** *Sofía was very sad when we left*, **Quedó viudo/viuda** *He/She lost his wife/her husband*.

e *to meet, arrange to meet*: ¿Dónde quedamos? *Where shall we meet?*, He quedado con Raúl *I've arranged to meet Raúl.*
f *to come to* (followed by **en**): Todo quedó en nada *Everything came to nothing.*
g *to be left without* (followed by **sin**): Quedamos sin luz/electricidad/agua *We were left without light/electricity/water.*

tener *to have*

a *age*: ¿Cuántos años tienes? *How old are you?*, Tengo treinta años *I'm 30 years old.*
b *measure*: Tiene dos metros de largo *It is two metres long*, Tiene veinte centímetros de ancho *It is 20 centimetres wide.*
c *to feel*: ¿Tienes hambre? *Are you hungry?*, Tengo sed *I'm thirsty*, Tengo frío/calor *I'm cold/hot*, Ella tiene miedo/vergüenza/rabia *She's afraid/ashamed/angry.*
d *to hear, receive*: ¿Has tenido noticias de Diego? *Have you heard from Diego?*, No he tenido carta de él desde hace mucho tiempo *I haven't had a letter from him for a long time.*
e *obligation* (followed by **que**): Tengo mucho que hacer *I have a lot to do*, Tienes que hacerlo *You have to do it.*
f *supposition* (followed by **que**): Tiene que estar muy triste después de lo que pasó *He/She must be very sad after what happened*, A esta hora tienen que estar en casa *At this time they must be at home.*
g *suggestion* (followed by **que**): Tendrías que estudiar más *You should study more*, Tendríais que contárselo *You should tell him/her.*

17 NUMBERS

Cardinal numbers
a Cardinal numbers – e.g. **dos, cuatro, veinte, cuarenta** – are adjectives, but they are invariable, except for forms involving **un(o)/a** and **cientos/as**, which agree in gender with the following noun, e.g. **una libra** *one pound*, **doscientos invitados** *200 guests.*

b Ciento is shortened to **cien** before a noun or an adjective, e.g. **cien dólares** *100 dollars*.

c Cien and **mil** are not preceded by the indefinite article, e.g. **cien kilómetros** *100 kilometres*.

d Un millón is preceded by the indefinite article and followed by de, e.g. **Tengo un millón de cosas que hacer** *I have a million things to do*.

Ordinal numbers

a Ordinal numbers agree in number and gender with the noun they refer to, e.g. **el segundo día** *the second day*, **las primeras acciones** *the first actions*.

b Primero and **tercero** drop the final -o before a masculine singular noun, e.g. **el tercer autobús** *the third bus*.

Irregular verbs

The following list includes only the most common irregular verbs. Only irregular forms are given (verbs marked with an asterisk are also stem-changing).

abrir *to open*
past particple: abierto

andar *to walk*
preterite: anduve, anduviste, anduvo, anduvimos, anduvisteis, anduvieron
imperfect subjunctive: anduviera/anduviese, anduvieras/anduvieses, anduviera/anduviese, anduviéramos/anduviésemos, anduvierais/anduvieseis, anduvieran/anduviesen

conducir *to drive*
present indicative: (yo) conduzco
present subjunctive: conduzca, conduzcas, conduzca, conduzcamos, conduzcáis, conduzcan
preterite: conduje, condujiste, condujo, condujimos, condujisteis, condujeron
imperfect subjunctive: condujera/condujese, condujeras/condujeses, condujera/condujese, condujéramos/condujésemos, condujerais/condujeseis, condujeran/condujesen

dar *to give*
present indicative: (yo) doy
present subjunctive: dé, des, dé, demos, deis, den
preterite: di, diste, dio, dimos, disteis, dieron
imperfect subjunctive: diera/diese, dieras/dieses, diera/diese, diéramos/diésemos, dierais/dieseis, dieran/diesen

decir* *to say*
present indicative: (yo) digo

present subjunctive: diga, digas, diga, digamos, digáis, digan
preterite: dije, dijiste, dijo, dijimos, dijisteis, dijeron
imperfect subjunctive: dijera/dijese, dijeras/dijeses, dijera/dijese, dijéramos/dijésemos, dijerais/dijeseis, dijeran/dijesen
future: diré, dirás, dirá, diremos, diréis, dirán
conditional: diría, dirías, diría, diríamos, diríais, dirían
imperative (familiar, singular): di
gerund: diciendo
past participle: dicho

escribir *to write*
past participle: escrito

estar *to be*
present indicative: estoy, estás, está, estamos, estáis, están
present subjunctive: esté, estés, esté, estemos, estéis, estén
preterite: estuve, estuviste, estuvo, estuvimos, estuvisteis, estuvieron
imperfect subjunctive: estuviera/estuviese, estuvieras/estuvieses, estuviera/estuviese, estuviéramos/estuviésemos, estuvierais/estuvieseis, estuvieran/estuviesen
imperative (familiar, singular): está

hacer *to do, make*
present indicative: (yo) hago
present subjunctive: haga, hagas, haga, hagamos, hagáis, hagan
preterite: hice, hiciste, hizo, hicimos, hicisteis, hicieron
imperfect subjunctive: hiciera/hiciese, hicieras/hicieses, hiciera/hiciese, hiciéramos/hiciésemos, hicierais/hicieseis, hicieran/hiciesen
future: haré, harás, hará, haremos, haréis, harán
conditional: haría, harías, haría, haríamos, haríais, harían
imperative: (Vd.) haga, (tú) haz
past participle: hecho

ir *to go*
present indicative: voy, vas, va, vamos, vais, van
present subjunctive: vaya, vayas, vaya, vayamos, vayáis, vayan
imperfect: iba, ibas, iba, íbamos, ibais, iban
preterite: fui, fuiste, fue, fuimos, fuisteis, fueron

imperfect subjunctive: fuera/fuese, fueras/fueses, fuera/fuese, fuéramos/fuésemos, fuerais/fueseis, fueran/fuesen
imperative: (Vd.) vaya, (tú) ve

leer *to read*
preterite: (él, ella, Vd.) leyó, (ellos, ellas, Vds.) leyeron
imperfect subjunctive: leyera/leyese, leyeras/leyeses, leyéramos/leyésemos, leyerais/leyeseis, leyeran/leyesen
gerund: leyendo

oír *to hear*
present indicative: oigo, oyes, oye, oímos, oís, oyen
present subjunctive: oiga, oigas, oiga, oigamos, oigáis, oigan
preterite: (él, ella, Vd.) oyó, (ellos, ellas, Vds.) oyeron
imperfect subjunctive: oyera/oyese, oyeras/oyeses, oyera/oyese, oyéramos/oyésemos, oyerais/oyeseis, oyeran/oyesen
imperative: (Vd.) oiga, (tú) oye
gerund: oyendo

poder* *to be able to, can*
preterite: pude, pudiste, pudo, pudimos, pudisteis, pudieron
imperfect subjunctive: pudiera/pudiese, pudieras/pudieses, pudiera/pudiese, pudiéramos/pudiésemos, pudierais/pudieseis, pudieran/pudiesen
future: podré, podrás, podrá, podremos, podréis, podrán
conditional: podría, podrías, podría, podríamos, podríais, podrían

poner *to put*
present indicative: (yo) pongo
present subjunctive: ponga, pongas, ponga, pongamos, pongáis, pongan
preterite: puse, pusiste, puso, pusimos, pusisteis, pusieron
imperfect subjunctive: pusiera/pusiese, pusieras/pusieses, pusiera/pusiese, pusiéramos/pusiésemos, pusieran/pusiesen
future: pondré, pondrás, pondrá, pondremos, pondréis, pondrán
conditional: pondría, pondrías, pondría, pondríamos, pondríais, pondrían
imperative: (Vd.) ponga, (tú) pon
past participle: puesto

querer* *to want*
preterite: quise, quisiste, quiso, quisimos, quisisteis, quisieron
imperfect subjunctive: quisiera/quisiese, quisieras/quisieses,
quisiera/quisiese, quisiéramos/quisiésemos, quisieran/quisiesen
future: querré, querrás, querrá, querremos, querréis, querrán
conditional: querría, querrías, querría, querríamos, querríais,
querrían

saber *to know*
present indicative: (yo) sé
present subjunctive: sepa, sepas, sepa, sepamos, sepáis, sepan
preterite: supe, supiste, supo, supimos, supisteis, supieron
imperfect subjunctive: supiera/supiese, supieras/supieses, supiera/
supiese, supiéramos/supiésemos, supierais/supieseis, supieran/supiesen
future: sabré, sabrás, sabrá, sabremos, sabréis, sabrán
conditional: sabría, sabrías, sabría, sabríamos, sabríais, sabrían
imperative: (Vd.) sepa

salir *to go out*
present indicative: (yo) salgo
present subjunctive: salga, salgas, salga, salgamos, salgáis, salgan
future: saldré, saldrás, saldrá, saldremos, saldréis, saldrán
conditional: saldría, saldrías, saldría, saldríamos, saldríais,
saldrían
imperative: (Vd.) salga, (tú) sal

ser *to be*
present indicative: soy, eres, es, somos, sois, son
present subjunctive: sea, seas, sea, seamos, seáis, sean
preterite: fui, fuiste, fue, fuimos, fuisteis, fueron
imperfect subjunctive: fuera/fuese, fueras/fueses, fuera/fuese,
fuéramos/fuésemos, fuerais/fueseis, fueran/fuesen
imperfect indicative: era, eras, era, éramos, erais, eran
imperative: (Vd.) sea, (tú) sé

tener* *to have*
present indicative: (yo) tengo
present subjunctive: tenga, tengas, tenga, tengamos, tengáis, tengan
preterite: tuve, tuviste, tuvo, tuvimos, tuvisteis, tuvieron

imperfect subjunctive: tuviera/tuviese, tuvieras/tuvieses, tuviera/
tuviese, tuviéramos/tuviésemos, tuvierais/tuvieseis, tuvieran/
tuviesen
future: tendré, tendrás, tendrá, tendremos, tendréis, tendrán
conditional: tendría, tendrías, tendría, tendríamos, tendríais,
tendrían
imperative: (Vd.) tenga, (tú) ten

traer *to bring*
present indicative: (yo) traigo
present subjunctive: traiga, traigas, traiga, traigamos, traigáis, traigan
preterite: traje, trajiste, trajo, trajimos, trajisteis, trajeron
imperfect subjunctive: trajera/trajese, trajeras/trajeses, trajera/
trajese, trajéramos/trajésemos, trajerais/trajeseis, trajeran/trajesen
imperative: (Vd.) traiga
gerund: trayendo

venir* *to come*
present indicative: (yo) vengo
present subjunctive: venga, vengas, venga, vengamos, vengáis, vengan
preterite: vine, viniste, vino, vinimos, vinisteis, vinieron
imperfect subjunctive: viniera/viniese, vinieras/vinieses, viniera/
viniese, viniéramos/viniésemos, vinierais/vinieseis, vinieran/viniesen
future: vendré, vendrás, vendrá, vendremos, vendréis, vendrán
conditional: vendría, vendrías, vendría, vendríamos, vendríais,
vendrían
imperative: (Vd.) venga, (tú) ven
gerund: viniendo

ver *to see*
present indicative: (yo) veo
present subjunctive: vea, veas, vea, veamos, veáis, vean
imperfect indicative: veía, veías, veía, veíamos, veíais, veían
imperative: (Vd.) vea
past participle: visto

volver* *to come back*
past participle: vuelto

Taking it further

Further study

There are a number of books on sale which may help you to expand your present knowledge of Spanish grammar. The following recommended textbooks may help you to achieve that.

Batchelor, R., *A Student Grammar of Spanish*, Cambridge University Press, 2006

Butt, J., *Spanish Grammar*, Oxford University Press, 2000

Butt, J. and Benjamin, C., *A New Reference Grammar of Modern Spanish*, Hodder Education, 4th edition, 2004

Kattán-Ibarra, J. and Howkins, A., *Spanish Grammar in Context*, Hodder Education, 2nd edition, 2008

Kattán-Ibarra, J. and Pountain, C. J., *Modern Spanish Grammar*, Routledge, 2nd edition, 2003

Muñoz, P. and Thacker, M., *A Spanish Learning Grammar*, Hodder Education, 2nd edition, 2006

Ortega, A., Beaven, T., Garrido, C. and Scrivener, S., *¡Exacto! A Practical Guide to Spanish Grammar*, Hodder Education, 2009

Turk, P. and Zollo, M., *¡Acción gramática!*, Hodder and Stoughton, 1993

Sources of authentic Spanish

SPANISH NEWSPAPERS AND MAGAZINES

El País (www.elpais.com); *El Mundo* (www.elmundo.es);
La Vanguardia (www.lavanguardia.es); *ABC* (www.abc.es);
El Periódico (www.elperiodico.com)

For general information, including Spanish current affairs and
world news, try the following magazines: *Cambio 16, Tiempo*.

For light reading and entertainment, you might like to look at
¡Hola!, Quo, Mía, Diez minutos, Lecturas, Semana, etc. These are
by far the most popular amongst Spaniards and, as a beginner, you
may find some of the articles easier to follow.

LATIN AMERICAN NEWSPAPERS AND MAGAZINES

Latin American newspapers and magazines will be more difficult to
find outside each country, but if you have internet access, you will be
able to visit their websites, although they may be special net versions.
The following is a list of some main Latin-American newspapers:

Argentina: *La Nación* (http://lanacion.com.ar); Clarín
(www.clarin.com)

Chile: *El Mercurio* (www.elmercurio.com)

Colombia: *El Espectador* (www.elespectador.com)

Cuba: *Granma* (www.granma.cu)

México: *El Universal* (www.eluniversal.com.mx)

Perú: *El Comercio* (elcomercio.pe); Correo
(www.correoperu.com.pe)

Radio, television and internet news

An excellent way to improve your understanding of spoken Spanish is to listen to the radio and watch television. On medium wave after dark (in Europe) and via satellite, you will be able to gain access to Radio Nacional de España, Televisión Española (TVE) and other stations. For Spanish-language news on the internet, you may like to go to BBC Mundo.com or to Podcast BBC Mundo Radio, which offers a 15-minute world news summary from Monday to Friday, with a special focus on Latin America. The main website is http://www.bbc.co.uk/mundo.

Travelling in Spain and Latin America

Travelling in a Spanish-speaking country is probably the best way to practise what you have learned and improve your command of the spoken language. If you are planning to do this, there are a number of good guidebooks which will help you to plan your journey. The well-known Lonely Planet series covers not just specific countries, but also main regions and cities, including Spain and Latin America. For the latter, the *Mexico and Central-American Handbook* and the *South-American Handbook* have a long tradition amongst travellers in the region. *Time Out*, Michelin and Fodor's, among several others, have also become well established in the travelling market.

For travellers in Spain, the following websites may prove useful, with information about tourist attractions, accommodation, travel, restaurants, etc.

Travelling to Spain: www.SiSpain.org/english/travelli/

Spain Today (local section of the Europe Today travel guide): www.worldtravelguide.net

All about Spain: www.red2000.com

Páginas amarillas del viajero (yellow pages for travellers):
www.spaindata.com/data/1index.shtml

Spanish National Tourist Office: www.tourspain.co.uk

Railway travel in Spain: www.renfe.es/horarios

Madrid metro: www.metromadrid.es

Travellers in Latin America will find useful information in:

www.travel.org/latin.html

www.travelnotes.org

Culture and history

Internet users interested in Spain may like to try the following sites:

Sí Spain: www.sispain.org/spanish/history

http://spanish.about.com

For those interested in Latin America, go to:

Internet Resources for Latin America:
http://lib.nmsu.edu/subject/bord/laguia

Latin American Network Information Center:
http://lanic.utexas.edu/las.html

A useful site for those interested in various aspects of Spanish,
including grammar, history of the language, dictionaries,

sports, press, radio, etc., is *La página del idioma español*:
www.elcastellano.org.

Spanish-language courses

For Spanish language, the Instituto Cervantes is a worldwide
organization that offers courses in Spanish and promotes
Spanish culture in general; in the United Kingdom, the Hispanic
Council, based in London, may be able to help you with enquiries
about Spanish-language courses and aspects of life in Spain.
For information on Latin-American Spanish, you can contact
the Hispanic Council or the embassy of the country you are
interested in.

For the Instituto Cervantes, go to: http://cervantes.es

For other related information, go to:

http://spanish.about.com

http://www.spanish-language.org

http://www.spanishabroad.com

http://planeta.com/schoolist.html

The publisher has used its best endeavours to ensure that the
URLs for external websites referred to in this book are correct
and active at the time of going to press. However, the publisher
has no responsibility for the websites and can make no guarantee
that a site will remain live or that the content is or will remain
appropriate.

Key to the exercises

1 a Me llamo (name). **b** Soy (nationality). **c** Soy de (town or city). **d** Soy (occupation). **e** Estoy/Soy (marital status).
2 ¿Cómo te llamas?/¿Eres español?/¿Eres de Buenos Aires?/¿Eres estudiante?
3 a A. Morales es taxista. **b** S. Pérez es peluquera. **c** A. Muñoz es mecánico. **d** J. González es camarero/mesero. **e** J. Díaz es médico. **f** F. Mella es estudiante.

Test yourself
1 Usted/yo/ella/vosotros
2 a nosotros/as **b** ella **c** ustedes **d** él **e** vosotros/as
3 son/somos/eres
4 a ingeniera **b** escritora **c** dependienta **d** actriz
5 a española **b** mexicana **c** francesa **d** alemana **e** andaluza
6 a americanos **b** árabes **c** irlandeses **d** andaluces **e** marroquíes **f** hindúes
7 ¿Usted es inglesa?/¿Es usted inglesa?/Usted es inglesa, ¿verdad?/¿no?
8 ¿Eres abogado? – No, no soy abogado. Soy dentista.
9 ¿Está soltera o casada? – Está divorciada.
10 te/Me/de

UNIT 2

1 a Quién **b** Cuál **c** Quiénes **d** Qué **e** Cuál **f** Cuáles
2 ¿Cómo estás?/presento/Este/gusto/Esta/estos

Test yourself
1 a Este/esta/estos/estas **b** esa/aquella **c** esto **d** ese/aquel
2 a la/el/la **b** las/la/el **c** el/las/el **d** la/la/las

3 a ¿Cuál es su email, señora Rojas? **b** ¿Cuáles son tus amigos?
c ¿Quién es esa señora? – Es mi madre. **d** ¿Qué es eso? – Estos son
mis billetes.

UNIT 3

1 a Paco y Pepe son (muy) gordos. **b** Paloma es (muy) alta. **c** Javier
está (muy) triste. **d** Rosa y Julio son/están (muy) elegantes. **e** El
coche está (muy) limpio. **f** La Tierra es redonda.
2 Es una ciudad muy bonita. La gente es muy simpática y el clima
es bastante bueno. No hace demasiado calor. El hotel es excelente.
Tiene un restaurante muy bueno y dos bares. También tiene una
playa estupenda. Estoy muy contento/a aquí.

Test yourself
1 a es/está **b** es/está **c** es/es/son/estoy **d** es/es/está
2 a difíciles **b** buena/buen/gran **c** preciosa/estupendas/amable/caros
d españoles/mexicanos/encantadora
3 a Hace frío hoy y hace un poco de viento. **b** ¿Cómo es el tiempo
en Chile?/¿Qué tiempo hace en Chile? **c** Tiene un clima templado.
d Hace mucho calor hoy, ¿verdad?/¿no?

UNIT 4

1 a ¿Tiene restaurante el hotel? **b** ¿Hay piscina? **c** ¿Tiene una/
alguna habitación doble? **d** ¿Tiene aparcamiento el hotel?
e ¿Hay un/algún supermercado por aquí? **f** ¿Hay museos en
la ciudad?
2 Follow example.
3 1 es 2 tiene 3 es 4 tiene/hay 5 es 6 hay 7 hay 8 tienen 9 es
10 tiene 11 tiene 12 es 13 tiene/hay 14 tiene

Test yourself
1 a Tienes/tengo **b** Tienen/tenemos **c** tenéis/Tenemos **d** tiene/
tienen
2 a algún/ninguno **b** alguna/ninguna **c** algo/nada **d** alguien/nadie
3 a ¿Cuánto dinero tienes? – No tengo nada. **b** ¿Cuánta gente/
Cuántas personas hay? – No hay mucha(s). **c** ¿Cuánta gasolina

tenemos? – Tenemos bastante. **d** ¿Cuántos invitados hay? – Hay muy pocos/poquísimos.

UNIT 5

1 a ¿Dónde está la catedral? **b** ¿Hay algún café por aquí? **c** ¿Dónde está el aparcamiento? **d** ¿Dónde está correos?
2 Ejemplos: **a** Sí, hay dos. Uno está en la calle Mayor, entre el cine y el restaurante, y el otro está en la calle Miramar, en la esquina, al lado del hotel Sol. **b** Está a la derecha, enfrente del café. **c** Está a la izquierda, al final de la calle Mayor. **d** Está en la próxima calle a la izquierda, al lado del museo.

Test yourself
1 a ¿Dónde está el museo? **b** ¿Dónde están los servicios? **c** Está al final de esta calle, a la derecha. **d** Están abajo, al lado del bar.
2 a es **b** es
3 a The market is a bit far. It's behind the station. **b** The bus terminal is two streets away from here, on the left, opposite the station. **c** Your passport is there, in(side) the black suitcase.
4 a ¿A qué distancia está Málaga? **b** Tus zapatos están debajo de la cama.

UNIT 6

1 a mía **b** De/de **c** su **d** mi/mis **e** mías **f** de/suya **g** pertenece **h** de
2 1 tu 2 tu 3 mía 4 tus 5 míos 6 su 7 tu 8 su 9 nuestro 10 tuyo
3 b Ana y Luis no tienen tarjetas de crédito. **c** Yo (no) tengo tarjetas de crédito. **d** Juan no tiene una casa. **e** Ana y Luis tienen una casa. **f** Yo (no) tengo una casa. **g** Juan tiene coche/carro. **h** Ana y Luis tienen coche/carro. **i** Yo (no) tengo coche/carro.

Test yourself
1 a Nuestro **b** Mi **c** su **d** Vuestra **e** Sus/suya.
2 a Este dinero es tuyo, ¿verdad? **b** No, ese dinero no es mío, es de José. **c** Esta es Carmen. Es una amiga mía. **d** Aquí está su pasaporte, señora Johnson, y aquí está el suyo, señor. **e** ¿De quién es esa chaqueta? ¿Es de María? – Sí, es suya/de ella.

UNIT 7

1 a Tenemos **b** Hay **c** debes **d** necesita **e** Hace falta **f** necesario
g necesita **h** imprescindible
2 a 5 **b** 4 **c** 6 **d** 3 **e** 1 **f** 2

Test yourself
1 a Tengo que **b** tienes que **c** Tenéis que **d** Debemos **e** Necesita
2 a No debes decir nada. **b** No hace falta comprar nada. **c** Hay
que ser muy puntual. **d** Es necesario esperar. **e** ¿Qué necesitan?

UNIT 8

1 a juega/sé **b** llueve/nieva **c** entiende **d** Conozco/voy **e** encuentro/
recuerdo **f** empieza/empezamos
2 a ¿Cuánto tiempo hace que vives en Madrid? Vivo en Madrid
desde hace diez años. **b** … trabajas …/Trabajo … ocho años. **c** …
estudias …/Estudio … cinco años. **d** … conoces …/Conozco … tres
años y medio. **e** … juegas …/Juego … dos años. **f** … haces …/Hago
… seis meses.
3 1 c 2 f 3 a 4 e 5 b 6 d

Test yourself
1 a Vivo/vive/viven/vives **b** sabe/sé/conozco **c** haces/hago **d** salgo/
sale/salís **e** Voy/vas
2 a ¿Cuánto tiempo hace que (ella) trabaja en Londres? **b** Carmen
y Agustín llevan un año aquí. **c** ¿Cuánto tiempo llevas estudiando
español? **d** Está preparando la cena para sus hijos. **e** Están jugando
al tenis. Llevan una hora jugando.

UNIT 9

1 1 hago 2 me levanto 3 desayuno 4 ayudo 5 voy 6 oigo 7 veo
8 juego 9 leo 10 salgo 11 vuelvo 12 escribo 13 llamo 14 me
acuesto
2 a ¿A qué hora te levantas normalmente? **b** ¿A qué hora sales de
la oficina? **c** ¿A qué hora tienes clase? **d** ¿Te acuestas tarde? **e** ¿Qué
haces los fines de semana? **f** ¿Qué sueles hacer en tus vacaciones?

3 a Se levanta **b** Se va al trabajo **c** habla por teléfono **d** vuelve a casa **e** prepara la cena **f** suele ver la televisión

Test yourself
1 a me acuesto/se acuesta/se acuestan **b** dormirme/me duermo **c** se va/va **d** Me despierto/me afeito/me baño/salgo **e** se alegra/vienen
2 a suele venir **b** sueles hacer **c** suelo olvidarme **d** acostumbran escuchar música o ver la televisión **e** no acostumbramos salir

UNIT 10

1 a ¿Puedes entender mi español? **b** ¿Puedes hablar más despacio? **c** ¿Puedes repetir, por favor? **d** ¿Sabes jugar al tenis? **e** Hoy no puedo jugar. Podemos jugar mañana. **f** No sé conducir. ¿Sabes conducir?
2 podemos/puede/pueden/puede/Pueden/puedo
3 a No se puede fumar. **b** No aparcar. **c** No se puede nadar. **d** No entrar. **e** No se puede girar/doblar a la izquierda. **f** No hacer/tomar fotografías.

Test yourself
1 a En Nueva York podemos ... **b** En la Metropolitan Opera House puedes ver ... **c** En Broadway podéis ir ... **d** ¿Cómo puedo reservar ...? **e** Puede reservar...
2 a ¿Puedo pasar/entrar? **b** ¿Podemos dejar nuestro equipaje aquí? **c** ¿Sabes tocar la guitarra? **d** ¿Puede venir esta tarde? **e** ¿Es posible hablar con la señora Rodríguez?

UNIT 11

1 Estudian/realizan/invitan/hacen/seleccionan/llaman/escogen
2 a se corta/se fríe/se le pone **b** se selecciona/se lleva/se envía **c** se eligen/se evalúan

Test yourself
1 a Más de 350 millones de personas hablan español. **b** Tres directores administran la empresa. **c** El padre lleva a los chicos al colegio. **d** Una empresa china fabrica estos coches.

2 a Las habitaciones se limpian por la mañana. **b** Las toallas se cambian todos los días. **c** Las reservas se hacen por internet y se confirman por email. **d** La cena se sirve a las 8:00.

3 a está **b** están **c** son **d** es

UNIT 12

1 Quisiéramos una habitación doble. ¿Tiene alguna?/Preferimos una exterior, pero quisiéramos verla. ¿Es posible?/Está bien, queremos tomar la habitación, pero quisiéramos saber cuánto cuesta./Queremos la habitación solamente. Preferimos comer fuera.

2 a 2 **b** 4 **c** 1 **d** 3

3 1 c 2 a 3 b 4 d

Test yourself

1 a quiero/prefiere **b** quiere **c** Preferimos **d** queréis **e** prefiere/prefiero

2 a lo **b** La **c** Las **d** Los **e** lo

UNIT 13

1 a le **b** nos **c** les **d** mí **e** ti **f** le **g** os **h** nos

2 a ¿Te gusta la habitación? **b** ¿Te gusta cocinar? **c** ¿Qué música te gusta? **d** ¿Qué programas de televisión te gustan? **e** ¿Te gustan los animales? **f** ¿Qué te gusta hacer los fines de semana?

3 1 **c**: A Rafael y su novia les gusta … 2 **f**: A Juan le gusta … 3 **a**: A Andrés le gusta … 4 **d**: A Ángeles le gusta … 5 **b**: A Paco le gusta … 6 **e**: A María y su familia les gusta …

Test yourself

1 a mí **b** ti **c** les **d** le **e** nos/les

2 a A Rebeca le fascina bailar salsa. **b** A vosotros también os gusta, ¿verdad? **c** Me gustan mucho las novelas de García Márquez. **d** Esos programas de televisión no me gustan nada. **e** A Ricardo y Cristina les encantan las películas de Almodóvar.

UNIT 14

1 a ¿Qué te parece la ciudad? **b** ¿Qué te parecen los museos?
c ¿Qué opinas de los parques? **d** ¿Qué piensas de la gente? **e** ¿Qué
opinas de mis amigos? **f** ¿Qué piensas de la vida en la ciudad?
2 1 parece 2 creo 3 En mi opinión 4 considero 5 a mi parecer 6 Pienso
3 El hotel es muy bueno, pero creo que la gente es un poco
ruidosa./La playa me parece excelente./Sí, estoy libre. ¿Qué te
parece si vamos a una disco?

Test yourself
1 a parece **b** Pienso que **c** creo que **d** crees **e** opinas **f** opino que/
parecen
2 a ¿Qué te parece el apartamento? **b** Es bonito/agradable, pero
pienso que es un poco pequeño. **c** Las vistas son maravillosas, ¿no
crees tú? **d** Sí, creo que sí. **e** Pero considero que es/está caro. **f** ¿Qué
te parece si vemos el apartamento de la calle Molina?

UNIT 15

1 a ¿Qué vas a hacer este verano? ¿Qué vais a hacer …? **b** Voy a
hacer un curso de inglés en Inglaterra. Vamos a viajar a la India.
c Miguel va a hacer un curso de inglés en Inglaterra. María y
Alberto van a viajar a la India. **d** Voy a (your plans).
2 1 será 2 Saldré 3 llegaré 4 Me quedaré 5 llamaré 6 podré
7 tendré 8 podremos 9 Vendrás 10 Tendrás
3 a 4: irá **b** 3: hará **c** 1: practicará **d** 2: estudiará

Test yourself
1 a llegará/vendrán **b** deberán **c** Llamaré/diré **d** habrá/Vendrás
e Nos quedaremos/miraremos **f** haréis/Iréis
2 a Diego llega mañana. Va a quedarse una semana. **b** Pensamos
ir a Cuenca. ¿Le gustará?/Me pregunto si le gustará. **c** ¿Quieres
venir con nosotros?/¿Vienes con nosotros? Mañana no trabajas,
¿verdad? **d** Lo siento, pero no puedo/podré. Voy a llevar a los
chicos/niños al dentista. **e** Voy a tomar un café. ¿Quieres uno
también? **f** Sí, gracias, pero tendré/tengo que irme pronto. Voy a
salir con Anita.

UNIT 16

1 a Por favor, ¿nos trae dos cafés? **b** … ¿me pasa …? **c** …¿nos despierta …? **d** … ¿nos envía …? **e** … ¿nos da …? **f** … ¿me llama …?
2 a ¿La ayudo? **b** ¿Le traigo una taza de café? **c** ¿La llevo a su hotel? **d** ¿La llamo mañana a las 9:00? **e** ¿Le enseño la ciudad? **f** ¿Le presento al gerente?
3 d

Test yourself
1 a ¿Me da la llave …? **b** ¿Me llevas …? **c** ¿Me dice …? **d** ¿Nos ayudáis …? **e** ¿Nos reservan una mesa …?
2 a ¿Te ayudo? **b** ¿Nos da la carta, por favor? **c** ¿Podría decirme dónde está? **d** ¿Te doy más café? **e** ¿Nos trae otra botella de vino, por favor?

UNIT 17

1 a 3: escribir **b** 5: decir **c** 1: romper **d** 6: volver **e** 7: hacer **f** 2: abrir **g** 4: poner
2 Hola, soy (your name). ¿Está Ana?/Hola Ana, ¿estás libre esta noche?/¿Has visto la nueva película de Almodóvar? Me han dicho que es muy buena./He llamado al cine y me han dicho que hay una sesión a las 9:00. ¿Qué te parece?
3 b Hemos ido **c** hemos alquilado **d** he nadado **e** hemos montado **f** hemos hecho

Test yourself
1 a he puesto **b** ha llamado/ha dicho **c** he escrito/ha contestado **d** Hemos pedido/han traído **e** habéis hecho/Habéis vuelto
2 a 4 **b** 5 **c** 2 **d** 1 **e** 3

UNIT 18

1 1 volví 2 pasé 3 Estuve 4 gustó 5 pareció 6 fui 7 conocimos 8 invitaron 9 fueron 10 traje

2 b Sí, lo escribí anteayer. **c** Sí, las hice el lunes. **d** Sí, la llamé ayer por la mañana. **e** Sí, lo compré la semana pasada. **f** Sí, lo mandé anoche. **g** Sí, la respondí anteanoche/antenoche (L.Am.).
3 a Carmen contestó el teléfono. **b** Pablo leyó la correspondencia. **c** Carmen envió faxes. **d** Pablo trabajó en el ordenador/la computadora (L.Am.). **e** Carmen atendió al público. **f** Pablo sirvió café a los clientes.

Test yourself
1 a trabajé/hizo/se fueron **b** llegó/oí **c** hiciste/Me fui/Estuve **d** quiso/se quedó **e** dio/gustó/pareció
2 a busqué/buscaste/buscaron **b** jugué/jugó/jugasteis **c** llegué/llegaste/llegaron **d** leí/leyó/leyeron **e** empecé/empezó/empezasteis

UNIT 19

1 1 Se llamaba 2 tenía 3 era 4 vestía 5 era 6 trabajaba 7 compartía 8 era 9 tenía 10 estudiaba 11 tocaba 12 gustaba
2 1 Llegué 2 tenía 3 hacía 4 había terminado 5 sabía 6 hice 7 fue 8 me quedé 9 encontré 10 era 11 tenía 12 ayudó 13 ganaba 14 trabajé
3 1 estaba 2 tenía 3 era 4 era 5 había 6 había 7 había 8 tenían 9 tenía 10 tenía 11 gustaba

Test yourself
1 a fue/Era **b** se llamaba/murió **c** quedamos/estaba **d** hablabas/Estaba **e** Iba/empezó
2 a Iban a España todos los años. Tenían muchos amigos allí.
b Salíamos de (la) casa a las 8:00 de la mañana y no volvíamos/regresábamos hasta las 7:00 de la tarde. **c** Su español era muy bueno. Había vivido en México (durante) cinco años. **d** La clase ya había empezado/comenzado cuando (él) llegó. **e** Agustín me dijo que quería verme.

UNIT 20

1 Dialogue 1: Sigue/gira/continúa
Dialogue 2: ven/ve/ingresa/ve/echa/pasa/tráeme/pregunta

2 a pongas/Ponla **b** dejes/Llévalas **c** traigas/Déjalas **d** cierres/Cierra
e limpies/Hazlo **f** vayas/Ve **g** hagas/Hazla **h** tires/Espera
3 Example: Sigue todo recto por esta calle y en la esquina gira/
dobla a la izquierda. En la segunda calle gira/dobla a la derecha.
Sigue/continúa todo recto hasta la segunda calle y allí gira/dobla a
la izquierda. La estación está al final de esa calle.

Test yourself
1 a Esté **b** Conduzca **c** Sigan **d** Espere **e** Tomen/Bájense
2 a No se lo digáis a nadie. **b** Ponlo en la cocina, por favor. **c** No
hagáis ruido. **d** Hazlo ahora mismo. **e** Por favor, llegad a la hora.

UNIT 21

1 1 hayas recibido 2 vaya 3 me quede 4 estaré 5 hayas conseguido
6 estés 7 pague 8 encuentre
2 a Es una lástima que se divorcie. **b** Me alegro de que vuelva a
España. **c** ¡Qué pena que no siga estudiando! **d** Me alegro de que
vayan a comprar una casa. **e** Siento que esté enfermo. **f** Espero que
vaya. **g** Me sorprende que lo deje. **h** ¡Qué lástima que se vayan!
3 a 3 **b** 4 **c** 2 **d** 1

Test yourself
a llegan/llegarán/confirmen **b** haga/llueva **c** vayas/traigas
d conozca/guste **e** viajemos/encontremos/sea **f** puedas/estés **g** hayáis
encontrado/necesiteis **h** sepa/diga **i** está/haya salido **j** hable

UNIT 22

1 a vayamos **b** nos quedáramos **c** saliéramos **d** invitáramos
e venga **f** la hagas
2 1 informara 2 llames 3 recordara 4 envíes 5 pases 6 lleves
3 a 4 **b** 3 **c** 1 **d** 2 **e** 6 **f** 5

Test yourself
1 a fuéramos/fuésemos **b** ayudara/ayudase **c** viera/viese – diera/
diese **d** acompañarais/acompañaseis **e** vinieran/viniesen

2 a Ella no quería que él supiera/supiese la verdad. **b** Nos ordenaron que nos marcháramos/marchásemos (or fuéramos/fuésemos). **c** Roberto me había pedido que le llamara/llamase. **d** Me gustaría que estuviera(s)/estuviese(s) aquí a la hora. **e** Nos rogó que no dijéramos/dijésemos nada.

UNIT 23

1 a 4 **b** 5 **c** 1 **d** 6 **e** 3 **f** 2
2 Querida Mari Carmen: Gracias por tu carta y tu invitación para visitarte en España. Desgraciadamente tengo que trabajar todo el verano, pero si estuviera libre, por supuesto te visitaría. Me encantaría verte otra vez. Quizá para las Navidades si puedo, a menos que tú quieras venir y quedarte conmigo entonces. ¡Sería fantástico!
Me alegro de que hayas encontrado trabajo. Sé que no es lo que querías, pero es un trabajo. Yo también lo habría/hubiera tomado. Espero que te guste.
3 1 c: construiría **2 e**: compraríamos/daríamos **3 a**: cambiaríamos
4 f: iríamos/aprenderíamos **5 b**: haríamos/invitaríamos
6 d: cambiaría/seguiría

Test yourself
1 a Si Alfonso me llama/me llama Alfonso, por favor dile/dígale que volveré/regresaré a las 5:00. **b** Si vienen a comer/almorzar, prepararé una paella. **c** Si pudiera, lo haría. **d** Si ella hablara/hablase español, ganaría más. **e** Si yo fuera/fuese rico, compraría esa casa.
2 a Si (yo) hubiera/hubiese tenido dinero, ... **b** Si (tú) nos lo hubieras/hubieses dicho, ... **c** Si (ellos) hubieran/hubiesen llegado ... **d** ... seguro que (ella) habría/hubiera venido. **e** ... os habría/hubiera encantado.

Spanish–English vocabulary

abajo   *downstairs*
abierto/a   *open*
abogado/a   *lawyer*
abuelo/a   *grandfather/ grandmother*
abuelos   *(m. pl.) grandparents*
aburrido   *boring*
acabar de   *to have just*
aceptar   *to accept*
acercarse   *to approach, come near*
acompañar   *to accompany*
acostarse   *to go to bed*
acostumbrar   *to be in the habit of*
acuerdo: de —   *all right*
además   *besides*
administrado/a   *administered, managed*
aeropuerto   *(m.) airport*
agencia   *(f.) agency*
agencia de viajes   *(f.) travel agency*
agradar   *to like, please*
agua   *(f.) water (but **el agua**)*
ahora   *now; — **mismo** right now*
aire acondicionado   *(m.) air conditioning*
alegrarse   *to be glad*
algo   *something, anything*
alguien   *somebody, anybody*
alguna vez   *ever*
alguno   *some, any*

allí   *there*
almorzar   *to have lunch*
alquilar   *to rent*
alquiler   *(m.) rent*
alto   *tall*
amable   *kind*
amigo/a   *friend*
andaluz   *Andalusian*
año   *(m.) year*
Año Nuevo   *(m.) New Year*
año pasado   *(m.) last year*
anoche   *last night*
antes   *before;* **lo — posible** *as soon as possible*
aparcamiento   *(m.) car park, parking lot (Am.E.)*
aparcar   *to park*
apartamento   *(m.) apartment*
aprender   *to learn*
aquí   *here*
argentino   *Argentinian*
arriba   *upstairs*
arte   *(f.) art*
artículo   *(m.) article*
asistir   *to attend*
asuntos exteriores   *(m. pl.) foreign affairs*
atardecer   *(m.) evening, dusk*
atender   *to look after*
aunque   *although, even though, even if*
auricular   *(m.) receiver*
autoridad   *(f.) authority*

avión (m.) aeroplane, airplane (Am.E.)

ayer yesterday

ayuda (f.) help

ayudar to help

ayuntamiento (m.) town hall

azul blue

bailar to dance

bajar to go down

bajarse to get off

bajo short

banco (m.) bank

baño (m.) bathroom

barato cheap

barrio (m.) district

bastante quite, enough

beber to drink

biblioteca (f.) library

bicicleta (f.) bicycle

bien well, good

billete (m.) ticket

blanco white

blusa (f.) blouse

bolígrafo (m.) ballpoint pen

bolso (m.) bag, handbag

bonito pretty, nice

botella (f.) bottle

británico British

bueno good, well

buenos días good morning

buscar to fetch, come for, look for

cabeza (f.) head

caer to fall

caja (f.) case

cajero automático (m.) cash point

caliente hot

calle (f.) street

calor (m.) heat; **hace —** it's warm, hot

caluroso hot (weather)

cama (f.) bed

camarero/a waiter

cambio (m.) change

camino (m.) way

camisa (f.) shirt

campo (m.) country, countryside

candidato/a candidate, applicant

cantante (m./f.) singer

carne (f.) meat

carnicería (f.) butcher's

caro expensive

carretera (f.) highway, main road

carta (f.) letter, menu

casa (f.) house

casado married

caso: en ese — in that case

catedral (f.) cathedral

católico catholic

cebolla (f.) onion

celebrado/a celebrated

cena (f.) dinner

centro (m.) centre

centro deportivo (m.) sports centre

cerrar to close

cerveza (f.) beer

chaqueta (f.) jacket

chico/a boy/girl

chicos/as children

chileno Chilean

chino (m.) Chinese (language)

chuleta de cerdo *(f.) pork chop*
cine *(m.) cinema*
cita *(f.) appointment*
ciudad *(f.) city*
clima *(m.) climate*
coche *(m.) car*
cocina *(f.) kitchen*
cocinar *to cook*
coger *to take, catch*
colega *(m./f.) colleague*
colegio *(m.) school*
colombiano *Colombian*
color *(m.) colour*
comedia *musical (f.) musical*
comedor *(m.) dining room*
comer *to eat*
comida *(f.) food, lunch, dinner
  (L.Am.)*
cómo *how*
cómodo *comfortable*
compartir *to share*
compra *(f.) shopping*
comprar *to buy*
comprimido *(m.) tablet*
conducir *to drive*
conmigo *with me*
conocer *to know, meet*
conseguir *to get*
considerar *to consider, think*
construido/a *built*
contaminado *polluted*
contar con *to have*
contar *to tell*
contestar *to answer, reply*
contigo *with you*
continuar *to continue*
contratar *to hire*
conversaciones *(f. pl.) talks*

copa *(f.) drink;* **irse de copas** *to
  go for a drink*
corbata *(f.) tie*
correos *(m.) post office*
correspondencia *(f.) mail*
cortar *to cut*
creer *to think*
cruzar *to cross*
cuál *which, what*
cuánto/s *how much/many*
cuarto de baño *(m.) bathroom*
cuenta *(f.) bill*
cuenta corriente *(f.) current
  account*
cuidado: con — *with care,
  carefully*
cumpleaños *(m.) birthday*
curso *(m.) course*

dar *to give*
datos personales *(m. pl.)
  personal information*
de nada *you're welcome*
de *of, from*
debajo *under, underneath*
deber *to have to, must*
deberes *(m. pl.) homework*
decir *to say, tell*
degraciadamente
  unfortunately
dejar *to leave*
delgado *thin*
demasiado/a *too, too much*
dentro *within, inside*
dependiente/a *shop assistant,
  sales clerk (Am.E.)*
deporte *(m.) sport*
derecha: a la — *on the right*

desayunar *to have breakfast*
desayuno *(m.) breakfast*
descansar *to rest*
desde *from*
despacho *(m.) study, office*
despertar *to wake up*
después *afterwards*
día *(m.) day*
difícil *difficult*
dinero *(m.) money*
dirección *(f.) address;* **en — a**
  towards
disponer de *to have*
disponible *available*
distancia *(f.) distance*
distinto *different*
doblar *to turn*
doble *double*
domingo *Sunday*
dormir *to sleep*
ducharse *to shower*
dudar *to doubt*
durante *during*

echar una carta *to post a letter*
edificio *(m.) building*
ejemplo *(m.) example*
embarcar *to board*
empresa *(f.) company, firm*
encantador(a) *lovely*
encantar *to like, love*
encontrar *to find*
encontrarse *to meet, be, be*
  situated
enfadarse *to get annoyed*
enfermarse *to become ill*
enfrente *opposite*
ensalada *(f.) salad*

enseñar *to teach*
entonces *then*
entrada *(f.) entrance, ticket*
  (show)
entrevistarse *to have talks*
enviar *to send*
equipaje *(m.) luggage,*
  baggage (Am.E.)
escocés *Scottish*
escribir *to write*
escritor(a) *writer*
escritorio *(m.) desk*
escuchar *to listen*
escuela *(f.) school*
esfuerzo *(m.) effort*
espacio *(m.) space*
español *Spanish*
esperar *to wait, hope, expect*
esquiar *to ski*
esquina *(f.) corner*
estación *(f.) station; —*
  de servicio *service station*
estar *to be*
estrella *(f.) star*
estresado/a *stressed, under*
  stress
estudiante *(m./f.) student*
estudiar *to study*
estupendo *great, fantastic*
exigir *to demand*
existir *to exist*
éxito *(m.) success*
expedir *to despatch*
exterior *facing the street*
extranjero *foreign; (m.) foreigner*

fábrica *(f.) factory*
fabricar *to manufacture, make*

fabricar   to manufacture
fácil   easy
factura   (f.) invoice, bill
falda   (f.) skirt
faltar   to miss, be absent
familia   (f.) family
farmacia   (f.) chemist's
fecha   (f.) date
feliz   happy
fijo   fixed
fin de semana   (m.) weekend
final: al — de   at the end of
finales: a — de   at the end of
fino   good
firma   (f.) firm, company
formulario   (m.) form
fotografía   (f.) photograph
freír   to fry
frío   cold; **hace —** it's cold
frito   fried
fruta   (f.) fruit
fuego   (m.) light
fuera   out, outside
fumar   to smoke

gafas   (f. pl.) glasses
galleta   (f.) biscuit
ganar   to earn
gasolinera   (f.) petrol station
gente   (f.) people
gerente   (m./f.) manager
girar   to turn
gobierno   (m.) government
gordo   fat
gótico   gothic
gracias   thank you
gran   big, large, great (before
  a noun)

grande   big, large
granjero   (m.) farmer
gratitud   (f.) gratitude
guapo   good looking, pretty
guía   (m./f.) guide (person)
gustar   to like

habitación   (f.) room
hablar   to speak
hacer falta   to need
hacer   to do, make
hallarse   to be situated
hambre   (f.) hunger; **tener —**
  to be hungry
hasta   until, as far as
hay que   one has to
hermano/a   brother/sister
hijo/a   son/daughter
hijos/as   children, sons and
  daughters
hindú   Indian, Hindu
hola   hello
hombre   (m.) man
hora   (f.) hour; **a la —** on time
horario de trabajo   (m.)
  working hours
húmedo   wet (climate)

idioma   (m.) language
iglesia   (f.) church
imaginar   to imagine
importar   to mind
indicar   to indicate
individual   single
inglés   English
iniciar   to start, begin
inmediato: de —   right away
instalar   to install, establish

instituto (m.) school
interesar to interest
interior at the back
invitado/a guest; — **de honor** guest of honour
irlandés Irish
irse to leave
izquierda: a la — on the left

jabón (m.) soap
japonés (m.) Japanese (language)
jardín (m.) garden
jefe/a de gobierno head of government
jefe/a de ventas sales manager
jefe/a manager, boss, head
jugar to play
juntos together
juventud (f.) youth, young people

lado: al — de next to
lana (f.) wool
largo long
lástima (f.) pity
lavarse to wash oneself
leche (f.) milk
leer to read
lejos far
levantar to lift
levantarse to get up
libertad (f.) freedom, liberty
libre free
libro (m.) book
limón (m.) lemon
limpio clean

listo ready
llamada (f.) call
llamar to call
llamarse to be called
llave (f.) key
llegada (f.) arrival
llegar to arrive
llevar to carry, take; — **+ gerund** to have been doing something
llover to rain
lluvia (f.) rain
luego then
lugar (m.) place
lunes Monday
luz (f.) light

madera (f.) wood
maleta (f.) suitcase
maletín (m.) small suitcase
malo bad
mañana tomorrow; (f.) morning
manera: de — que so that; **de esta —** in this way
mano (f.) hand
manzana (f.) block; apple
marcharse to leave
marido (m.) husband
marrón brown
más o menos more or less
más more, else
material de oficina (m.) office material
mayor elderly
medianoche (f.) midnight
medicina (f.) medicine
médico/a doctor
mediodía (m.) midday

mejor   *better;* **a lo —** *perhaps*
mentira   *(f.) lie*
menudo: a —   *often*
mercado   *(m.) market*
mes   *(m.) month*
mesa   *(f.) table*
mexicano   *Mexican*
mientras   *while, whilst*
ministro/a   *minister*
minuto   *(m.) minute*
mirar   *to watch, look*
molestarse   *to be annoyed*
moneda   *(f.) currency*
montañismo   *(m.) mountain climbing*
moreno   *tanned*
morir   *to die*
motivo   *(m.) reason*
muchacho/a   *boy/girl*
mucho   *much, a lot;* **— gusto** *pleased to meet you*
muerto   *dead*
mujer   *(f.) woman, wife*
mundo   *(m.) world*
museo   *(m.) museum*
muy   *very*

nacer   *to be born*
nada   *nothing*
nadar   *to swim*
nadie   *nobody*
naranja   *(f.) orange*
Navidades   *(f. pl.) Christmas*
necesitar   *to need*
nevera   *(f.) refrigerator*
ninguno   *none, any*
niño/a   *boy/girl, child*
noche   *(f.) night*

normalmente   *normally*
norte   *(m.) north*
noticia   *(f.) news*
novio/a   *boyfriend/girlfriend, fiancé/fiancée*
nuevamente   *again*
nuevo   *new*
número   *(m.) number*

obligar   *to force*
obtener   *to obtain*
ocupado   *busy, occupied, engaged*
ocupar   *to occupy*
ocurrir   *to happen*
odiar   *to hate*
oferta   *(f.) offer;* **de —** *special offer*
oficina   *(f.) office*
oficio   *(m.) trade*
oír   *to hear*
ojalá   *let's hope so, I hope so*
ojo   *(m.) eye*
olvidarse   *to forget*
opinar   *to think*
orden   *(m.) order, kind*
ordenador   *(m.) computer*
ordenar   *to order*
oro   *(m.) gold*
otra vez   *again*
otro   *other, another*

padre   *(m.) father*
padres   *(m.pl.) parents*
pagar   *to pay*
país   *(m.) country*
pan   *(m.) bread*
panadería   *(f.) baker's*

pantalones   (m. pl.) trousers
papelería   (f.) stationer's
paquete   (m.) parcel, package
par   (m.) pair
para   for, in order to
parecer   to seem
pariente   (m.) relative
pasado   last, past; — **mañana** the day after tomorrow
pasajero/a   passenger
pasar   to come in, come by, spend (time), to pass
pasarlo bien   to have a good time
paseo   (m.) walk
pedir   to ask for, order
película   (f.) film
peluquería   (f.) hairdresser's
pensar   to think
pensión   (f.) guest/boarding house
perdonar   to forgive
perdone   excuse me
periódico   (m.) newspaper
permiso de trabajo   (m.) work permit
perro   (m.) dog
persona   (f.) person
personalmente   personally
pertenecer   to belong
peruano   Peruvian
pescado   (m.) fish
piscina   (f.) swimming pool
piso   (m.) flat, apartment (Am.E.); floor
plancha: a la —   grilled
plato   (m.) dish, plate
playa   (f.) beach

pobre   poor
poco   little
poder   to be able to, can
pollo   (m.) chicken
poner   to put
por favor   please
por supuesto   certainly
por   for, by, per, at; — **aquí** this way
portero   (m.) porter
precio   (m.) price
precioso   beautiful
preguntar   to ask
preocupado   worried
preocuparse   to worry
preparar   to prepare
presentar   to introduce
primero   first
primo/a   cousin
príncipe   (m.) prince
privado   private
probarse   to try on
problema   (m.) problem
producir   to produce
profesor/a   teacher
propiedad   (f.) property
propio   own
próximo/a   next
publicar   to publish
pueblo   (m.) town, village
puerta   (f.) door, gate
puerto   (m.) port
pues   well, then, because
puesto   (m.) post, job

qué   what, which; ¿— **tal?** how are you?
quedarse   to stay

quejarse to complain
querer to want, love
quién who
quitarse to take off (clothes)
quizá perhaps

raro strange
rato (m.) while, moment
razón (f.) reason; **tener —** to be right
recado (m.) message
recibir to receive
recoger to pick up
recto straight; **todo —** straight on
redondo round
referencia (f.) reference
regresar to return
reiterar to reiterate
rellenar to fill in
reparar to repair
reserva (f.) reservation
resfriado: estar — to have a cold
reunión (f.) meeting
revista (f.) magazine
rico rich
robo (m.) theft
rojo red
ruido (m.) noise
ruidoso noisy

sábado Saturday
saber to know, know how to
sabroso tasty
sacar to get, buy (tickets), take out
sal (f.) salt

saludar to greet
secretario/a secretary
seguir to follow, continue
segundo second
seguro: estar — to be sure; sure, certain
semáforo (m.) traffic light
semana (f.) week
Semana Santa (f.) Holy Week
señor (m.) Mr, sir, gentleman
señora (f.) Mrs, madam, lady
señorita (f.) Miss, young lady
sentir to be sorry
ser to be
servicio (m. pl.) toilet, washroom, restroom (Am.E.)
siempre always
sierra (f.) mountain
simpático nice
solamente only
soler to be in the habit of, to usually
solicitar to request
solicitud (f.) application, application form
solo alone
sólo only
soltero single
sonar to ring
sopa de verduras (f.) vegetable soup
sostener to hold
suceder to happen
sucio dirty
supermercado (m.) supermarket
supuesto: por — of course, certainly

tal vez *perhaps*
talla *(f.) size (clothes)*
tamaño *(m.) size*
también *also*
tarde *late;* **buenas tardes**
 good afternoon/evening
té *(m.) tea*
teatro *(m.) theatre, theater*
 (Am.E.)
televisor *(m.) television set*
tema *(m.) subject, theme*
temer *to fear*
templado *temperate*
temprano *early*
tener *to have;* **— que** *to*
 have to
terminar *to finish*
tiempo *(m.) time, weather;*
 a — *on time*
tienda *(f.) shop, store*
Tierra *(f.) Earth*
tímido *shy*
tinto *red (wine)*
tío/a *uncle/aunt*
tipo *(m.) type*
tirar *to throw away*
tocar *to play (an instrument)*
todavía *still, yet*
todo *everything;* **— recto**
 straight on
todos *all*
tomar notas *to take notes*
tono de marcar *(m.) dialling*
 tone, dial tone (Am.E.)
tonto/a *fool*
trabajar *to work*
traer *to bring*
tráfico *(m.) traffic*

tranquilidad *(f.) peace*
tranquilo *quiet, relaxed*
trasladar *to take, transfer*
tratar *to deal with*
tren *(m.) train*
triste *sad*
trono *(m.) throne*
trozo *(m.) piece*

última vez *last time*
último *last*
universidad *(f.) university*
unos *some, about*

vacaciones *(f. pl.) holiday(s),*
 vacation (Am.E.)
vale *OK*
valer *to cost*
vamos *let's go*
vender *to sell*
ventana *(f.) window*
ver *to see*
verano *(m.) summer*
verdad *(f.) truth*
verde *green*
vestido *(m.) dress*
vez *(f.) time;* **de — en cuando**
 from time to time; **otra —**
 again; **una —** *once;* **a veces**
 sometimes
viajar *to travel*
viaje *(m.) trip, journey, travel;*
 — de negocios *business trip*
viajero/a *traveller, traveler*
 (Am.E.)
viento *(m.) wind;* **hace —** *it's*
 windy
vino *(m.) wine*

visado *(m.) visa*
visita *(f.) visit*
vista *(f.) view*
volver *to return, come back*
vuelo *(m.) flight*

ya *already*

zapatería *(f.) shoe shop*
zapato *(m.) shoe*
zumo *(m.) juice*

English–Spanish vocabulary

able (to be — to) **poder**
accept (to) **aceptar**
accompany (to) **acompañar**
address **dirección** *(f.)*
aeroplane **avión** *(m.)*
airplane **avión** *(m.)*
after **después**
afterwards **después**
again **otra vez, nuevamente**
agency **agencia** *(f.)*
airport **aeropuerto** *(m.)*
all **todo(s)/a(s)**
all right **de acuerdo**
alone **solo/a**
also **también**
although **aunque**
always **siempre**
Andalusian **andaluz(a)**
annoyed (to be) **estar enfadado/a**
annoyed (to get) **enfadarse, molestarse**
annoyed **enfadado/a**
another **otro/a**
any **alguno/a(s)**
any (not) **ninguno/a**
anybody **alguien**
anything **algo**
apartment **apartamento** *(m.)*
apple **manzana** *(f.)*
application form **solicitud** *(f.)*
appointment **cita** *(f.)*
approach (to) **acercarse**

April **abril**
Argentinian **argentino/a**
arrive (to) **llegar**
art **arte** *(f.)*
article **artículo** *(m.)*
as far as **hasta**
as soon as possible **lo antes posible**
ask (to) **preguntar**
at **en**
attend (to) **asistir**
August **agosto**
aunt **tía** *(f.)*
authority **autoridad** *(f.)*
autumn **otoño** *(m.)*

bad **malo/a**
bag **bolso** *(m.)*
baker's **panadería** *(f.)*
ballpoint pen **bolígrafo** *(m.)*
bank **banco** *(m.)*
bathroom **baño** *(m.)*
be (to) **ser, estar**
be glad (to) **alegrarse**
be in the habit of (to) **acostumbrar**
beach **playa** *(f.)*
beautiful **bonito/a, precioso/a**
because **porque**
bed **cama** *(f.)*
before **antes**
begin (to) **empezar, comenzar**
belong (to) **pertenecer**

besides **además**

better **mejor**

bicycle **bicicleta** (f.)

big **grande**

bill **cuenta** (f.); **factura** (f.) (invoice)

birthday **cumpleaños** (m.)

biscuit **galleta** (f.)

bit: a **— un poco**

black **negro/a**

block **manzana** (f.); **cuadra** (f.) (L.Am.)

blouse **blusa** (f.)

blue **azul**

book **libro** (m.)

boring **aburrido/a**

born (to be) **nacer**

boss **jefe/a**

bottle **botella** (f.)

boy **niño, muchacho, chico** (m.)

bread **pan** (m.)

breakfast (to have) **desayunar**

breakfast **desayuno** (m.)

bring (to) **traer**

British **británico/a**

brother **hermano**

brown **marrón**

building **edificio** (m.)

business **negocio** (m.)

busy **ocupado/a**

butcher's **carnicería** (f.)

buy (to) **comprar**

by **por**

call (to) **llamar**

call **llamada** (f.)

called (to be) **llamarse**

can (to be able to) **poder**

car park **aparcamiento** (m.), **estacionamiento** (Southern Cone, L. Am.)

car **coche** (m.); **carro** (m.), **auto** (m.) (L. Am.)

carry (to) **llevar**

case **caja** (f.)

case (in that) **en ese caso**

cash dispenser **cajero automático** (m.)

cash point **cajero automático** (m.)

catch (to) **coger**

cathedral **catedral** (f.)

Catholic **católico/a**

center **centro** (m.)

centre **centro** (m.)

certainly **por supuesto**

change (to) **cambiar**

change **cambio** (m.)

cheap **barato/a**

chemist's **farmacia** (f.)

chicken **pollo** (m.)

children **niños** (m.pl.), **hijos** (m.pl.)

Chilean **chileno/a**

Christmas **Navidad** (f.sing.), **Navidades** (f.pl.)

church **iglesia** (f.)

cinema **cine** (m.)

city **ciudad** (f.)

city hall **ayuntamiento** (m.), **municipalidad** (f.) (L.Am.)

clean **limpio/a**; to — **limpiar**

climate **clima** (m.)

cold; it is **— hace frío**

cold **frío/a**

color **color** (m.)

colour **color** (m.)
come (to) **venir**
come back (to) **volver, regresar**
come in (to) **pasar, entrar**
comfortable **cómodo/a**
company **compañía** (f.),
  empresa (f.), **firma** (f.)
complain (to) **quejarse**
computer **ordenador** (m.);
  computadora (f.) (L.Am.)
confirm (to) **confirmar**
consider (to) **considerar;**
  pensar
continue (to) **continuar, seguir**
cook (to) **cocinar**
corner **esquina** (f.); **rincón** (m.)
cost (to) **valer, costar**
country **país** (m.); **campo** (m.)
countryside **campo** (m.)
course **curso** (m.)
cousin **primo/a**
cross (to) **cruzar**
currency **moneda** (f.)
current account **cuenta**
  corriente (f.)
cut (to) **cortar**

dance (to) **bailar**
date **fecha** (f.)
daughter **hija** (f.)
day after tomorrow (the)
  pasado mañana
day before yesterday (the)
  anteayer, antes de ayer,
  antier (Mexico)
day **día** (m.)
dead **muerto/a**
deal with (to) **tratar**

December **diciembre**
demand (to) **exigir**
dentist **dentista** (m./f.)
desk **escritorio** (m.)
despatch (to) **despachar,**
  enviar, expedir
dial tone **tono de marcar** (m.)
dialling tone **tono de marcar**
  (m.)
die (to) **morir**
different **diferente, distinto/a**
difficult **difícil**
dining room **comedor** (m.)
dinner **cena** (f.)
dirty **sucio/a**
distance **distancia** (f.)
district **barrio** (m.)
divorced **divorciado/a**
do (to) **hacer**
doctor **médico/a, doctor/a**
dog **perro/a**
door **puerta** (f.)
double **doble**
doubt (to) **dudar**
downstairs **abajo**
dress **vestido** (m.)
drink (to) **beber; tomar**
  (L.Am.)
drink **copa** (f.); **bebida** (f.)
drive (to) **conducir**
during **durante**
dusk **atardecer** (m.)

each **cada**
early **temprano, pronto**
earn (to) **ganar**
Earth **Tierra** (f.)
easy **fácil**

eat (to)   comer
effort   esfuerzo (m.)
eighth   octavo/a
elderly   mayor
else   más
e-mail   email (m.)., correo
  electrónico (m.)
end (at the — of)   al final de
  (location); a finales de (time)
English   inglés/inglesa;
  inglés (m.) (language)
enough   bastante, suficiente
entrance   entrada (f.)
establish (to)   instalar, establecer
evening   atardecer (m.)
ever   alguna vez
every   todos/as
everyday   todos los días
everything   todo
example   ejemplo (m.)
excuse (to)   perdonar
exist (to —)   existir
expect (to)   esperar
expensive   caro/a
eye   ojo (m.)

factory   fábrica (f.)
fall (Am.E.)   otoño (m.)
fall (to)   caer
family   familia (f.)
far   lejos
farmer   granjero (m.)
fat   gordo/a
father   padre (m.)
fear (to)   temer
February   febrero
fetch (to)   buscar
fifth   quinto/a

fill in (to)   rellenar
film   película (f.)
find (to)   encontrar
finish (to)   terminar
firm   firma (f.), empresa (f.),
  compañía (f.)
first   primero/a
fish   pescado (m.)
fixed   fijo/a
flat piso (m.),   apartamento (m.)
follow (to)   seguir
food   comida (f.), alimento (m.)
fool   tonto/a
for   por, para
force (to)   obligar
foreign   extranjero/a
foreigner   extranjero/a
forgive (to)   perdonar
form   formulario (m.)
fourth   cuarto/a
free   libre
Friday   viernes (m.)
fried   frito/a
friend   amigo/a
from time to time   de vez en
  cuando
from   de, desde
fruit   fruta (f.)
fry (to)   freír

garden   jardín (m.)
gas station   gasolinera (f),
  estación de servicio (f.)
gentleman   señor   (m.)
get (to)   conseguir
get up (to)   levantarse
girl   niña, muchacha, chica (f.)
give (to)   dar

glasses **gafas** (f.pl.)

go down (to) **bajar**

go to bed (to) **acostarse**

gold **oro** (m.)

good afternoon **buenas tardes**

good evening **buenas tardes, buenas noches**

good looking **guapo/a**

good morning **buenos días**

good night **buenas noches**

good **bueno/a; fino/a**

government **gobierno** (m.)

grandfather **abuelo**

grandmother **abuela**

grandparents **abuelos** (m.pl.)

great **estupendo/a** (fantastic); **gran** (important)

green **verde**

greet (to) **saludar**

grilled **a la plancha**

guest **invitado/a; huésped** (hotel) (m./f.)

guide **guía** (m./f.) (person); **guía** (f.) (book)

hairdresser's **peluquería** (f.)

hand **mano** (f.)

handbag **bolso** (m.)

happen (to) **ocurrir, suceder, pasar**

happy **feliz, contento/a**

have (to — to) **tener que, deber**

have (to) **tener, contar con, disponer de**

have a cold (to) **estar resfriado, estar constipado** (Spain)

have just (to) **acabar de**

have lunch (to) **almorzar**

head of government **jefe/a de gobierno**

head **cabeza** (f.)

hear (to) **oír**

heat **calor** (m.)

hello **hola**

help (to) **ayudar**

help **ayuda** (f.)

here **aquí**

highway **carretera** (f.)

hire (to) **contratar** (a person); **alquilar** (a house, a car)

hold (to) **sostener**

holiday **vacaciones** (f.pl.)

homework **deberes** (m.pl.)

hope (to) **esperar**

hot **caliente, caluroso** (weather)

hour **hora**

house **casa** (f.)

how are you? **¿qué tal?, ¿cómo está(s)?**

how many **cuántos/as**

how much **cuánto/a**

how **cómo**

hunger **hambre** (f.)

husband **marido, esposo** (m.)

ill (to become) **enfermarse**

imagine (to) **imaginar**

in **en**

Indian **indio/a, hindú**

indicate (to) **indicar**

inside **dentro**

install (to) **instalar, establecer**

interest (to) **interesar**

introduce (to) **presentar**
invoice **factura** *(f.)*
Irish **irlandés/irlandesa**

jacket **chaqueta** *(f.)*
January **enero**
journey **viaje** *(m.)*
juice **zumo; jugo** *(L.Am.)*
July **julio**
June **junio**

key **llave** *(f.)*
kind **amable**
kitchen **cocina** *(f.)*
know (to) **conocer, saber**
know how to (to) **saber**

lady **señora, señorita** *(f.)*
large **grande**
last year **año pasado** *(m.)*
last **pasado/a; último/a**
late **tarde**
lawyer **abogado/a**
learn (to) **aprender**
leave (to) **irse, marcharse, dejar**
left (on the) **a la izquierda**
left **izquierdo/a**
letter **carta** *(f.)*
library **biblioteca** *(f.)*
lie **mentira** *(f.)*
lift (to) **levantar**
light **fuego** *(m.);* **luz** *(f.)*
like (to) **gustar**
like **como**
listen (to) **escuchar**
little **poco/a** *(amount);* **pequeño/a** *(size)*

long **largo/a**
look after (to) **cuidar, atender**
look for (to) **buscar**
lot (a) **mucho/a**
love (to) **gustar mucho, encantar**
luggage **equipaje** *(m.)*
lunch **almuerzo** *(m.),* **comida** *(f.)*

madam **señora**
magazine **revista** *(f.)*
mail **correspondencia** *(f.)*
mail (to) **enviar (una carta, un paquete);** — *a letter* **echar una carta**
make (to) **hacer**
man **hombre**
manager **gerente, jefe/a**
March **marzo**
married **casado/a**
mild **templado**
morning **mañana** *(f.)*
manufacture (to) **fabricar**
market **mercado** *(m.)*
married **casado/a**
May **mayo**
meat **carne** *(f.)*
medicine **medicina** *(f.)*
meet (to) **encontrarse;** **conocer** *(to get to know)*
meeting **reunión** *(f.)*
menu **menú** *(m.),* **carta** *(f.)*
message **recado** *(m.),* **mensaje** *(m.)*
Mexican **mexicano/a**
midday **mediodía** *(m.)*
mind (to) **importar**

minister **ministro/a**

minute **minuto** (m.)

miss (to) **faltar** (to be absent);
perder (transport); **echar
de menos/extrañar** (L.Am.)
(nostalgia)

Miss **señorita**

moment **momento** (m.), **rato** (m.)

Monday **lunes** (m.)

money **dinero** (m.)

month **mes** (m.)

more or less **más o menos**

more **más**

mother **madre**

mountain **montaña** (f.),
sierra (f.)

Mr **señor**

Mrs **señora**

much **mucho/a**

museum **museo** (m.)

must **deber, tener que**

near **cerca**

need (to) **necesitar, hacer
falta**

never **nunca, jamás**

New Year **Año Nuevo** (m.)

new **nuevo/a**

news **noticia** (f.)

newspaper **periódico** (m.),
diario (m.)

next to **al lado de**

next **próximo/a**

nice **bonito/a;
simpático/a** (person)

night **noche** (f.)

ninth **noveno/a**

nobody **nadie**

noise **ruido** (m.)

noisy **ruidoso/a**

none **ninguno/a**

normally **normalmente**

north **norte** (m.)

nothing **nada**

November **noviembre**

now **ahora**

number **número** (m.)

obtain (to) **obtener**

occupy (to) **ocupar**

October **octubre**

of course **por supuesto**

of **de**

offer **oferta** (f.)

offer (special) **de oferta**

office **oficina** (f.),
despacho (m.)

often **a menudo**

OK **vale** (especially Spain)

on **en**

once **una vez**

onion **cebolla** (f.)

only **sólo, solamente**

opposite **enfrente**

orange **naranja** (f.) (fruit);
naranja (m./f.) (colour)

order (in — to) **para**

order (to) **ordenar**

order **orden** (m.)

others **otros/as**

out **fuera**

outside **fuera**

own **propio/a**

package **paquete** (m.)

pair **par** (m.)

pants **pantalón** *(m.sing.)*, **pantalones** *(m.pl.)*

parcel **paquete** *(m.)*

parking lot **aparcamiento** *(m.)*, **parking** *(m.)*; **estacionamiento** *(m.) (Southern Cone, L.Am.)*

park (to) **aparcar, estacionar** *(Southern Cone, L.Am.)*

past **pasado/a**

pay (to) **pagar**

peace **tranquilidad** *(f.)*

people **gente** *(f.sing.)*

per **por**

perhaps **a lo mejor, tal vez, quizá(s)**

persona **person** *(f.)*

personally **personalmente**

Peruvian **peruano/a**

petrol **gasolina** *(f.)*

petrol station **gasolinera** *(f.)*

photograph **foto** *(f.)*, **fotografía** *(f.)*

pick up (to) **recoger**

piece **trozo** *(m.)*

pity **lástima** *(f.)*

place **lugar** *(m.)*, **sitio** *(m.)*

play (to) **jugar; tocar** *(an instrument)*

plead (to) **rogar**

please **por favor**

pleased to meet you **mucho gusto, encantado/a**

polluted **contaminado/a**

poor **pobre**

pork chop **chuleta de cerdo** *(f.)*

pork **cerdo** *(m.)*

port **puerto** *(m.)*

porter **portero/a**

post office **(oficina de) correos** *(f.)*

post (to — a letter) **echar una carta**

prepare (to) **preparar**

pretty **bonito/a**

price **precio** *(m.)*

prince **príncipe** *(m.)*

private **privado**

problem **problema** *(m.)*

produce (to) **producir**

property **propiedad** *(f.)*

publish (to) **publicar**

purse **bolso** *(m.)*, **cartera** *(f.) (L.Am.)*

put (to) **poner**

question **pregunta** *(f.)*

quiet **tranquilo/a**

quite **bastante**

rain **lluvia** *(f.)*

rain (to) **llover**

read (to) **leer**

ready **listo/a**

reason **motivo** *(m.)*, **razón** *(f.)*

receive (to) **recibir**

receiver **auricular** *(m.)*

red **rojo/a; tinto** *(wine)*

relative **pariente** *(m./f.)*

rent (to) **alquilar**

rent **alquiler** *(m.)*

repair (to) **reparar**

request (to) **solicitar**

reservation **reserva** *(f.)*; **reservación** *(f.) (L.Am.)*

rest (to) **descansar**

restroom **servicio** *(m.)*, **lavabo** *(m.)*, **baño** *(m.)*

return (to) **regresar, volver; devolver** *(something)*

rich **rico/a**

right (on the) **a la derecha**

right (to be) **tener razón**

right away **de inmediato, ahora mismo**

right now **ahora mismo**

right **derecho/a**

ring (to) **sonar**

room **habitación** *(f.)*, **cuarto** *(m.)*

round **redondo/a**

sad **triste**

salad **ensalada** *(f.)*

sales clerk **dependiente/a** *(m./f.)*

sales manager **jefe/a de ventas**

salt **sal** *(f.)*

Saturday **sábado** *(m.)*

say (to) **decir**

school **colegio** *(m.)*, **escuela** *(f.); **instituto** *(m.) (secondary school, Spain)*

Scottish **escocés/escocesa**

second **segundo/a**

secretary **secretario/a**

see (to) **ver**

seem (to) **parecer**

sell (to) **vender**

send (to) **enviar, mandar**

September **septiembre, setiembre**

serve (to) **servir**

seventh **séptimo/a**

share (to) **compartir**

shirt **camisa** *(f.)*

shoe shop **zapatería** *(f.)*

shoe **zapato** *(m.)*

shop assistant **dependiente/a**

shop **tienda** *(f.)*

short **bajo/a**

shower (to) **ducharse**

shower **ducha** *(f.)*

shy **tímido/a**

single **soltero/a** *(marital status);* **individual** *(room)*

sir **señor**

sister **hermana** *(f.)*

situated (to be) **estar situado/a, encontrarse, hallarse**

sixth **sexto/a**

size **tamaño** *(m.) (volume);* **talla** *(f.) (clothing)*

ski (to) **esquiar**

skirt **falda** *(f.)*

sleep (to) **dormir**

smoke (to) **fumar**

soon **pronto**

so that **de manera que**

some **unos/as, algunos/as**

somebody **alguien**

something **algo**

sometimes **a veces**

son **hijo** *(m.)*

sorry: I am — **lo siento**

soup **sopa** *(f.)*

south **sur** *(m.)*

space **espacio** *(m.)*

Spanish **español/a; español** *(m.) (language)*

speak (to) **hablar**
spend (to) **pasar** (time); **gastar**
(money)
sport **deporte** (m.)
sports centre **centro**
deportivo (m.)
spring **primavera** (f.)
star **estrella** (f.)
start (to) **empezar, comenzar**
station (service) **estación de**
servicio (f.), **gasolinera** (f.)
station **estación** (f.)
stationer's **papelería** (f.)
stay (to) **quedarse**
still **todavía**
store **tienda** (f.)
straight on **todo recto**
strange **raro/a**
street **calle** (f.)
student **estudiante**
study (to) **estudiar**
study **despacho** (m.)
subject **tema** (m.) (topic)
success **éxito** (m.)
suitcase **maleta** (f.)
summer **verano** (m.)
Sunday **domingo** (m.)
sunglasses **gafas de sol** (f.pl.)
supermarket **supermercado** (m.)
sure (to be) **estar seguro/a**
swim (to) **nadar**
swimming pool **piscina** (f.);
alberca (f.) (Mexico)

table **mesa** (f.)
tablet **comprimido** (m.),
tableta (f.), **pastilla** (f.)
take (to) **tomar, coger**

take off (to) **quitarse** (clothes);
despegar (aeroplane)
talks (to have) **entrevistarse**
talks **conversaciones** (f.pl.)
tall **alto/a**
tanned **moreno/a**
tasty **sabroso/a**
tea **té** (m.)
teach (to) **enseñar**
teacher **profesor/(a), maestro/a**
television **televisión** (f.)
tell (to) **decir, contar**
temperate **templado/a**
tenth **décimo/a**
thank you **gracias**
that **ese/esa** (demonstrative);
que (relative pronoun)
theatre **teatro** (m.)
theft **robo** (m.)
then **entonces; en seguida,**
después
there is/are **hay**
there **allí**
thin **delgado/a**
think (to) **opinar; creer;**
pensar; considerar
third **tercero/a**
throw away (to) **tirar**
Thursday **jueves** (m.)
ticket **billete** (m.), **boleto** (m.)
(L.Am.), **entrada** (show) (f)
tie **corbata** (f.)
time (last —) **última vez**
time (on —) **a la hora**
time (to have a good —)
pasarlo bien
time **tiempo** (m.)
today **hoy**

together **juntos/as**

toilet **lavabo** *(m.)*, **servicios** *(m.pl.)*

tomorrow **mañana**

towards **en dirección a**

towel **toalla** *(f)*

town hall **ayuntamiento** *(m.)*, **municipalidad** *(f.) (L.Am.)*

town **ciudad** *(f.)*, **pueblo** *(m.)*

trade **oficio** *(m.)*

traffic light **semáforo** *(m.)*

traffic **tráfico** *(m.)*

train **tren** *(m.)*

travel (to) **viajar**

travel agency **agencia de viajes** *(f.)*

traveler **viajero/a**

traveller **viajero/a**

trip **viaje** *(m.)*

trousers **pantalón** *(m.sing.)*, **pantalones** *(m.pl.)*

truth **verdad** *(f.)*

try (to — on) **probarse**

Tuesday **martes** *(m.)*

turn (to) **girar, doblar**

twice **dos veces**

uncle **tío** *(m.)*

unfortunately **desgraciadamente, desafortunadamente**

university **universidad** *(f.)*

until **hasta**

upstairs **arriba**

usually **generalmente, normalmente**

vegetable **verdura** *(f.)*

very **muy**

view **vista(s)** *(f. sing./pl.)*

village **pueblo** *(m.)*

visa **visado** *(m.)*, **visa** *(f.) (L.Am.)*

visit **visita** *(f.)*

wait (to) **esperar**

waiter **camarero, mesero** *(L.Am.)*

waitress **camarera, mesera** *(L.Am.)*

wake (to — up) **despertar(se)**

walk **paseo** *(m.)*

walk (to) **andar, caminar**

want (to) **querer**

warm (it is —) **hace calor**

washroom **servicio** *(m.)*, **lavabo** *(m.)*, **baño** *(m.)*

wash (to — oneself) **lavarse**

watch (to) **mirar, ver**

way (in this) **de esta manera**

way (this) **por aquí**

way **camino** *(m.); **manera** *(f.)*, **modo** *(m.)*

weather **tiempo** *(m.)*

Wednesday **miércoles** *(m.)*

week **semana** *(f.)*

weekend **fin de semana** *(m.)*

welcome (you're —) **de nada, no hay de qué**

well **bien**

wet **húmedo/a** *(climate)*

what **qué, cuál/cuáles** *(sing./pl.)*

which **cuál/cuáles** *(sing./pl.)*

while **mientras; rato** *(m.)*

whilst **mientras**

white **blanco/a**

who **quien/quienes**

why? **¿por qué?**
wife **mujer, esposa** *(f.)*
wind **viento** *(m.)*
windy: it's — **hace viento**
window **ventana** *(f.)*
wine **vino** *(m.)*
winter **invierno** *(m.)*
with me/you **conmigo/contigo**
  *(familiar)/***con usted** *(formal)*
with **con**
within **dentro**
woman **mujer** *(f.)*
wonderful **maravilloso/a**
wood **madera** *(f.)*

wool **lana** *(f.)*
work (to) **trabajar**
work permit **permiso de**
  trabajo *(m.)*
working hours **horario de**
  trabajo *(m.)*
worried **preocupado/a**
worry (to) **preocuparse**
worse **peor**

year **año** *(m.)*
yellow **amarillo/a**
yesterday **ayer**
yet **todavía**

Grammatical index

Key to three-part references

05:GS:3 = Unit 5, Grammar summary, paragraph 3
KS = Key sentences
GR = Grammar reference

Credits